DATE DUE

DEMCO 38-296

JOHN McCABE

John McCabe. Photograph courtesy of Reg Wilson.

John McCabe_____

_____A Bio-Bibliography

STEWART R. CRAGGS

Bio-Bibliographies in Music, Number 32
Donald L. Hixon, Series Adviser

GREENWOOD PRESS
New York • Westport, Connecticut • London

Library of Congress Cataloging-in-Publication Data

Craggs, Stewart R.
  John McCabe : a bio-bibliography / Stewart R. Craggs.
    p.   cm.—(Bio-bibliographies in music, ISSN 0742-6968 ; no.
  32)
  Includes bibliographical references and index.
  Discography: p.
  ISBN 0-313-26445-7 (alk. paper)
    1. McCabe, John, 1939-   —Bibliography. 2. McCabe, John, 1939-
  —Discography. I. Title. II. Series.
  ML134.M48C7 1991
  016.78′092—dc20   90-20135

British Library Cataloguing in Publication Data is available.

Library of Congress Catalog Card Number: 90-20135
ISBN: 0-313-26445-7
ISSN: 0742-6968

First published in 1991

Greenwood Press, 88 Post Road West, Westport, CT   06881
An imprint of Greenwood Publishing Group, Inc.

Printed in the United States of America

The paper used in this book complies with the
Permanent Paper Standard issued by the National
Information Standards Organization (Z39.48-1984).

10 9 8 7 6 5 4 3 2 1

TO
Georgina and Monica

Contents

viii   Contents

Preface

John McCabe is regarded as one of Britain's leading composers and has an international reputation, both as a composer and as a pianist. His compositions, which cover most of the established forms, have received wide acclaim and performances in many countries.

This volume, which constitutes a first attempt to document McCabe's output, is arranged in the following manner:

(1) A brief <u>biography</u> of the composer, prepared with his kind assistance.

(2) A list of <u>works and performances</u> classified by genre and then arranged alphabetically by title of composition. Following each title are details about a work including its first and other selected performances, each work being prefaced by a mnemonic "W." Reference is made to commentaries and reviews cited in the "Bibliography."

Derived works and arrangements follow the original work, retaining the work number with the addition of a further subsidiary letter to distinguish them from the original work. Main titles are given in upper case letters, without reference to any subsidiary works in lower case.

(3) A selected <u>discography</u> of commercially produced long-playing records, cassettes and compact discs.

This is divided into two sections:

(a) McCabe as a composer

Recordings are listed alphabetically by title, each work prefaced by a mnemonic "D".

(b) McCabe as a performer

Recordings are listed alphabetically by composer name and again prefaced by a mnemonic "D."

Reference is made to reviews of some recordings cited in the "Bibliography."

(4) A <u>bibliography</u>, divided into two sections:

   (a) Articles and features about (both as composer and pianist) and by John McCabe, arranged alphabetically by author, with annotations often taking the form of brief quotations from this material.

   (b) Gramophone record reviews written by John McCabe for the British journal <u>Records and Recordings</u> between 1967 and 1974. These are arranged alphabetically by composer and then chronologically with brief details supplied but no annotations.

Each citation is preceded by the mnemonic "B", entries in the Bibliography refer to the "Works and Performances" and "Discography" sections by their entry codes.

In addition, appendices provide alphabetical and chronological listings of McCabe's works. A general <u>index</u> of names (personal and corporate) concludes the volume.

Acknowledgments

I must thank John McCabe and his wife Monica who helped in so many ways and who welcomed me into their home so many times while I consulted and had free access to the many papers and manuscripts that are kept under their roof. Thanks to the unfailing warmth of their welcome and their generosity, my task was a delightful one. I must also thank John's agent, Georgina Ivor, for her help, generosity and her many other kindnesses.

Many other people helped me in a number of ways, in particular: Kathleen ATKINS, General Manager of the Guildford Philharmonic Orchestra; Jean BAMPTON, Halle Concerts Society; Roger BEACHAM, Cheltenham Library; Charles BOWDEN, Assistant Director, Bristol Entertainments Department; Clare BROWN, formerly of the BBC Written Archives Centre; Ros BROWN, Archivist, Borders Regional Library; Eveyln BRYSON, Scottish Ballet; Kieran BURKE, Cork City Library; Marion BUTLER, Fishguard Music Festival; Bruce CARR, Pittsburgh Symphony Society; N. CARRICK, Liverpool Record Office; Lesley COPPELL, Liverpool Daily Post; Malcolm COTTLE, London Concord Singers; Jacky COWDREY, Records Room, Royal Albert Hall; Roger CRUDGE, County Music Librarian, Avon; Tim DAY, National Sound Archive; Departmental Librarian (Music), Glasgow City Libraries; Kate ENDERSBY, Malvern Concert Club; Brian FAWCETT, the University of Reading; Patricia F. GILLIES, Concerts Manager, Scottish National Orchestra; John GULLEY, Huddersfield Polytechnic; Gill HANCOCK, Cardiff Festival of Music; Karensa HARRISON, Norwich Festival; Barbara HEAS, Cork International Festival; Bryan HESFORD; Sheila HODGE, Birmingham Chamber Music Society; Paula HOWARD, Dublin Public Libraries; Patrick HOWGILL, IMP; Anthony JOHN, Stonyhurst College; M. JOYCE, Avon Leisure Department; Beresford KING-SMITH, CBSO; Brian KIRTLEY, Music Librarian, University of Lancaster; Rosemary LOBBAN, Staffordshire Polytechnic Libary; Kenneth LOVELAND; Bryan MARSON-SMITH; Margaret MATICKA, University of New England, NSW; Michael MESSENGER, County Librarian, Hereford and Worcester; Duncan MIRYLEES, Guildford Public Library; Music Librarian, Manchester Central Library; National Youth

Orchestra of Scotland; Celia NEWMAN, RFH; Michael PEGG, Alice Ottley School; Carolyn RAMSDEN, BBC, Manchester; Anne RANSLEY, Henry Watson Music Library; Reference Librarian, Shrewsbury Public Library; Michael J. ROGAN, Boston (USA) Public Library; John RUSSELL, Head of Concert Planning, English Heritage; Margaret SANDERS, Librarian, Information Services, Hereford and Worcester; Scottish Theatre Archives; Daniel SHAW, Senior Arts Officer, London Borough of Camden; Lawrence TAGG, Newcastle City Libraries; Tim TAYLOR, University College, Cardiff; Susan THOMPSON, Northampton Philharmonic Choir; John THORN, Portsmouth Central Library; Alan THURLOW, Organist and Master of the Choristers, Chichester Cathedral; Kathleen TURTLE, Deputy Librarian, IBA; Jeff WALDEN, BBC Written Archives Centre; Linda WALLACE of the Minnesota Orchestal Asociation; B.M. WEST, Local History Librarian, Macclesfield Public Library.

I must also record my thanks to my wife, Valerie, for help and support, to Pauline LOMAX for typing much of my correspondence, to my colleagues Anne BUNDOCK and Jane MOORE for obtaining much material for me, and to Helen CRUTE and her staff for producing a beautifully typed manuscript.

JOHN McCABE

Biography

John McCabe was born in Huyton, Liverpool, in April
1939, the son of Frank McCabe, a physicist of Irish-Scottish
stock, and his German-born mother, Elisabeth. The arts and
sciences were strong influences in both families. His
paternal grandfather, Joseph McCabe, was the author of a
large number of books on a wide range of subjects, including
astronomy, history, popular science, and religion. (He had
in his younger years been a monk in Ireland.) John's mother
had German, Swedish, Finnish and Spanish ancestry, and her
great-uncle's family (named Gottschalk) included several
musicians. (Her uncle Franz pursued a successful career as
a zither-player and orchestral conductor in the United
States in his later years.) She herself was an accomplished
amateur violinist.

When John was nearly three, he fell into a fire and
was so badly burned that he suffered from severe ill health
for eight years, during which time he was only able to
attend school for a total of three weeks. He had
meningitis, mastoiditis and pneumonia and at one time lost
his hearing. He spent the eight years "reading, being ill,
having a good time." McCabe recalls that his parents had a
lot of good books and a large stock of 78s. "I remember
vividly the impact of works I heard at this time, such as
Elgar's Violin Concerto with Menuhin, the first broadcast of
Bartok's Concerto for Orchestra and Vaughan Williams' Sixth
Symphony. I always was interested in relatively modern
music." (1)

At the age of seven, he was saving up pocket money
to buy records of Alan Rawsthorne's Symphonic Studies; at
10, he knew all the Mozart Koechel catalogue numbers by
heart. It was not a lonely life he says as the house was
always full of children. By this time, McCabe had written
13 symphonies and part of an opera based on themes from
Mussorgsky. (2)

In 1950, he enrolled in the Liverpool Institute
where he began to study composition seriously, taking the
"A" level music course; fortunately his health started to
improve at this time. He continued his studies at
Manchester University with Humphrey Procter-Gregg, a

professor with a passion for opera, and he graduated with a
Bachelor of Music degree on 15 June 1960. McCabe recalls
that he "was kicked out of the composition classes at
University, like Maxwell Davies three years before, because
I was too modern. They were very anti-modern." (3) One term
of a post-graduate teaching course was enough to convince
him that he would not make a good teacher.

Instead, he entered the old Royal Manchester College
of Music studying composition with Thomas Pitfield and piano
with Gordon Green, the latter his teacher since the age of
eight.   McCabe obtained a performer's diploma with
distinction in pianoforte on 16 July 1962. It was during
this period that he made his solo debut as a pianist playing
Turina's Rapsodia Sinfonica with the strings of the
Merseyside Youth Orchestra, conducted by William Jenkins.
The breadth of his modern repertoire at this time is
revealed in a list of works which is still in existence: it
ranges from pieces by Richard Rodney Bennett, Elliot Carter,
Copland, Christopher Headington, Hoddinott, Lutoslawski to
Tippett, Peter Dickinson, Malcolm Lipkin and Willem Pijper.
(4)

A life-long ambition of the young composer was to
study in Europe, and this was fulfilled on completion of his
course at the RMCM.   In 1964, he went to the Munich
Hochschule to study composition with Harald Genzmer on a
German Government Scholarship. McCabe had, however, very
much hoped to study with Karl Amadeus Hartmann: a letter,
written in May 1959, reveals that Hartmann told McCabe that
he did not take pupils, but recommended that he either
approach Boris Blacher in Berlin or Wolfgang Fortner in
Freiberg. (5) The two composers finally met in 1963 when
Hartmann agreed to supervise his work.   However before
McCabe was able to take up this arrangement, Hartmann died.
The Variations on a Theme of Hartmann (W37) form a sort of
tribute to him, though it is lively, rather than requiem, in
feeling. McCabe has admitted that his studies in Munich
were not entirely successful.   "They wanted me to be a
German composer writing imitation Hindemith." (6)

On his return to England in 1965, McCabe worked in
an office until Alun Hoddinott telephoned and offered him
the job of resident pianist at University College, Cardiff.
Gerald Larner also suggested that he should do some
reviewing for the Guardian newspaper.

McCabe stayed at Cardiff for three years, where,
besides teaching and writing, he learned new chamber works
for piano as well as many solos. At this time, he was
coming to the fore as a composer: while at Cardiff he wrote
his first symphony, a piano concerto, three chamber
concertos, an opera and several major chamber works. Almost
all were written on commission. The First Symphony (W33)
was very much championed by Sir John Barbirolli who
introduced it at the Cheltenham Festival. Canto for guitar
(W76) was a commission from the Cardiff Festival of 20th
Century Music. It is reported that McCabe borrowed a guitar

from his landlady's son and sat up all night working out how
to play the instrument so that he could write this piece for
it.

McCabe moved to London in 1968 where he worked as a
recital pianist and soloist, besides maintaining and
consolidating his reputation as a leading British composer.
He also continued in freelance musical criticism until 1974.
His career as a pianist has subsequently taken him all over
the world, and his repertoire still shows his wide range of
interests, from Pinto and Clementi to contemporary works.
His recordings of the complete sonatas of Haydn and the
complete piano music of Nielsen have received wide acclaim;
he has also given the British premiere of the difficult
piano concerto by John Corigliano and the Danish premiere of
the Delius Piano Concerto.

He has in recent years found increasing inspiration
in landscapes such as the English Lake District, which
resulted in his brass band piece Cloudcatcher Fells (W168).
During the last few years he has also written a series of
works inspired by deserts: Scenes in America Deserta (W124)
was commissioned by the King's Singers and performed in the
United States. Rain forests form another inspiration:
Rainforest II (W101) was performed by Hakan Hardenberger at
the 1987 Harrogate Festival.

The composer's fascination with fire reappeared in
his most recent orchestral work, Fire at Durilgai (W26),
written in response to a commission from the BBC in 1988.
His inspiration was in fact a bush fire, which was featured
in Patrick White's Australian novel The Tree of Man.

Further evidence of McCabe's practical approach to
music is also manifest in other ways. He has chaired the
Association of Professional Composers, presided over the
Incorporated Society of Musicians, and sat on the Performing
Right Society's general council. In August 1991, he will
have completed eight years as Director of the London College
of Music, which has offered further scope.

In conclusion, it is worth quoting a paragraph from
a 1973 interview which aptly summarises his present status:

> McCabe has never belonged to one of
> the nebulous groups which composers
> are apt to form, or in which they tend
> to be placed, and it is possible that
> the unorthodox nature of his education
> and musical studies may have contributed
> to the artistic independence, but not
> isolation, of his present position. (7)

Notes

1.   "McCabe — man of music."   Interview   with   John
        Falding: Birmingham Post, 22 September 1973, p.6.

2.   The (short) score of Symphony No. 2 in C still exists
        in the composer's archive.   It is in four
        movements, the last consisting of a theme and six
        variations.   The duration of the whole work is
        indicated as 54 minutes.

3.   "McCabe — man of music."

4.   Contemporary works...list now in the BBC Written
        Archives Centre, Caversham.

5.   Letter from Hartmann to McCabe, dated 15 May 1959, now
        in the composer's archive.

6.   "McCabe — man of music."

7.   Ibid.

Works and Performances

"See" references, e.g., SEE: B133, identify citations in the
"Bibliography" section.

OPERA

W1.   THE PLAY OF MOTHER COURAGE (1974)

        Chamber opera in five scenes. Libretto by Monica
        Smith from the book by Grimmelshausen.

        Prologue (Allegro)

        Scene 1: Interior of a military tent, or lonely
                  field lodgings. In a curtained or draped
                  bed, Courage and her husband of one night
                  are sleeping off the effects of their
                  wedding party the evening before.

        Scene 2: Courage as a whore. This can be the same
                  setting as before, but now is the scene of
                  a drinking party and debauch, with
                  officers   ...   and   whores.   (Allegro
                  Marcato)

        Interlude (Agitato)

        Scene 3: A battle field in the aftermath of battle.
                  Corpses, signs of fire - blasted, like a
                  scene in Flanders in World War 1.

        Parenthesis (Allegro Deciso)

        Interlude

        Scene 4: A room in a castle prepared for a banquet,
                  with a high table and lower
                  one (s). Various courtiers of both sexes
                  are scattered about, in conversation while
                  waiting for the appearance of the Court.

        Scene 5: Introduction (Adagio)

Curtain up. The edge of a desolate, half-ruined hamlet, on a snow-covered heath. The cottages are fire-blackened with scorched thatch. They look deserted .... (Allegretto)

Commissioned by Opera Nova

1 principal role (mezzo-soprano), 39 other parts and orchestra: 1.1.1.1/1.1.1.0/2 perc piano/ strings: 1.1.1.1.1

Duration: 1 hour 55 minutes

Publication: unpublished, but handled by Novello

Premiere: Middlesbrough, Little Theatre, 3 October 1974; Opera Nova, conducted by Iris Lemare.

SEE: B340, B364

BALLETS

Dance Macabre: Ballet

See under SYMPHONY NO.1 (W33a)

Die Fenster: Ballet

See under THE CHAGALL WINDOWS (W5a)

W2.   MARY, QUEEN OF SCOTS (1975)

Ballet in two acts. Scenario by Nöel Goodwin. Choreography by Peter Darrell.

ACT ONE

Scene 1: A danced tennis 'match' between four male courtiers (Allegro) who wield the small racquets of the period (Giocoso)

Interlude: The Voyage to Scotland (Moderato, con movimento)

Scene 2: The Palace of Holyrood (Andantino Soave)

An Entertainment (Allegro Moderato)

Interlude (Andante)

Scene 3: The Queen's Chamber
(L'istesso tempo)

ACT TWO

Scene 1: An open, non-specific, location suggesting a park or meadow....

Country Dance (Andante)

Pantomime (Allegretto Giocoso)

Scene 2: A Courtyard of the Palace of Holyrood (Allegro moderato)

Mary/Bothwell Pas de Deux (Andante)

Double Pas de Trois (Vivo Decisamente)

Interlude (Andante Ruvido)

Scene 3: An enclosed castle chamber (Andante)

Vision of Elizabeth

Vision of James in Scots Court (Allegro ironico)

Threnody (Lento)

<u>Scene 4</u>:   A bare stage.... (Adagio)

Commissioned by Scottish Ballet

1.1+1.1.1/2.2.1.0/2 perc celesta harp/strings

Duration : 2 hours 15 minutes

Publication: unpublished, but handled by Novello

Premiere: Glasgow, Theatre Royal, 3 March 1976; the
          Scottish Ballet; Orchestra conducted by
          Terence Kern.

SEE: B66, B383

DERIVED WORKS:

W2a   <u>MARY, QUEEN OF SCOTS</u>: Orchestral Suite

No. 1 (1976)

Consisting of:

1. Introduction and Tennis Match (Lento)
2. Courtly Dance for Mary (L'istesso tempo)
3. Mary and Bothwell (Andante)
4. Dance of the Four Maries (Allegro leggiero)
5. Mourning Dance (Lento)
6. Mary and the Conspirators (Vivo)

1.1.1.1 (or 2.2.2.2)/2.2.1.0 (or 4.2.3 or 2.1)/
timp(opt) 2 perc celesta harp/strings

Duration: 19 minutes

Publication: unpublished, but handled by Novello

Premiere: London, Queen Elizabeth Hall, 16 March
          1987; the Purcell School Orchestra,
          conducted by Colin Durrant.

W2b   <u>MARY, QUEEN OF SCOTS</u>: Orchestral Suite

No.2 (1976)

Consisting of:

1. Crowd Dance (Allegro Moderato)
2. Mary in Captivity (Andante)
3. The Courtiers (Andantino Suave-Allegro Pesante)
4. Riccio's Lute Dance (Allegro Leggiero)
5. Mary and Darnley (Lento)
6. Double Pas de trois (Vivo Decisamente)

1.1.1.1 (or 2.2.2.2)/2.2.1.0 (or 4.2.3 or 2.1)/timp
(opt) 2perc celesta harp/strings

Duration: 22 minutes

Publication: unpublished, but handled by Novello

Premiere: Harlow (Essex), Mark Hall School, 23 October 1988; the Harlow Youth Orchestra, conducted by George Caird.

W2c   TWO DANCES FOR STRINGS AND HARP FROM MARY, QUEEN OF SCOTS (1977)

Duration: 5½ minutes

Publication: unpublished, but handled by Novello

Notturni ed Alba: Ballet

See under NOTTURNI ED ALBA (W30a)

Shadow Reach: Ballet

See under SYMPHONY NO.2 (W34a)

W3.   THE TEACHINGS OF DON JUAN (1973)

Ballet, with baritone and chamber ensemble. Text by Monica Smith, from the book by Carlos Castenada. Choreography by Suzanne Hywel.

Pupil is seated or kneeling in front of Don Juan (Adagio)
Dance with Fear (Tempo primo)
Dance with Self Assurance (Allegro deciso)
Dance with Power (Vivo)
Dance with Old Age (Lento)
Pupil starts to search for benevolent spot
Pupil finds benevolent spot
Pupil searches for enemy spot
Fear attacks - Old Age attacks
Power attacks
Enemies converge in united attack on pupil
Devil's Weed appears
Dance with the Devil's Weed (Allegro)
Crow spirits of Don Juan and pupil emerge from shadows behind them and dance in imitation flight (Vivo)
Crow spirits are joined by three other crows
Crow spirits merge back into shadows
Entry of sorceress
Pupil is offered payote but refuses (Allegro)
Pupil eats payote as Don Juan and sorceresses start this dance, slowly increasing in intensity
The eye of a great bee appears, in gold and black (Andante)

Blackness, and then the appearance of a black lake
and rushing water
The sourceresses worships Mescalito (Largo)
The sorceresses resumes dancing, and dances off with
Mescalito (Vivace)
Mescalito is suddenly picked out by spotlight....
(Andante)
Pupil dances increasingly ecstatic dance (Vivo)
The pupil collapses
A vision of the pupil as an old man separates from
his body and shuffles off-stage (Lento)

Commissioned by the Northern Dance Theatre

1.0.1.0/1.1.0.0/2 perc/strings

Duration: 36 minutes

Publication: unpublished, but handled by Novello

Premiere: Manchester, Northern College, 30 May 1973;
          Northern Dance Theatre; Chamber Orchestra
          and Patrick McGuigan (baritone), conducted
          by Christopher Robins.

SEE: B179

ORCHESTRAL

Basse Danse: version for orchestra

See under   BASSE DANSE (W39a)

W4.   BURLESQUE (1966)

Overture for Orchestra

2.2.2.2/2.2.3.0/timp. 2 perc/strings

Duration: c. 7 minutes

Publication: British and Continental Music Agencies Ltd., 1968

Premiere: Lewisham; Lewisham Philharmonic Orchestra, conducted by Barry Freer.

Notes: See also W27

W5.   THE CHAGALL WINDOWS (1974)

For Orchestra

Consisting of:

Reuben (Largo)
Simeon
Levi
Judah (Allegro deciso)
Zebulun (Andante con moto)
Issachar
Dan (Lento)
Gad (Allegro feroce)
Asher (Andante)
Naphtali (Vivo e Leggiero)
Joseph (Moderato)
Benjamin (Allegro strepitoso)

Commissioned by the Halle Concerts Society

3+1.3+1.3+1.3+1/4.4.3.1/ 4 perc piano + celesta harp/strings

Dedicated to Jimmie and Nancy

Duration: c. 30 minutes

Publication: Novello & Co. Ltd., 1975

Premiere: Manchester, Free Trade Hall, 9 January 1975; the Halle Orchestra, conducted by James Loughran.

First London: Royal Festival Hall, 21 March 1975;
       the Halle Orchestra, conducted by James
       Loughran.

RECORDINGS: D5

SEE: B43, B114, B175, B328, B334

DERIVED WORK:

W5a   DIE FENSTER (1980)

       Ballet to music of The Chagall Windows.

       Choreography by Rosemary Hellewell.

       Premiere: Stuttgart (West Germany), 16 February
             1980; the Stuttgart Ballet.

W6.   CHAMBER CONCERTO FOR VIOLA, CELLO AND ORCHESTRA
       (1965)

       1. Aria and Dance (Lento)
       2. Toccata and Trio (Allegro vivo Andantino)
       3. Finale (Lento)

       Commissioned by Andrew Thomas and Martin Robinson

       2+1.1.2.2/4.2.3.1/ 4 perc piano + celesta/strings
       (min.) 0.0.4.4.6

       Dedicated to my good friends Andrew and Martin

       Duration: c. 30½ minutes

       Publication: unpublished, but handled by Novello

       Premiere: unable to trace

       Manuscript: it is signed by the composer and dated:
       München November 1964 – February 1965. It is
       described as "Opus 36".

W7.   CONCERTANTE FOR HARPSICHORD AND CHAMBER ENSEMBLE
       (1965)

       1. Elegia (Adagio)
       2. Capriccio (Lento)
       3. Toccata (Allegro Moderato ma Vigoroso)

       Commissioned by the Sandon Studios Society,
       Liverpool

1.1.1.1/1.1.0.0/2 perc/strings (1.1.1.1.1)

Dedicated to the Sandon Club, Liverpool

Duration: 18 minutes

Publication: unpublished, but handled by Novello

Premiere: Liverpool, Bluecoat Hall (School Lane), 18
          December 1965; Thomas Wess (harpsichord)
          and the Sandon Ensemble, conducted by
          David Connolly.

SEE: B35, B84, B168, B310

W8.   <u>CONCERTANTE MUSIC</u> (1968)

       For Orchestra

       1. Prelude (Allegretto Pesante)
       2. Capriccio (Giocoso)
       3. Chorale with Variations: In Memoriam M.L.K.
          (Lento)
       4. Rondo (Allegro)

Commissioned by Newton Park College of Education,
for performance at their Bath Festival concert, 1968

3+1.3.3.2/4.3.3.0/ 6 perc piano/strings

Dedicated to Penny and George

Duration: 24 minutes

Publication: Novello & Co. Ltd., 1970

Premiere: Bath, the Abbey, 24 June 1968; Newton Park
          College of Education Orchestra, conducted
          by George Odam.

SEE: B1, B164, B174, B190, B228, B326, B330

W9.   <u>CONCERTANTE VARIATIONS ON A THEME OF NICHOLAS MAW</u>
       (1970)

       For String Orchestra (4.4.2.2.1)

       The theme is derived from Nicholas Maw's song
       cycle for voice and piano <u>The Voice of Love</u>

       Moderato – Allegro marcato – Lento – Largo –
       Allegro leggiero – Andante – Allegro deciso –
       Maestoso

Duration: 18 minutes

Publication: Novello & Co. Ltd., 1976

Premiere: Bristol, Colston Hall, 3 March 1971;
Bournemouth Symphony Orchestra, conducted
by Zdenek Macal.

SEE: B331

OTHER VERSION:

W9a   CONCERTANTE VARIATIONS ON A THEME OF NICHOLAS MAW:
Arrangement for 11 Solo Strings (1987)

    (3.3.2.2.1)

Publication: unpublished but handed by Novello

Premiere: Southampton, the Guildhall, 7 February
1989; the Guildhall String Ensemble,
directed by Robert Salter.

First London: Wigmore Hall, 9 February 1989, the
Guildhall String Ensemble, directed by
Robert Salter.

W10.   CONCERTINO FOR PIANO DUET AND ORCHESTRA (1968)

    Andante – Giocoso – Andantino – Giocoso

Commissioned by Mr and Mrs Norman Patrick for the
1969 Farnham Festival

2.2.2.1/2.2.2.0/timp 2 perc/strings

Dedicated to Christopher Latham and the orchestra of
Frensham Heights School, Farnham

Duration: 10 minutes

Publication: Novello & Co Ltd., 1970

Premiere: Farnham, Frensham Heights School, 11 May
1969; Frank Wibaut and Christian
Rutherford (piano duet) with the School
Orchestra, conducted by Christopher
Latham.

SEE: B381

W11.   CONCERTO FOR CHAMBER ORCHESTRA (1962)

    1.   Introduzione (Allegro Moderato)
    2.   Capriccio   (Allegro)
    3.   Scherzo   (Giocoso)
    4.   Notturno   (Andante – Lento)
    5.   Toccata

1.2.2.2/2.0.0.0/perc(opt)/strings

Duration: 13 minutes

Publication: unpublished

Premiere: Doncaster; Royal Manchester College of Music Chamber Orchestra, conducted by David Jordan.

REVISED VERSION:

W11a   Minor amendments were made to the score by the composer in 1968.

Premiere: London, Royal Festival Hall, 5 July 1968, the New Cantata Orchestra, conducted by James Stobart.

SEE: B74, B319, B380

W12.   <u>CONCERTO FOR CLARINET AND ORCHESTRA</u> (1977)

1. Moderato
2. Andante
3. Moderato
4. Vivo

Commissioned by the Scottish Philharmonic Society for the Scottish Chamber Orchestra with funds from the Scottish Arts Council

2.1.1.1/2.0.0.0/timp harp/strings

Dedicated to Janet Hilton

Duration: c. 13 minutes

Publication: unpublished, but handled by Novello

Premiere: Glasgow, the Kelvin Hall, 26 June 1978; Janet Hilton (clarinet) and the Scottish Chamber Orchestra, conducted by Roderick Brydon.

First London: Royal Albert Hall, 7 September 1979; Janet Hilton (clarinet) and the Scottish Chamber Orchestra, conducted by Tamas Vasary.

SEE: B186

W13.   <u>CONCERTO FOR FLUTE AND ORCHESTRA</u> (1989-90)

Allegro vivo - Maestoso -
Adagio

Moderato – Andante flessibile – Moderato –
Andante flessibile – Vivo – Moderato –
Andante flessibile – Andante con moto –
Allegro deciso

Commissioned by the London Symphony Orchestra with
funds provided by Shell UK

3.3.3.3/4.3.3.1/timp 3   perc/harp/strings

Dedicated to James Galway

Duration: 24 minutes

Publication: unpublished, but handled by Novello

Premiere: London, Barbican Hall, 20 September 1990;
James Galway (flute) and the London
Symphony Orchestra, conducted by Michael
Tilson Thomas

W14.   CONCERTO FOR OBOE D'AMORE AND CHAMBER ORCHESTRA
(1972)

1. Andante
2. Vivo
3. Lento

Commissioned by the 1972 Portsmouth Festival

1+1.2.2.2/2.1.1.0/strings

Dedicated by Jennifer Paull

Duration: 14 minutes

Publication: unpublished, but handled by Novello

Premiere: Portsmouth, Central Hall, 26 April 1972;
Jennifer Paull (oboe d'amore) and the
Havant Chamber Orchestra, conducted by
Peter Craddock.

SEE: B119, B339

W15.   CONCERTO FOR ORCHESTRA (1982)

Deciso – Adagio –
Scherzino (Allegro vivo) –
Romanze (Andante) –
Intermezzo (Giocoso) –
Largo – Allegro deciso – Allegro marcato –
Pesante

Commissioned by the London Philharmonic Orchestra
for their 50th anniversary season, with the aid of
funds provided by the Arts Council of Great Britain

3+1.3.3.3/4.3.3.1/timp 3perc piano + celesta harp/
strings

Dedicated to the London Philharmonic Orchestra, in
celebration of their 50th anniversary

Duration: c. 24 minutes

Publication: Novello & Co. Ltd., 1987

Premiere: London, Royal Festival Hall, 10 February
          1983; the London Philharmonic Orchestra,
          conducted by Georg Solti.

First USA:Chicago, Orchestra Hall (Michigan Ave), 3
          May 1984; Chicago Symphony Orchestra,
          conducted by Georg Solti.

SEE: B31, B299, B313, B320, B333, B360

W16.   CONCERTO NO.1 FOR PIANO AND ORCHESTRA (1966)

1. Largo
2. Vivo
3. Lento – Cadenza – Allegretto – Maestoso –
   Tempo 1
4. Giocoso – Danzato – Giocoso

Commissioned by the Southport Festival Committee for
the 1967 Festival

2+1.2.2.2/4.2.3.1/timp 3 perc harp/strings

Dedicated to the people of the Borough of Southport

Duration: c. 30 minutes

Publication: Novello & Co. Ltd., 1967

Premiere: Southport, Floral Hall, 19 May 1967; John
          McCabe (piano) and the Royal Liverpool
          Philharmonic Orchestra, conducted by
          Charles Groves.

The work is described as "Opus 43" on the printed
full score

SEE: B22, B34, B153, B166, B181

W17.   CONCERTO NO.2 FOR PIANO AND ORCHESTRA – 'SINFONIA
       CONCERTANTE' (1970)

    In seven sections played without a break

Commissioned by the Northern Sinfonia with funds
provided by the Calouste Gulbenkian Foundation

1.2.2.2/2.0.0.0/strings (this orchestration includes a concertino of 9 instruments)

Duration: c. 22 minutes

Publication: unpublished, but handled by Novello

Premiere: Middlesbrough, the Town Hall, 23 November 1971; John McCabe (piano) and the Northern Sinfonia, conducted by Rudolf Schwarz.

First London: Queen Elizabeth Hall, 26 November 1971; John McCabe (piano) and the Northern Sinfonia, conducted by Rudolf Schwarz.

SEE: B72, B98, B347

OTHER VERSION:

W17a   ARRANGEMENT FOR 3 PIANOS

Publication: unpublished but handled by Novello

W18.   CONCERTO NO.3 FOR PIANO AND ORCHESTRA (DIALOGUES) (1976)

Part One: Moderato - Allegro -
          Andante (Intermezzo) -
          Tempo comenciato

Part Two: Andante fessible -
          Allegro moderato

Commissioned by and dedicated to Ilan Rogoff

3+1.3.3+1.3+1/4.3.3.1/timp 3perc celesta harp/strings

Duration: c. 37 minutes

Publication: Novello & Co Ltd., 1981

Premiere: Liverpool, Philharmonic Hall, 5 August 1977; Ilan Rogoff (piano) and the Royal Liverpool Philharmonic Orchestra, conducted by Charles Groves.

SEE: B37, B42, B338

REVISED VERSION:

W18a   The concerto was revised in 1977 - percussion being added to the beginning of the last movement.

W19.   CONCERTO No.1 FOR VIOLIN AND ORCHESTRA - 'SINFONIA CONCERTANTE' (1959)

1.   Fantasia: Lento - Allegro moderato -
                 Lento Maestoso - Allegro
2.   Capriccio: Vigoroso
3.   Chaconne: Largo e mesto
4.   Epilogue with variants: Allegro comodo e
     piacevole - Feroce - Lento - Epilogue

2+1.2.2.2/4.2.3.1/timp 3 perc harp/strings

Duration: c. 29 minutes

Publication: Novello & Co. Ltd., 1968
   (Solo part with piano reduction)

Premiere: Manchester, Free Trade Hall, 5 March 1963;
          Martin Milner (violin) and the Halle
          Orchestra, conducted by Maurice Handford.

The work is described as "Opus 2" on the printed
score

SEE: B13, B103

W20.   CONCERTO No.2 FOR VIOLIN AND ORCHESTRA (1979)

1.   Moderato
2.   (Dances) - Lento
              - Vivo, ma non troppo presto
              - Presto
              - Tempo primo
              - Giocoso
3.   Con moto, poco pesante - Lento

Commissioned by (and dedicated to) Erich Gruenberg
with the aid of funds provided by the Arts Council

3.3+1.3.3/4.3.3.1/timp 3 perc celesta harp/strings

Duration: 38 minutes

Publication: unpublished, but handled by Novello

Premiere: Birmingham, the Town Hall, 20 March 1980;
          Erich Gruenberg (violin) and the City of
          Birmingham Symphony Orchestra, conducted
          by Christopher Seaman.

First London: Royal Festival Hall, 21 March 1980;
          Erich Gruenberg (violin) and the City of
          Birmingham Symphony Orchestra, conducted
          by Christopher Seaman.

SEE: B58, B82, B108, B118, B305, B312, B361

REVISED VERSION:

W20a   The   concert   was   revised   after   the   first performances : the doubling was taken out and adjustments made to the orchestration.

W21.   CONCERTO FUNEBRE FOR VIOLA AND SMALL ORCHESTRA (1962)

1. Prefazione   (Lento)
2. Elegia I   (Lento Rapsodico)
3. Notturno   (Allegretto Misterioso)
4. Elegia II   (Largo - Lento Espressivo)
5. Cadenza   (Molto Rubato)
6. Elegia III   (Lento Rapsodico)

0.2.0.0/2.0.0.0/strings

Duration: 13 minutes

Publication: unpublished

Premiere: Glasgow, September 1971; James Durant (viola) and the BBC Scottish Symphony Orchestra, conducted by Andrew Davies.

Manuscript: It is signed by the composer and dated 16 April 1962.

W22.   DIVERTIMENTO No.1.

For Clarinet and Double String Orchestra (1958-59)

1. Toccata - Fantasia (Lento)
2. Chaconne (Andante con moto)
3. Rondo Burlesca (Allegro giocoso)

Duration: c. 13 minutes

Publication: unpublished

Premiere: unable to trace

W23.   DIVERTIMENTO No.2.

For Flute, Oboe (or 2nd flute or clarinet) and Strings (1959)

1. Fantasia (Andante)
2. Chorale   (Feroce - Calmo)
   leading into
3. Finale   (Allegro giocoso)

Commissioned by the Liverpool Institute Chamber Group

Duration: unable to trace

Publication: unpublished

Premiere: Liverpool, Institute Music Club, 25 March 1960; Liverpool Institute Chamber Group, conducted by John McCabe.

REVISED VERSION:

W23a   The Divertimento was revised by the composer in 1961

Premiere: Liverpool, Institute Music Club, 29 March 1962; Liverpool Institute Chamber Group.

W24.   DOUBLE CONCERTO FOR OBOE, CLARINET AND ORCHESTRA (1987-88)
        Largo - Vivo - Andante - Allegro - Lento - Allegro Deciso - Lento

Commissioned by English Heritage for performance at their open air summer concerts in 1988

2.2.2.2/2.2.0.0/timp/strings

Dedicated to Michael Webber

Duration: c. 20 minutes

Publication: unpublished, but handled by Novello

Premiere: Hampstead (London), Kenwood Lakeside and Marble Hill Waterside, 25 June 1988; Nicholas Daniel (oboe), Joy Farrell (clarinet) and the London Mozart Players, conducted by Nicholas Cleobury.

Manuscript:"Night with her train of stars" (W.E. Henley) appears at the head of the score.

W25.   ELEGY FOR STRING ORCHESTRA (1958)

        Lento

1st and 2nd violins, violas, cellos and double basses

Duration: c. 6½ minutes

Publication: unpublished

Premiere: unable to trace

Manuscript: The following note appears on the score: 'This work was composed on Good Friday 1958, and scored during June 1958.'

W26.   FIRE AT DURILGAI (1988)

     For Orchestra

Commissioned by the British Broadcasting Corporation

3.3.3.3/4.3.3.1/timp 3 perc harp/strings

Dedicated to Edward Downes and the BBC Philharmonic
Orchestra

Duration: c. 20 minutes

Publication: unpublished, but handled by Novello

Premiere: Manchester, the Free Trade Hall, 13
            January 1989; the BBC Philharmonic
            Orchestra, conducted by Edward Downes.

First London: Royal Albert Hall, 15 August 1989; the
            BBC Philharmonic Orchestra, conducted by
            Edward Downes.

SEE: B67, B96, B156, B176, B303, B308

W27.   HOLIDAY OVERTURE (1958)

     For Orchestra

     Allegro con brio

2.2.2.2/4.2.3.1/3 perc/strings

Duration: c. 6½ minutes

Publication: unpublished

Premiere: unable to trace

Notes: The second subject of this work was later
           used in Burlesque (W4)

W28.   JUBILEE SUITE (1977)

     For Orchestra

     1. Prelude   (Allegro Giocoso)
     2. Lullaby   (Andantino Soave)
     3. Jig   (Giocoso)
     4. Fugue   (Andante)
     5. Finale   (Allegro Vigoroso)

The Prelude was commissioned by the Cultural
Committee for the London Celebrations of the Silver
Jubilee of H.M. Queen Elizabeth II. It was
afterwards suggested to the composer that he should
make it the first movement of a little Suite, and

the same Committee commissioned him to do so —
however, by the time all this had been accomplished
the celebrations were over, so the remaining
movements remained unperformed until 1986.

3+1.3.3.3/4.3.3.1/timp   3   perc   celesta   (opt.)/
strings

Duration: Prelude — c.   1¼ minutes (version for
brass and percussion)
        — c.   2½ minutes (version for
full orchestra)
   Whole   — c.   12 minutes

Publication: unpublished, but handled by Novello

Premiere: Prelude — London, Royal Festival Hall, 17
April 1977; the London Symphony Orchestra,
conducted by Andre Previn.

Suite   — Hampstead (London), Kenwood
Concert Bowl, 14 June 1986; the London
Philharmonic Orchestra, conducted by
Norman del Mar.

SEE: B64

The Lion, the Witch and the Wardrobe:

Orchestral suite

See under THE LION, THE WITCH AND THE WARDROBE
(W146a)

Mary, Queen of Scots: ORCHESTRAL SUITES

See under Ballets (W2a and W2b)

W29.   METAMORPHOSEN FOR HARPSICHORD AND ORCHESTRA (1968)

Andante —
Adagio Movendo —
Allegro Marcato —
Presto

Commissioned by the Royal Liverpool Philharmonic
Society

2+1.2+1.2.2/2.2.2.1/4 perc celesta harp/strings

Dedicated to Charles Groves and the Royal
Philharmonic Orchestra

Duration: c.   22 minutes

Publication: unpublished, but handled by Novello

Premiere: Liverpool, Philharmonic Hall, 19 February
1972; John McCabe (harpsichord) and the
Royal Liverpool Philharmonic Orchestra,
conducted by Charles Groves.

SEE: B36, B194, B318, B337

W30.   NOTTURNI ED ALBA (1970)

For Soprano and Orchestra
Text: Medieval Latin. English version by Helen
Waddell.

1. Hymnus ante sommus - Predentius (Andante)
2. Te vigilans oculis - MS of Beauvais (Lento)
3. Somnia - Petronius Arbiter (Agitato)
4. Alba - 10th Century MS (Lento)

Commissioned by the Herefordshire Arts Association
with funds made available by the Midlands
Association for the Arts for the 1970 Three Choirs
Festival

3+2.3+1.3+2.3/4.2.3.1/harp   3   perc   piano   +
celesta/strings

Dedicated to Sheila Armstrong

Duration: 21 minutes

Publication: Novello & Co Ltd., 1971

Premiere: Hereford, the Cathedral Choir of Our Lady
and St. Ethelbert, 26 August 1970; Sheila
Armstrong (soprano) and the City of
Birmingham Symphony Orchestra, conducted
by Louis Fremaux.

First London: Royal Festival Hall, 9 December 1971;
Sheila Armstrong (soprano) and the London
Symphony Orchestra, conducted by Andre
Previn.

First USA:Minnesota, Orchestra Hall, 19 February
1975; Barbara Brandt (soprano) and the
Minnesota Orchestra, conducted by Yehudi
Menuhin.

RECORDINGS: D17

SEE: B63, B95, B98, B187, B199, B352, B377

DERIVED WORK:

W30a   NOTTURNI ED ALBA

Ballet performed by the Munster State Ballet in April 1976, at Westfallen, West Germany

Sam: theme music

see under SAM (W163a)

W31.   THE SHADOW OF LIGHT (1978)

For Orchestra

Lento

1. Dances - Gavot
            Hornpipe
            Jigg (Giocoso)
            Minuet (Andante)

2. Sports (Hunting) (Deciso)
   Cards   (Leggiero)
   Horse Racing   (Vivo)

   Adagio

3. Scenes   Pastorale
            Alla Marcia (Recruiting March)
            Romance (Grazioso)

4. Fugue and Quodlibet (Energico)

Commissioned by the Royal Philharmonic Orchestra to celebrate the Bicentenary of the death of William Boyce, 1979

3+1.3.3.2/4.3.3.1/timp 3 perc harp/strings

Dedicated to the memory of Charles Cudworth, formerly Curator of the Pendlebury Music Library, Cambridge

Duration: 23 minutes

Publication: unpublished, but handled by Novello

Premiere: London, the Royal Festival Hall, 6 December 1979; the Royal Philharmonic Orchestra, conducted by John Pritchard.

Manuscript:A note in the manuscript says: The title is taken from Atalanta in Calydon by Swinburne:
"Night, the shadow of light,
And Life, the shadow of death."

SEE: B5, B125

W32.   SONATA ON A MOTET (1976)

   For String Orchestra (minimum 4.3.2.2.1).

   The theme is derived from Thomas Tallis's 40-part
   motet Spem in Alium

   Adagio-Allegro Marcato-Lento-Vivo e leggiero –
   Lento-Vivo e leggiero –
   Lento-Adagio-Allegro deciso
   (fugue)-Adagio

Commissioned by the Manchester Camerata, with
financial assistance from the Gulbenkian Foundation

Duration: 19 minutes

Publication: Novello & Co Ltd., 1977

Premiere: Manchester, Royal Northern College of
          Music, 20 March 1976; the Manchester
          Camerata, conducted by Frank Cliff.

See: B93, B177, B356

W33.   SYMPHONY No. 1 (ELEGY) (1965)

   For Orchestra

   Prelude: Lento moderato
   Dance: Allegro molto
   Elegy: Adagio-Allegro vivo-Adagio

Commissioned by the Halle Concerts Society

3+1.3.3.3/4.3.3.1/timp 3 perc celesta harp/strings

Dedicated to Sir John Barbirolli and the members of
the Halle Orchestra

Duration: 20 minutes

Publication: Novello & Co Ltd., 1966

Premiere: Cheltenham, the Town Hall, 4 July 1966;
          the Halle Orchestra, conducted by John
          Barbirolli.

First London: Royal Festival Hall, 8 July 1966; the
              Halle Orchestra, conducted by John
              Barbirolli.

Manuscript: The symphony is described as 'Opus 40'

RECORDINGS: D23

SEE: B14, B26, B29, B77, B142, B146, B169, B343,
     B368, B375, B384

DERIVED WORK:

W33a   DANCE MACABRE (1968)

Ballet to music of Symphony No. 1

Choreography by Peter Wright

Premiere: London, Sadlers Wells Theatre, 6 March
1968; members of the Western Theatre
Ballet. Music director and conductor:
Kenneth Alwyn.

SEE: B116

W34.   SYMPHONY No.2 (1971)

For Orchestra

Vivo – Andante – Allegrissimo – Lento – Vivo

Commissioned by the John Feeney Trust for the City
of Birmingham Symphony Orchestra.

3+1.3+1.3+1.3+1/4.3.3.1/timp perc piano + celesta
harp/strings

Dedicated to Louis Fremaux and the City of
Birmingham Symphony Orchestra

Duration: 22 minutes

Publication: Novello & Co Ltd., 1973

Premiere: Birmingham, the Town Hall, 25 September
1971; the City of Birmingham Symphony
Orchestra, conducted by Louis Fremaux.

First London: Royal Festival Hall, 10 March 1972;
the City of Birmingham Symphony Orchestra,
conducted by Louis Fremaux.

First USA:Troy (New York), Music Hall of Troy Second
Bank, 20 May 1983; Albany Symphony
Orchestra, conducted by Julius Hagyi.

RECORDINGS: D24

SEE: B83, B99, B185, B353

DERIVED WORK:

W34a   SHADOW REACH (1978)

Ballet to music of Symphony No.2, with small
additions from the Hartmann Variations (W37),
based on Henry James's novel The Turn of the
Screw.

Choreography by Dormy Reiter-Soffer

Premiere: Dublin, the Abbey Theatre, 19 June 1978;
          members of the Irish Ballet Company.

SEE: B117, B154, B275

W35.   SYMPHONY No.3 (HOMMAGES) (1977-78)

    For Orchestra

Flessibile
Adagio [Fantasia]
Moderato [Fugue-Variations]

Commissioned by the Royal Philharmonic Orchestra

3+1.3.3.3+1/4.3.3.1/timp 3 perc piano+celesta harp/
strings

Dedicated to Charles Dutoit

Duration: 24 minutes

Publication: Novello & Co Ltd., 1983

Premiere: London, the Royal Festival Hall, 11 July
          1978; the Royal Philharmonic Orchestra,
          conducted by Charles Dutoit.

Notes: A note in the printed score mentions that
          the symphony contains direct quotations
          from two composers – Haydn (the slow
          movement of the String Quartet, Opus 76,
          No.6) and Carl Nielson (Suite for Piano,
          Opus 45).

SEE: B50, B122

W36.   TUNING (1984-85)

    For Orchestra

Commissioned by the Carnegie United Kingdom Trust
for performance by the National Youth Orchestra of
Scotland in recognition of the 150th Anniversary of
the Birth of Andrew Carnegie and of European Music
Year 1985

4.4.4.4/6.5.4.2/timp 4 perc harp/strings

Dedicated to David and Sally Sternbach

Duration: 18 minutes

Publication: unpublished, but handled by Novello

Premiere: Holland,   the   Casino   theater,
          S'Hertogenbosch,   27   July   1985;   the
          National   Youth   Orchestra   of   Scotland,
          conducted by Nicholas Braithwaite.

UK Premiere:Ripon, the Cathedral Church of St. Peter
          and St. Wilfred, 5 August 1985; the
          National   Youth   Orchestra   of   Scotland,
          conducted by Nicholas Braithwaite.

RECORDINGS: D27

W37.   VARIATIONS ON A THEME OF HARTMANN (1964)

          For Orchestra

          Theme: Lento Assai - Con Passione

          Variation I   :   Elegia   (Lento)
          Variation II   :   Scherzo   (Vivo)
          Variation III   :   Intermezzo (Andante)
          Variation IV   :   Capriccio (Giocoso)
          Variation V   :   Sarabande (Andante Moderato)
          Variation VI   :   Fugue with Epilogue (Allegro -
                              Lento assai : con passione)

          The theme is taken from Symphony No.4 by Karl
          Amadeus Hartmann (1905-1963), and used by kind
          permission of Scholt's Söhne, Mainz.

          3+1.3.3.3/4.3.3.1/3 perc piano + celesta harp/
          strings

          Dedicated to the composer's mother

          Duration: 20 minutes

          Publication: Novello & Co Ltd., 1967

          Premiere: Manchester,   the   Free   Trade   Hall,   24
                    November   1965;   the   Halle   Orchestra,
                    conducted by Maurice Handford.

          First London: Royal Festival Hall, 1 November 1968;
                    the Halle Orchestra, conducted by Maurice
                    Handford.

          First USA:Pittsburgh, Heinz Hall for the Performing
                    Arts,   4   February   1977;   the   Pittsburgh
                    Symphony   Orchestra,   conducted   by   Andre
                    Previn.

          Manuscript: The work is described as "Opus 28"

          RECORDINGS: D30

          SEE: B81, B157, B162, B178, B336, B348, B357

CHAMBER AND INSTRUMENTAL

W38.   AUBADE (STUDY No 4)

>   for solo piano (1970)

>   Written for the 1970 Harrogate Festival

Duration: 7 minutes

Publication: Novello & Co Ltd., 1972

Premiere: Harrogate, the Festival Club, 10 August
          1970. John McCabe (piano).

RECORDINGS: D1

SEE: B55, B345

W39.   BASSE DANSE

>   for two pianos (1970)

Commissioned by University College, Cardiff, with
funds made available by the Welsh Arts Council

Dedicated to Ian Bruce

Duration: 12 minutes

Publication: Novello & Co Ltd., 1974

Premiere: Cardiff, the Reardon Smith Lecture
          Theatre, 12 January 1971; John McCabe and
          Ian Bruce (piano).

SEE: B47, B188

First London: Cartoon Gallery (Victoria and Albert
          Museum), 4 April 1971; John McCabe and
          Malcolm Troup (pianos).

SEE: B65, B97

DERIVED WORK:

W39a   BASSE DANSE: version for orchestra (1973)

3+1.3.3+1.3+1/4.3.3.1/timp 3 perc piano + celesta
harp/strings

Publication: unpublished, but handled by Novello

Premiere: Guildford, Civic Hall, 3 May 1975; the
Guildford Philharmonic Orchestra,
conducted by Vernon Handley.

SEE: B363

W40.   CAPRICCIO (STUDY No. 1)

for solo piano (1969)

Dedicated to Anthony Goldstone

Duration: 7 minutes

Publication: Novello & Co Ltd., 1970

Premiere: Dublin, Trinity College, 6 January 1969;
John McCabe (piano).

RECORDINGS: D4

SEE: B2, B316

Chaconne: for piano

See under FANTASIA FOR ORGAN (W66a)

Concerto No. 3 for Piano and Orchestra

– arranged for 3 pianos

See under CONCERTO NO. 3 FOR PIANO AND ORCHESTRA
(W17a)

Couples: arranged for solo piano

See under COUPLES (W152a)

W41.   FANTASY ON A THEME OF LISZT

for solo piano (1967)

Dedicated to Bernard Herrmann

Duration: 10 minutes

Publication: Novello & Co Ltd., 1968

Premiere: Cheltenham, the Town Hall, 20 July 1967;
John McCabe (piano). (A performance of
the Fantasy had been broadcast the
previous day).

First London: Purcell Room, 18 March 1975; John
   McCabe (piano).

Manuscript: The theme is the 12-note theme from the
  Faust Symphony's first movement

RECORDINGS: D12

SEE: B55, B80, B126, B376

W42. <u>FIVE BAGATELLES</u>

   for solo piano (1964)

1. Capriccio (Allegro vivo)
2. Aria (Andantino)
3. Elegia (Lento alla breve)
4. Toccata (Con brio)
5. Notturno (Adagio)

Commissioned by Robin Elkin

Dedicated to Isobel

Duration: c. 3½ minutes

Publication: Elkin & Co Ltd., 1964

Premiere: unable to trace

First London: Great Drawing Room (4 St. James's
   Square), 27 February 1967. John McCabe
   (piano).

RECORDINGS: D2

SEE: B4, B27, B127

W43. <u>FIVE IMPROMPTUS</u>

   for solo piano (1959-1960)

1. Vivo   (dated 25.12.59)
2. Lento Malincolico (dated 19. 1.60)
3. Allegro Marcato (" 29. 1.60)
4. Adagio   (" 5. 2.60)
5. Allegro con brio (" 22.11.59)

Dedicated to John Ogdon

Duration: c. 5½ minutes

Publication: Oxford University Press, 1963

  (Numbers 1 to 3 only)

Premiere: Manchester, the Royal Manchester College
of Music, 5 July 1960; John McCabe
(piano). (An examination concert)

W44.   GAUDI (STUDY No. 3)

for solo piano (1970)

Commissioned by the Cardiff Festival of 20th-Century
Music, with funds provided by the Welsh Arts Council

Dedicated to Valerie Tryon

Duration: 15 minutes

Publication: Novello & Co Ltd. 1973

Premiere: Cardiff, Festival of 20th-Century Music, 8
March 1970. Valerie Tryon (piano).

RECORDINGS: D13

SEE: B48, B139, B195

W45.   GAVOTTE

for solo piano (1950s)

Publication: unpublished

Premiere: unable to trace

W46.   HAYDN VARIATIONS

for solo piano (1982-83)

Commissioned by the City Music Society, London

Dedicated to Philip Fowke

Duration: 26 minutes

Publication: Novello & Co Ltd., 1988

Premiere: London, Goldsmith's Hall, 26 October 1983;
Philip Fowke (piano).

W47.   INTERMEZZO

for solo piano (1968)

Moderato deciso

1. Andantino
2. Con moto
3. Allegro
4. Maestoso
5. Allegro

Commissioned by Priory Boys' School Music Society, Shrewsbury, for the 1968 Shropshire Schools' Music Festival

Dedicated to David Wilde

Duration: c. 9 minutes

Publication: Novello & Co Ltd., 1971

Premiere: Shrewsbury, Priory Boys' School Hall, 26 March 1968; David Wilde (piano).

W48.   LAMENTATION RAG

for solo piano (1982)

A contribution to Homage to Haydn, the other contributors being George Benjamin, Richard Rodney Bennett, Lennox Berkeley, Robert Sherlaw Johnson and Edmund Rubbra.

Commissioned by the BBC for 1982, in celebration of the 250th Anniversary of the birth of Haydn

Duration: c. 1¼ minutes

Publication: unpublished, but handled by Novello

Premiere: London, Broadcasting House, 18 March 1982; John McCabe (piano). This recording was subsequently broadcast in Radio 3 on 31 March 1982

First USA: New York, Merkin Concert Hall, 4 January 1983; Dorothy Lewis – Griffith (piano).

Manuscript: A note by the composer is included in the manuscript – The melodic line of this short piece is entirely derived from the musical transliteration of the name FRANZ JOSEPH HAYDN. The slightly lugubrious title was chosen for two reasons:

(i) it seems to suit the nature of the piece, and

(ii) it refers to one of my favourites among early Haydn symphonies.

W49.   <u>LANDSCAPE</u>

for solo piano (1978)

Dedicated to Irit Rogoff on her birthday

Duration: unable to trace

Publication: unpublished, but handled by Novello

Manuscript: It is dated 17.11.78 and the landscape
            in question indicated as "Hills near
            Jerusalem".

W50.   <u>MOSAIC (STUDY No.6)</u>

for solo piano (1980)

Commissioned for the 1980 North Wales Festival with
the aid of funds provided by the Welsh Arts Council

Dedicated to William Mathias

Duration: c. 14 minutes

Publication: Novello & Co. Ltd., 1985

Premiere: Wales, St. Asaph's Cathedral, 25 September
          1980; John McCabe (piano).

First London: St. John's Smith Square, 25 October
              1980; John McCabe (piano).

SEE: B332

W51.   <u>MUSIC FOR PIANO</u> (1958)

1. Allegro con fuoco
2. Andantino
3. Allegretto Malincolia
4. Lento
5. Epilogue (Lento)

Duration: c. 9 minutes

Publication: unpublished

Premiere: unable to trace

Manuscript: It is signed by the composer and the
            piece composed "March, April and August
            1958".

W52.   <u>NOTHING TO IT</u> (An exercise in fives)

for solo piano (1988)

Dedicated to John Holt, on his 50th birthday

Duration: unable to trace

Publication: unpublished

Manuscript: It is dated 22 December 1988; the tempo
            indicated as "do whatever you can manage"
            and an indication that each bar should be
            repeated five times.

W53.   PARAPHRASE ON MARY, QUEEN OF SCOTS (STUDY No.5)

for solo piano (1979)

Commissioned by Kelso Music Society with the aid of
funds provided by the Scottish Arts Council

Dedicated to the Kelso Music Society

Duration: 9 minutes

Publication: Novello & Co Ltd., 1982

Premiere: Kelso, Music Society, 11 January 1980;
          John McCabe (piano).

SEE: B30

W54.   PASSACAGLIA FOR 2 PIANOS (1957)

Duration: unable to trace

Publication: unpublished

Premiere: Liverpool, Institute Music Club, 14 March
          1958; John McCabe and L.A. Naylor
          (pianos).

SEE: B20

W55.   PIANO VARIATIONS (1958)

The composer describes this piece as very
minimalist, with the main theme being a single
note - and not even finally copied out.

Duration: c. 8 minutes

Rivals, The: suite for solo piano

see <u>under</u> THE RIVALS (W162a)

W56.   <u>SONATA FOR PIANO (No.1)</u> (1957)

1. Andante
2. Andante con moto
3. Moderato

Duration: c. 13 minutes

Publication: unpublished

Manuscript: It is described as "Opus 1" and was
            written between mid June – July 1957.

W57.   <u>SONATA FOR PIANO (No.2)</u> in E minor (1957)

1. Allegro Moderato
2. Adagio Mesto

Duration: unable to trace

Publication: unpublished

Manuscript: It was written in August 1957.

W58.   <u>A SORT OF FANFARE</u>

        for solo piano (1986)

Dedicated to Richard Rodney Bennett, on his 50th
birthday (give or take a day or two)

Duration: unable to trace

Publication: unpublished

Manuscript: It is dated 25 March 1986 and marked
            'very fast'. The composer describes this
            piece as "... a take-off of one of the
            <u>Diabelli Variations</u>".

W59.   <u>SOSTENUTO (STUDY No.2)</u>

        for solo piano (1969)

Duration: 8 minutes

Publication: Novello & Co Ltd., 1972

Premiere: Bath, the Little Theatre, 25 June 1969;
          John McCabe (piano).

RECORDINGS: D21

SEE: B317

W60.   STUDY IN B-FLAT

for solo piano (1950s)

Duration: unable to trace

Publication: unpublished

Premiere: unable to trace

W61.   STUDY OF C-FLAT

for solo piano (1950s)

Duration: unable to trace

Publication: unpublished

Premiere: unable to trace

Manuscript: It is described as "Opus 11, number 3".

W62.   TOCCATA IN C

for solo piano (1950s)

Duration: unable to trace

Publication: unpublished

Premiere: unable to trace

Manuscript: It is described as 'Opus 10'.

W63.   VARIATIONS FOR PIANO (1963)

Lento - Doppio movimento - Lento maestoso - Lento
(con rubato) - Adagio - Pochissimo - piu mosso -
Poco meno mosso - Piu mosso - Grandioso - Cadenza
: rubato : maestoso

Dedicated to Gordon Green, with affection and
gratitude

Duration: c. 10 minutes

Publication: Novello & Co. Ltd., 1966

Premiere: Newcastle Upon Tyne, People's Theatre Arts
          Centre (Tyneside Music Society), 18
          February 1964; John McCabe (piano).

First London: Great Drawing Room (4 St. James's

Square), 14 March 1966; Ronald Lumsden (piano).

RECORDINGS: D29

SEE: B138, B167

W64.   DIES RESURRECTIONIS

for organ (1963)

Introduction (Maestoso)
Filius mortuus (Allegretto)
Filius in sepulchro (Andante soave)
Filius resurrectus (Vivo)

Commissioned for the inaugural recital series on the new Manchester University organ

Duration: 7 minutes

Publication: Oxford University Press, 1964
    (Assigned to Novello & Co. Ltd. in 1986)

Premiere: Manchester, Whitworth Hall (University of Manchester), 1 March 1963; Gordon Thorne (organ).

First London: Priory Church of St. Bartholomew – the – Great (Smithfield), 26 November 1963; Simon Preston (organ).

RECORDINGS: D10

SEE: B79, B104, B346

W65.   ELEGY FOR ORGAN (1965)

Commissioned by Bryan Hesford, to whom the piece is dedicated

Duration: 4 minutes

Publication: Novello & Co. Ltd., 1967

Premiere: Brecon, the Cathedral, June 1965; Bryan Hesford (organ).

Manuscript: It is described as "Opus 34".

RECORDINGS: D11

W66.   FANTASIA FOR ORGAN (1959)

Introduction (Lento)

Interlude - Come Pastorale
Allegro
Chaconne (Adagio con moto)

Commissioned by Brian Fawcett

Duration: unable to trace

Publication: unpublished

Premiere: Leeds, Parish Church, 1959 or 1960; Brian
Fawcett (organ).

DERIVED WORK:

W66a   CHACONNE

arranged for piano solo (1983)

Duration: unable to trace

Publication: unpublished

Premiere: unable to trace

W67.   JOHANNIS - PARTITA

for organ (1964)

1. Overture (Grave-Allegro vivo-Grave)
2. Intermezzo (Lento malincolica)
3. Ritornello (Vivo) Tempo I
            (Allegro giocoso) Tempo II
            (Vivo) Tempo I
            (Allegro giocoso) Tempo II
            Tempo I (Vivo)
            Grave (tempo comenciato)

Written for the Pershore Abbey Organ Week, October
1965

Dedicated to Rodney Baldwyn, who prepared the
registration

Duration: c. 10 minutes

Publication: Novello & Co. Ltd., 1965

Premiere: Pershore Abbey (Worcester) 23 October
1965; Rodney Baldwyn (organ).

First London: Parish Church of St. Mary of Eton
(Hackney), 6 April 1967; Rodney Baldwyn
(organ).

W68.   MINICONCERTO

for organ, percussion and 485 penny-whistles (1966)

Commissioned by Peter Hurford for the <u>Organ in sanity and madness</u>

Percussion includes vibraphone, 4 car horns, cymbal, Chinese block, tenor drum and 3 bongos

Duration: 8 minutes

Publication: unpublished, but handled by Novello

Premiere: London, the Royal Albert Hall, 24 September 1966; Gillian Weir (organ), James Blades and Jack Westrup (percussion) and audience, conducted by David Willcocks.

RECORDINGS: D15

W69.   <u>NOCTURNE</u>

for organ (1964)

Commissioned by Oxford University Press for <u>Modern Organ Music, Book 1</u>

Dedicated to Simon Preston

Duration: c. 5 minutes

Publication: Oxford University Press, 1965

Premiere: Cambridge, King's College, July 1965, David Willcocks (organ).

W70.   <u>PASTORALE SOSTENUTO</u>

for organ (1960)

Commissioned by Oxford University Press for <u>Easy Modern Organ Music</u>

Duration: c. 3 minutes

Publication: Oxford University Press, 1967

Premiere: unable to trace

W71.   <u>LE POISSON MAGIQUE (MEDITATION AFTER PAUL KLEE</u>)

for organ (1964)

Dedicated to Brian Runnett

Duration: c. 6 minutes

Publication: unpublished

Premiere: Bradford, St. George's Hall, 15 February
          1965; Brian Runnett (organ).

Manuscript: It is described as "Opus 32" and is
            dated 11/10/64.

RECORDINGS: D19

W72.   <u>PRELUDE</u>

for organ (1964)

Commissioned by Novello & Co. Ltd., for <u>Music Before</u>
<u>Service : 5 modern pieces for organ</u>

Duration: c. 4 minutes

Publication: Novello & Co. Ltd., 1969

Premiere: unable to trace

W73.   <u>SINFONIA FOR ORGAN</u> (1961)

Introduzione - Passacaglia - Cadenza 1-Notturno
Interludium I - Elegia - Capriccio - Cadenza II
Interludium II - Toccata

Dedicated to Gordon Thorne who commissioned the work

Duration: 17 minutes

Publication: Novello & Co. Ltd., 1966

Premiere: Armley (Leeds), Parish Church of St.
          Bartholomew, 26 June 1961; Gordon Thorne
          (organ).

Manuscript: It is described as "Opus 6".

W74.   <u>WEDDING MUSIC</u>

for organ (1963)

Written for the wedding of Mr. Gordon Sill and
Miss Beryl Wood, friends of the composer

Music for the following:

Entrance of the Bride

Interlude during the signing of the register
Exit of the Bride and Bridegroom

Duration: unable to trace

Premiere: Stretford, All Saint's Church, 10 August
1963; Brian Fawcett (organist).

W75.   BAGATELLES FOR 2 CLARINETS IN B-FLAT (1965)

1.   Con fuoco, ma non troppo allegro
2.   Andante
3.   Allegro Giocoso
4.   Fugatississimo (Allegro marcato)
5.   Adagio
6.   Bossa Nova (Allegretto soave)
7.   Crescendo (Presto possible e ritmico)
8.   Fantasy (Andantino)

Duration: 8 minutes

Publication: unpublished, but handled by Novello

Premiere: unable to trace

W76.   CANTO FOR GUITAR (1968)

Andante – Giocoso – Serenade (Lento) – Allegro e
ritmico – Andante

Commissioned by the 1968 Cardiff Festival of 20th
Century Music

Duration: 7-8 minutes

Publication: Novello & Co. Ltd., 1970

Premiere: Cardiff, the Castle, 22 April 1968;
William Gomez (guitar).

RECORDINGS: D3

SEE: B46, B115, B197

W77.   CARAVAN

for string quartet (1987-1988)

Commissioned by the Universtiy of Essex with funds
provided by the Eastern Arts Association and members
of the University's regular concert audience to
celebrate the 20th anniversary of the Gabrieli
String Quartet

Duration: 8 minutes

Publication: unpublished, but handled by Novello

Premiere: Colchester, University of Essex, 23
          February 1988; the Gabrieli String
          Quartet.

Concertante Variations on a theme of Nicholas Maw –
arr. for 11 solo strings

>   See under CONCERTANTE VARIATIONS ON A THEME OF
>   NICHOLAS MAW (W9a)

W78.   CONCERTO FOR PIANO AND WIND QUARTET (1969)

>   Maestoso – Allegro deciso – Maestoso – Lento –
>   Vivo – Lento – Allegro Marcato – Maestoso

Commissioned by the Birmingham Chamber Music Society

1.1.1.1/1.0.0.0/piano

Dedicated to Alun and Rhiannon Hoddinott

Duration: 21 minutes

Publication: Novello & Co Ltd., 1977

Premiere: Birmingham, the City Art Gallery, 21
          February 1970; the Venturi Ensemble and
          John McCabe (piano).

First London: Purcell Room, 17 April 1970; the
          Venturi Ensemble and John McCabe (piano).

SEE: B62, B86

W79.   DANCE MOVEMENTS FOR HORN, VIOLIN AND PIANO (1967)

>   1. Lento moderato
>   2. Allegro
>   3. Maestoso – Andante con moto – Maestoso
>   4. Allegro vigoroso – Andantino – Allegro vigoroso

Dedicated to the Ifor James Horn Trio

Duration: c.20 minutes

Publication: Novello & Co. Ltd., 1972

Premiere: London, Wigmore Hall, 4 December 1967; the
          Ifor James Trio.

SEE: B335

W80.   DANCE-PRELUDE FOR OBOE D'AMORE (OR CLARINET) AND
         PIANO (1971)

         Lento - Allegro giocoso

         Dedicated to Jennifer Paull

         Duration: c.4 minutes

         Publication: Novello & Co. Ltd., 1973

         Premiere: Liverpool, Empire Theatre, 24 June 1971
                   (in the presence of HM Queen Elizabeth
                   II); Jennifer Paull (oboe d'amore) and
                   John McCabe (piano).

W81.   DESERT I: LIZARD

         for flute, oboe, clarinet, bassoon and percussion
         (1981)

         Vivo - Lento - Vivo - Lento - Vivo - Lento

         Commissioned by the New Music Ensemble, Redlands
         University, California

         Dedicated to Barney Childs

         Duration: c.10 minutes

         Publication: unpublished, but handled by Novello

         Premiere: unable to trace

         First U.K.: London, The Place, 14 March 1983; the
                     Endymion Ensemble.

W82.   DESERT III: LANDSCAPE

         for violin, cello and piano (1982)

         Lento - Vivo - Lento - Deciso - Allegro - Vivace
         - Maestoso

         Commissioned by and dedicated to Earle Page College
         of the University of New England, Armidale, NSW and
         the New England Ensemble of Australia

         Duration: c.22 minutes

         Publication: Novello & Co. Ltd., 1987

         Premiere: Armidale, University Hall, 17 June 1982;
                   the New England Ensemble and John McCabe
                   (piano).

First USA: New York, the Guggenheim Museum, 24 April
        1983; the Music Group of London.

First UK: Cheltenham, the Town Hall, 6 July 1983;
        the Music Group of London.

RECORDINGS: D9

W83.   <u>DESERT IV: VISTA</u>

   for solo recorder (1983)

Dedicated to Tom Pitfield, with great affection, for
his 80th birthday, and for John Turner, whose idea
it was

Duration: c.7 minutes

Publication: unpublished, but handled by Novello

Premiere: Altrincham (Cheshire), All Saints Church,
        6 May 1983; John Turner (recorder)

SEE: B28

W84.   <u>THE GODDESS TRILOGY</u>

   for horn and piano (1973-75)

1. The Castle of Arianrhod (Allegro Vivo)
2. Floraison (Largo)
3. Shape-Shifter (Maestoso)

Dedicated to Ifor James

Duration: 28 minutes (11;9;8)

Publication: Novello & Co. Ltd., 1978

Premiere:

1. Pennsylvania, State University, 7 November 1973;
   Ifor James (horn) and John McCabe (piano).

First UK: London, Bishopsgate Institute, 4 March
        1975; Ifor James (horn) and John McCabe (piano).

2+3. Worcester, Alice Ottley School, 25 August
     1975; Ifor James (horn) and John McCabe
     (piano).

First London: Bishopsgate Institute, 4 March 1975;
     Ifor James (horn) and John McCabe (piano).

SEE: B191, B201, B353

W85. THE GREENSLEEVES GROUND

for harpsichord (1969)

Commissioned by Igor Kipnis

Duration: 7 minutes

Publication: unpublished, but handled by Novello

Premiere: unable to trace

W86. LITTLE SUITE

for trumpet and piano (1959)

1. Fanfare (Allegro)
2. Serenade (Lento malincolico)
3. Burlesque (Allegro giocoso)

Dedicated to Michael McCabe [the composer's cousin]

Duration: unable to trace

Publication: unpublished

Premiere: unable to trace

W87. MAZE DANCES

for solo violin (1973)

Allegro Deciso – Adagio – Vivo – Lento – Allegro
deciso

Commissioned by Michael Davis

Dedicated to Sue and Mike

Duration: c.13 minutes

Publication: Novello & Co. Ltd., 1976

Premiere: London, the Wigmore Hall, 15 May 1974;
Michael Davis (violin).

W88. MOVEMENTS

for clarinet, violin and cello (1964)

Lento
Allegretto
Allegro agitato
Adagio
Allegro agitato
Allegretto

Lento

Dedicated to the Gabrieli Ensemble who commissioned
the work

Duration: 12 minutes

Publication: Novello & Co. Ltd., 1967

Premiere: London, Great Drawing Room (4 St James's
        Square), 25 January 1965; Keith Puddy
        (clarinet), Kenneth Sillito (violin) and
        Keith Harvey (cello).

SEE: B44, B69, B344

REVISED VERSION:

W88a   Minor adjustments were made to the score in 1966 by
        the composer

        SEE: B85

W89.   MUSICA NOTTURNA

            for violin, viola and piano (1964)

            Lento - Andante molto - Allegro

        Dedicated to Martin Milner who commissioned the work

        Duration: c.14 minutes

        Publication: Novello & Co. Ltd., 1971

        Premiere: Manchester, Houldsworth Hall, 24 March
                1964; Martin Milner (violin), Ludmilla
                Navratil (viola) and John McCabe (piano).

        RECORDINGS: D16

        SEE: B101

W90.   NOCTURNAL

            for piano quintet (1966)

            Introduction - Nocturne 1 - Cadenza 1 - Interlude
            - Cadenza II - Nocturne II - Epilogue

        Commissioned by the Park Lane Group

        Duration: c.13 minutes

        Publication: Novello & Co. Ltd., 1967

Premiere: Lancaster, the University Concert Hall, 8 October 1970; the Lancaster Ensemble.

Manuscript: It is described as "Opus 42" and the title is a deliberate reference to John Donne's poem A Nocturnal upon St. Lucie's Day.

SEE: B92

W91.   PARTITA

for solo cello (1966)

Theme (Lento)
Marcia giocoso (Allegretto Giocoso)
Aria (Lento)
Reprise (Lento con rubato)
Jig (Vivo)
Canons (Mesto)
Marcia funebre (Lugubre)
Finale (Allegro comodo)

Dedicated to Christopher Gough who commissioned the work

Duration: c.11½ minutes

Publication: unpublished, but handled by Novello

Premiere: London the Wigmore Hall, 6 December 1966; Christopher Gough (cello).

Manuscript: It is described as "Opus 44".

RECORDINGS: D18

SEE: B57, B70, B91

W92.   PARTITA FOR STRING QUARTET (1960)

1. Lamento (Lento)
2. Fantasia (Maestoso)
3. Arioso (Lento, ma con moto)
4. Capriccio (Vivo e articulato)
5. Epilogue (Lento con movimento)

Duration: c.21 minutes

Publication: Novello & Co. Ltd., 1965

Premiere: Manchester, Contemporary Music Centre, 9 June 1961; the Royal Manchester College of Music Quartet.

Notes: The composer now regards this work as String Quartet No. 1. The first movement

(Lamento) was originally written in 1959 as a separate piece, the other four were added the following year.

SEE: B100, B304

W93.   PUEBLO

for solo double bass (1986)

Commissioned by Northwestern Arts for performance by Leon Bosch

Duration: unable to trace

Publication: unpublished, but handled by Novello

Premiere: unable to trace

W94.   QUARTET FOR OBOE AND STRINGS (1968)

Vivo –
Lento –
Fantastico –
Lento –
Agitato

Commissioned by University College, Cardiff for their weekly term-time Chamber Concerts

Dedicated to my friends and colleagues at University College, Cardiff

Duration: c.12 minutes

Publication: Novello & Co. Ltd., 1970

Premiere: Cardiff, Reardon Smith Lecture Theatre, 11 February 1969; Philip Jones (oboe) and the University Ensemble.

Manuscript: It is dated 15/12/68.

SEE: B52, B196, B198

W95.   QUARTET No. 2 FOR STRINGS (1972)

Flessible –
Vivo –
Largo –
Deciso

Commissioned by Ernest Scragg and Sons Ltd., for performance by the Delme String Quartet at the Macclesfield Arts Festival, 1972

Dedicated to Pat and Neil Chaffrey

Duration: c.12 minutes

Publication: Novello & Co. Ltd., 1975

Premiere: Macclesfield, Parish Church of St. George, 17 July 1972; the Delme Quartet.

SEE: B304

W96.   QUARTET No. 3 FOR STRINGS (1979)

1. Variants [a tribute to Alun Hoddinott who celebrated his 50th birthday in 1979]
2. Scherzo I
3. Romanza
4. Scherzo II
5. Passacaglia

Commissioned by the Fishguard Festival with funds provided by the Welsh Arts Council

Dedicated to the Gabrieli String Quartet

Duration: c.31 minutes

Publication: Novello & Co. Ltd., 1983

Premiere: Goodwick, Parish Church of St. Peter, 23 July 1979; the Gabrieli String Quartet.

SEE: B53, B304

W97.   QUARTET No. 4 FOR STRINGS (1982)

Adagio - Vigoroso - Andante - Vivo - Andante - Vivo - Lento - Moderato - Allegro - Lento

Commissioned by the Delme Quartet, with the aid of funds provided by the Arts Council of Great Britain, to celebrate the Delme Quartet's 20th Anniversary and the 250th Anniversary of the birth of Josef Haydn

Dedicated to the Delme Quartet, in honour of their 20th anniversary, and to the shade of Josef Haydn, for his 250th

Duration: 18 minutes

Publication: unpublished, but handled by Novello

Premiere: London, the Wigmore Hall, 20 October 1982; the Delme String Quartet.

SEE: B304

W98.   QUARTET No. 5 FOR STRINGS (1989)

This work is strongly influenced by Graham Sutherland's series of acquatints The Bees. There are 14 acquatints in the series and the Quartet divides into that number of sections:

LENTO FLESSIBILE: Metamorphosis: Egg, Larvae, Pupae (concluding with a kind of free cadenza)
Hatching I (marked by rising, flowing violin scales)
Hatching II
Nuptial flight (contrasting forceful chords and decoration)
The Court (with climatic chords of thematic importance)

ALLEGRO LEGGIERO: Figure of Eight Dance: Orientation to Sources of Nectar and Pollen (a light, dance-like scherzo)

ALLEGRO VIVO: Round Dance: Orientation to Sources of Nectar and Pollen (another, slightly faster scherzo)

ANDANTE: Bee and Flower (a lyrical interlude or trio)

ALLEGRETTO DECISO E MARCATO: Wild Nest Primitve Hive I (Skep) (a doomed beehive)
Primitve Hive II (these three sections marked by shared material and strong rhythmic content)

ALLEGRO DECISO: Bee Keeper (an obsessive, slightly faster movement), linking to the finale-

ALLEGRO NERVOSO: Expulsion and Killing of an Enemy (marked by irregular rhythms and a growth from piano to forte)

Fight between Workers and Drones: a vigorous, virtuosic final movement, ending with two references to the climactic chords from The Court and a final flourish.

Commissioned by the Fishguard Music Festival with funds provided by the Welsh Arts Council

Dedicated to John Davies

Duration: c.20 minutes

Publication: unpublished, but handled by Novello

Premiere: Fishguard, School Concert Hall, 23 July 1989; the Gabrieli String Quartet.

SEE: B304

W99.   QUINTET FOR STRINGS (1962)

        Prefazione (Lento moderato)
        Aria (Lento)
        Toccata (Allegro energico)
        Elegia (Lento)
        Interludium
        Scherzo (Allegro giocoso)
        Chaconne (Andante – Allegro energico – Molto
        moderato – Allegro)

        Duration: unable to trace

        Publication: unpublished

        Premiere: Manchester, Art Gallery (Institute of
                  Contemporary Arts) 5 November 1962; the
                  Turner String Quartet.

        SEE: B342

W100.   RAINFOREST I

        for flute, clarinet, glockenspiel, string quartet
        and piano trio (1984)

        Commissioned by the Chamber Music Society of Lincoln
        Center, New York

        Dedicated to Charles Wordsworth and the Chamber
        Music Society of Lincoln Center

        Duration: c. 19-20 minutes

        Publication: unpublished, but handled by Novello

        Premiere: New York, Alice Tully Hall, 30 November
                  1984; members of the Chamber Music
                  Society, including Charles Wordsworth
                  (piano).

        First UK: London, St. John's Smith Square, 4
                  February 1987; the Endymian Ensemble,
                  conducted by J. Whitfield.

        SEE: B87

W101.   RAINFOREST II

        for trumpet and strings (3.3.2.2.1) (1987)

        Commissioned for the 1987 Harrogate International
        Festival with the aid of funds provided by the
        Yorkshire Arts Association

        Duration: c. 20 minutes

Publication: unpublished, but handled by Novello

Premiere: Ripon, Cathedral Church of St. Peter and
          St. Wilfred, 3 August 1987; Hakan
          Hardenberger (trumpet) and the Guildhall
          String Ensemble.

SEE: B75

W102.   SAM VARIATIONS

for piano quartet and double bass (1989)

Deciso - Vivo - Allegro Marcato - Quasi
Recitativo - Lento - Quasi Recitativo - Vivo -
Lento - Vivace - Allegro Moderato e Marcatissimo
- Lento

Commissioned by the Schubert Ensemble with the aid
of funds provided by the Holst Foundation

Dedicated to the Schubert Ensemble

Duration: c. 13 minutes

Publication: unpublished, but handled by Novello

Premiere: London, the Wigmore Hall, 15 June 1989;
          the Schubert Ensemble of London.

W103.   SONATA FOR CLARINET, CELLO AND PIANO (1969)

Lento - poco - agitato - Allegro - Andante -
Trisamente - Vivo - Andante

Commissioned by Brocklehurst-Whiston Amalgamated for
the 1969 Macclesfield Festival

Dedicated to the de Peyer, Pleeth and Wallfisch Trio

Duration: c.12 minutes

Publication: Novello & Co. Ltd., 1972

Premiere: Macclesfield, the King's School Hall, 22
          May 1969; the de Peyer Trio.

SEE: B170

W104.   STAR PRELUDES

for violin and piano (1978)

1. Lento (Pleiades)
2. Andantino (Andromeda)
3. Vivo (Sirius)

4. Andante lirico (White Dwarf)
5. Vivo (...suiris)
6. Lento, come prima (...sedaielP)

Dedicated to Erich Gruenberg who commissioned the work

Duration: c. 14 minutes

Publication: Novello & Co. Ltd., 1981

Premiere: Los Angeles, Schoenberg Hall (University of California), 28 April 1978; Erich Gruenberg (violin) and John McCabe (piano).

First UK: London, the Wigmore Hall, 17 January 1978; Erich Gruenberg (violin) and John McCabe (piano).

SEE: B12

W105.   STRING TRIO (1965)

1. Allegro con fuoco
2. Mesto, senza espressione
3. Lento

Dedicated to Alan Rawsthorne, on his 60th birthday

Duration: 23 minutes

Publication: Novello & Co. Ltd., 1969

Premiere: unable to trace. It may have been performed in Mannheim during 1966 by the Berlin Philharmonic Trio.

Manuscript: It is described as "Opus 37" and was written in Munich.

RECORDINGS: D22

W106.   THREE PIECES FOR CLARINET AND PIANO (1964)

1.   Nocturne: Aria (Lento)
2.   Improvisation: Bossa Nova (Con moto)
3.   Fantasy (Lento)

Dedicated to Keith Puddy

Duration: c.8½ minutes (3½; 2; 3)

Publication: Novello & Co. Ltd., 1967

Premiere: Cheltenham, the Town Hall, 8 July 1964; Keith Puddy (clarinet) and Vivian Troon (piano).

Manuscript: It is described as "Opus 26" and the
pieces were originally meant for a
clarinet sonata.

RECORDINGS: D26

SEE: B10, B145

VOCAL

W107.   ASPECTS OF WHITENESS

Cantata for double mixed chorus (SSAATTBB) and piano (1967)

Text by Herman Melville, adapted from Moby Dick by John McCabe

Dedicated to the Aeolian Singers who commissioned the work

Duration: c. 27¼ minutes

Publication: unpublished

Premiere: London, Queen Elizabeth Hall, 21 June 1967; the Aeolian Singers and John McCabe (piano), conducted by Sebastian Forbes.

SEE: B78, B349

REVISED VERSION:

W107a   Extensive revisions and cuts were made to the work in 1969; the importance of the piano part was also increased.

Duration: c. 19 minutes

Publication: Novello & Co. Ltd., 1972

Premiere: Manchester, Houldsworth Hall, 16 June 1973; the BBC Northern Singers and John McCabe (piano), conducted by Stephen Wilkinson. This recording was subsequently broadcast in the BBC's Radio 3 on 22 April 1974.

W108.   BEHOLD A SILLY TENDER BABE

Carol for mixed chorus (SATB) and organ (1975)

Text By Robert Southwell

Commissioned by Trinity Parish Church, Southport, Connecticut for its 250th anniversary

Duration: 7 minutes

Publication: Novello & Co. Ltd., 1975

Premiere: Southport (Connecticut), Trinity Parish Church; unable to trace date, organist and conductor.

W109.   <u>COVENTRY CAROL</u> (1960)

> Arranged for soprano solo (or a few voices), mixed chorus (SATB) and organ (optional)

> Text: 15th century anonymous

> Duration: unable to trace

> Publication: Oxford University Press, 1965

> Premiere: unable to trace

> OTHER VERSION:

W109a   Arrangement with orchestral accompaniment

> 2.2.2.2/2.2.1.0/harp (opt.)/strings

> Publication: unpublished

> Notes: See also W122

> RECORDINGS: D7

W110.   <u>ENGLISH SONGS</u> 1963

> for unaccompanied mixed chorus (SATB)

> My Love in her attire (Anon)
> O gentle love (George Peele)
> My Daphne's hair is twisted gold (John Lyly)
> Shall I compare thee to a summer's day
>   (Shakespeare)

> Duration: unable to trace

> Publication: unpublished

> Premiere: Chester, the College, 3 January 1964; the Northern Consort (The Annual Dinner of the Incorporated Society of Musicians for which these songs were specially composed).

> First public performance: Manchester, the Renold Theatre (College of Science and Technology), 20 January 1965; the Northern Consort.

> SEE: B180

W111.   <u>EVENING CANTICLES FOR NORWICH</u> (1970)

> for unaccompanied mixed chorus (SATB)

Magnificat (Andante)
Nunc Dimittis (Lento)

Commissioned for the 1970 Norwich Triennial Festival
and dedicated to the memory of Brian Runnett

Duration: 10 minutes

Publication: Novello & Co. Ltd., 1972

Premiere: Norwich, the Cathedral Church of the Holy
         and Undivided Trinity, 24 October 1970;
         the Cathedral Choirs of Ely, Peterborough
         and Norwich.

W112.   EVENING CANTICLES FOR SALISBURY (1966)

         for mixed chorus (SATB) and organ

Magnificat (Allegro deciso)
Nunc Dimittis (Andante)

Commissioned for the Southern Cathedrals Festival
1967

Duration: 10 minutes

Publication: Novello & Co. Ltd., 1967

Premiere: Salisbury, the Cathedral Church of the
         Blessed Virgin Mary, 24 July 1967; the
         Cathedral Choirs of Chichester, Salisbury
         and Winchester with Michael Smith (organ),
         conducted by Christopher Dearnley.

Manuscript: It is described as "Opus 45".

W113.   GREAT LORD OF LORDS (1966)

         Anthem for mixed chorus (SATB) and organ, or
         brass (1.2.1.1), timpani and organ

         Text: Anonymous

Commissioned by the Holy Trinity Church, Southport

Dedicated to David Bowman

Duration: 6 minutes

Publication: Novello & Co. Ltd., 1967

Premiere: Southport, Holy Trinity Church, unable to
         trace date; choir conducted by David
         Bowman.

W114.   A HYMN TO GOD THE FATHER (1966)

> Anthem for unaccompanied mixed chorus (SATB)
>
> Text by John Donne
>
> Commissioned by St. Matthew's Church, Northampton
>
> Dedicated to Michael Nicholas and the Choir of St. Matthew's, Northampton
>
> Duration: 5 minutes
>
> Publication: Novello & Co. Ltd., 1966
>
> Premiere: Northampton, St. Matthew's Church, 20 September 1967; St. Matthew's Church Choir; conducted by Michael Nicholas.

W115.   A LUTE-BOOK LULLABY (1977)

> Carol for female voices (SSA) and flute
>
> Text by W. Ballett (17th century)
>
> Commissioned by and dedicated to Wendy Edwards and the Choir of the Alice Ottley School, Worcester
>
> Duration: 4 minutes
>
> Publication: Novello & Co. Ltd., 1979
>
> Premiere: Worcester, Cathedral Church of Christ and St. Mary, 16 December 1977; the School Senior Choir, unable to trace flute player, conducted by Wendy Edwards. According to the programme this performance was given in memory of Miss Roden.

W116.   MANGAN TRIPTYCH (1979-83)

> Text by James Clarence Mangan comprising:
>
> 1. Motet (1979) for unaccompanied double mixed chorus (SSAATTBB)
>
> Commissioned by the Chichester 904 Festivities
>
> Dedicated to George Guest and the Choir of St. John's College, Cambridge
>
> Duration: 10 minutes
>
> 2. Siberia (1980) for unaccompanied mixed chorus (SATB)

Commissioned by the Cork International Festival

Dedicated to Stephen Wilkinson

Duration: 7 minutes

3. _Visions_ (1983) for unaccompanied double mixed chorus (SSAATTBB)

Commissioned by the 1984 Harrogate Festival

Dedicated to Clive Wilson

Duration: 9 minutes

Publication: Novello & Co. Ltd.

> 1 - 1979
> 2 - 1988
> 3 - unpublished

Premieres: 1 - Chichester, Cathedral Church of the Holy Trinity, 11 July 1979; the Choir of St. John's College, Cambridge, conducted by George Guest.

2 - Cork, Aula Maxima, U.C.C., 9 May 1980; the William Byrd Singers, conducted by Stephen Wilkinson.

Complete Work (1-3) - Harrogate, Parish Church of St. Wilfred, 10 August 1984; the BBC Northern Singers, conducted by Stephen Wilkinson.

First London:(complete work) - Parish Church of St. Paul (Covent Garden), 9 April 1987; the London Concord Singers, conducted by Malcolm Cottle.

SEE: B314

W117.   MARY LAID HER CHILD (1964)

Carol for unaccompanied mixed chorus (SATB)

Text by Norman Nicholson

Duration: 4 minutes

Publication: Novello & Co. Ltd., 1965 (MT 1470)

Premiere: unable to trace

Manuscript: It is dated 11/10/64.

RECORDINGS: D14

W118.   MISSA MEDITATIONIS (1961)

      for mixed chorus (SATB) and organ

    Prefazione - per organo (Lento)
    Kyrie (Moderato, con espressione)
    Gloria (Con moto)
    Sanctus (Allegro moderato)
    Osanna I (Moderato)
    Benedictus (Lento)
    Osanna II (Allegro moderato)
    Agnus Dei (Moderato)
    Postludium - per organo (Lento)

    Duration: unable to trace

    Publication: unpublished

    Premiere: Islington (London), Parish Church of St.
          John, 12 April 1964. Unable to trace
          performers.

    Manuscript: it is described as "Opus 7".

W119.   THE MORNING WATCH (1968)

      Anthem for mixed chorus (SATB) or organ

      Text by Henry Vaughan

    Dedicated to David Patrick and the Choir of Barnet
    Parish Church, Herts

    Duration: c. 4 minutes

    Publication: Novello & Co. Ltd., 1968

    Premiere: unable to trace

    Motet: see under MANGAN TRIPTYCH (W116)

W120.   MUSIC'S EMPIRE (1981)

      for 16 soloists (SSSS, AAAA, TTTT, BBBB) or four
      soloists (SATB) with chorus or chorus only,
      orchestra or piano reduction

      Text by Andrew Marvell (from The Complete Poems)

    Commissioned, with the aid of funds provided by the
    Arts Council of Great Britain, by the Incorporated
    Society of Musicians, as part of the celebrations
    for their Centenary in 1982

    2.2.2.2/3.2.2.1/timp 2 perc harp/strings

Dedicated to the Incorporated Society of Musicians for their Centenary

Duration: c.11½ minutes

Publication: Novello & Co. Ltd., 1982

Premiere: London, Royal Festival Hall, 6 October 1982; 16 'ISM Young Artists' and the Halle Orchestra, conducted by James Loughran.

W121.   PROUD SONGSTERS (1989)

   for unaccompanied mixed chorus (SSAATTBB)

   Text by Thomas Hardy

Commissioned by the BBC Northern Singers and the North West Arts to celebrate the 70th birthday of Stephen Wilkinson and to thank him for 35 years of major contribution to the well-being of English choral music in general. 6 other composers also contributed settings:

The Spacious Firmament	Alan Bullard
Wild Air	Michael Ball
Invocation	Stephen Dodgson
Sonnet (Op.123)	John Joubert
On Stephenses Day	Elizabeth Maconchy
Do not go gentle	David Gow

Dedicated to Stephen, on his 70th birthday

Duration: c. 2 minutes

Publication: unpublished, but handled by Novello

Premiere: Manchester, BBC Studio 7 (Oxford Road), 9 September 1989, the BBC Northern Singers conducted by Stephen Wilkinson.

W122.   PUER NATUS IN BETHLEHEM (1961)

   A triptych of Christmas songs for mixed chorus (SATB) and organ

1. 'Eia, eia' (To us in Bethlem city)
2. Coventry Carol (Lullay, Lullay')
3. 'In Bethlehem that fair city'

Duration: unable to trace

Publication: unpublished

Premiere: Liverpool, Institute School Hall, 18 December 1961; members of the Liverpool Institute Choral Society and David

Williams (organ), conducted by Noel Evans.

Notes: See also W109, W129

SEE: B366

W123.   REFLECTIONS OF A SUMMER NIGHT (1977)

Cantata for mixed chorus (SATB) and small orchestra

The Lotus-eaters (Tennyson) Moderato
Evening (H.D. [Hilda Doolittle]) Allegro flessible
Evangeline (Longfellow) Lento
The Moth (Walter de la Mare) Vivo
Ode to a Nightingale (Keats) Andante

Commissioned for the 1978 Fishguard Festival with funds made available by the Welsh Arts Council

1.1+1.0.1/1.0.0.0/2 perc harpsichord/strings

Dedicated to the John Davies Singers

Duration: c. 15 minutes

Publication: Novello & Co. Ltd., 1983

Premiere: Fishguard, School Concert Hall, 26 July 1978; the John Davies Singers and Orchestra conducted, by John Davies.

First London: St. Paul's Church (Covent Garden), 21 June 1979; the London Concord Singers and Orchestra, conducted by Malcolm Cottle.

SEE: B54, B193

W124.   SCENES IN AMERICA DESERTA (1986)

for 6 voices: 2 countertenors
              tenor
              2 baritones
              bass

Text by Reyner Banham

Dedicated to the King's Singers who commissioned the work

Duration: c. 14 minutes

Publication: unpublished, but handled by Novello

Premiere: unable to trace, but presumably performed on one of the King's Singers American tours.

First UK: London, Queen Elizabeth Hall, 29 January
          1988; the Kings's Singers.

SEE: B68, B307

Siberia: see under MANGAN TRIPTYCH (W116)

W125.   STABAT MATER (1976)

         for soprano solo, mixed chorus (SATB) and
         orchestra

Commissioned by the Northampton Philharmonic Choir
[to celebrate its 80th season] with funds made
available by the East Midlands Arts Association

2.2.2.2/2.2.0.0/timp perc/strings

Dedicated to the Northampton Philharmonic Choir

Duration: c. 15 minutes

Publication Novello & Co. Ltd., 1981

Premiere: Northampton, St. Matthew's Church, 28
          October 1976; Felicity Lott (soprano), the
          Northampton Philharmonic Choir and the
          Midland Chamber Orchestra, conducted by
          Graham Mayo.

First London: unable to trace

SEE: B25

W126.   STUDY IN LIMERICKS No. 1 (1959)

         for unaccompanied double mixed chorus (SSAATTBB)

         Text by Edward Lear ('There was a young lady in
         white')

Duration: unable to trace

Publication: unpublished

Premiere: unable to trace

Manuscript: It is dated 17 April 1959

W127.   TE DEUM (1963)

         for mixed chorus (SATB), 4 trumpets (optional)
         and organ

Introduction (Con Moto)

We praise (Allegro giocoso)
When thou tookest (Andante)
Thou sittest (Allegro giocoso)
O Lord, save (Andante)

Duration: 6-7 minutes

Publication: unpublished

Premiere: Canterbury, the Cathedral Church of Christ, 19 October 1963; the Cathedral Choir, conducted by Alan Wicks.

W128.   TO US IN BETHLEM CITY (1969)

Carol for unaccompanied mixed chorus (SATB)

Text from Cölner Psalter, 1638; English translation by Percy Dearmer

Duration: 4 minutes

Publication: Novello & Co. Ltd., 1969

Premiere: unable to trace

W129.   UPON THE HIGH MIDNIGHT (1973)

3 Nativity carols for SATB soli and unaccompanied mixed chorus (SATB)

1. A little child there is y-born

for SATB soli and unaccompanied mixed chorus.

Text: Anonymous, 15th century

Moderato, ma con moto

2. Dormi, Jesu!

for soprano solo and unaccompanied mixed chorus.

Text: Anonymous

Andante

3. In Bethlehem, that fair city

for mixed chorus and organ (opt.)

Text: Anonymous, 14th century

Giocoso

Duration: c. 7 minutes (2½.2½.2)

Publication: Novello & Co. Ltd., 1974

Premiere: unable to trace

Notes: see also W122

RECORDINGS: D28

Visions: see under MANGAN TRIPTYCH (W116)

W130.   VOYAGE (1972)

Cantata for soprano, mezzo-soprano, countertenor, baritone and bass soli, boy's choir, mixed chorus (SATB) and orchestra

Libretto by Monica Smith

1. Barinthus describes the Land of Promise (Lento)
2. Brendan decides to search for the land
3. Boat-building song (Deciso)
4. Why do you seek...? (Lento)
5. Orchestral interlude, with one vocal section (L'istesso tempo [Lento])
6. Christmas in the Monastery of the Fiery Arrow
7. Orchestral interlude (Allegro Agitato)
8. The Barren Land and the Meeting with the Steward (Andante)
9. Orchestral Interlude (Vivo)
10. The Isle of Singing Birds (Allegro)
11. Interlude; seven years pass (Lento)
12. The Meeting with Judas on the Rock (Molto Allegro)
13. The Voice of Crystal
14. Brief orchestral section
15. Conclusion

Commissioned by the 1972 Three Choirs Festival with funds made available by the Arts Council of Great Britain

3+1.3+1.3.3/4.4.3.1/timp 3 perc celesta organ harp/strings

Dedicated to Shirley and Christopher Robinson

Duration: c. 42 minutes

Publication: unpublished, but handled by Novello

Premiere: Worcester, the Cathedral Church of Christ and St. Mary, 29 August 1972;
Jane Manning (soprano),
Meriel Dickinson (mezzo-soprano),
Charles Brett (countertenor),
Brian Raynor Cook (baritone),
Brian Kay (bass),
Richard Lloyd (organ),
the 3-Choirs Festival Chorus and the Royal

Philharmonic   Orchestra,   conducted   by
Christopher Robinson.

SEE: B189, B200, B354, B355, B378

SONGS

W131.   DAS LETZTE GERICHTE (1973)

    for Voce Umana, Guitar and Percussion

Text by Andreas Gryphius

Dedicated to Siegfried and Claudia Behrend

Duration: c. 15 minutes

Publication: unpublished, but handled by Novello

Premiere: Nuremberg   (Germany),   1978;   Claudia
        Brodzinska-Behrend, Siegfried Behrend and
        Siegried Fink.

1st UK: unable to trace

W132.   FIVE ELEGIES FOR SOPRANO AND CHAMBER ORCHESTRA
(1962)

1. Adieu, farewell earth's bliss (Thomas Nashe)
Lento

2. The Hour-Glass (Ben Johnson) Vivo

3. Eyes that last I saw in tears (T.S. Elliott)
Andantino

4. The Hag (Robert Herrick) Con Fuoco

5. Do not got gentle into that good night (Dylan
Thomas)

1.1.1.1/1.0.0.0/timp 2 perc/strings

Dedicated to Thomas Pitfield, with deep gratitude

Duration: 16 minutes

Publication: unpublished, but handled by Novello

Premiere: Liverpool, Philharmonic Hall, 18 June
        1963; Marie Collier (soprano) and members
        of the Royal Liverpool Philharmonic
        Orchestra, conducted by Robert Wolf.

Notes: This composition won the Royal
        Philharmonic Prize for Composition in
        1962.

W133.   FOLK SONGS

    Arranged for high voice, clarinet or horn and

piano (1963/1976)

1. The Water of Tyne (English) Andantino
2. Weaving Song (Scottish) Allegretto moderato
3. Johnny has gone for a soldier (American) Lento,
   ma con moto
4. Hush-a-ba-birdie, croon, croon (Scottish)
   Andantino
5. John Peel (English) Allegro giocoso

Nos 3-5 were arranged in 1963 for voice, clarinet
and piano (and classed as Opus 19); these were
re-arranged in 1976 for voice, horn and piano with
nos 1 and 2 added.

Nos 2 was also re-arranged in 1986 for voice and
piano duet: see below -

Dedicated (Nos 3-5) to Catriona and Barry

Duration: 13 minutes (total)

Publication: Nos 3-5 only: Novello & Co. Ltd., 1967

Premiere:

Nos 3-5:   Irvine (Scotland), Music Club, 11 December
           1963; Cationa Gordon (soprano), Keith
           Puddy (clarinet) and John McCabe (piano).

Nos 1-5:   Derby, ISM Centre, 7 July 1979; Ann Archer
           (soprano), Dennis Kiddy (piano); unable to
           trace the horn player.

No 2:   (arr. for voice and piano duet): London,
           Merchant Taylor's Hall, 9 June 1986; Jill
           Gomez (soprano) with Richard Rodney
           Bennett and John McCabe (pianos).
           (Arranged as an encore at a fund-raising
           soiree for the London College of Music)

RECORDINGS: D25

W134.   LES SOIRS BLEUS

for soprano, recorders (1 player), cello and
harpsichord (1979)

Text by Rimbaud

Dedicated to John Turner

Duration: 3 minutes

Publication: unpublished, but handled by Novello

Premiere: Sussex, Petworth House, 15 September 1980;
          the Legrand Ensemble.

W135.   RAIN SONGS (1966)

Scherzo for soprano, countertenor (or alto), cello and harpsichord

1. Rain (Mo-ch'i Yung) Allegro Moderato
2. Keep indoors by the rain (Lu Yu)
3. The rain is not controlled (for the Book of Songs)

Songs translated for the Chinese by Robert Kotewall and Norman Smith

Dedicated to the Lydian Ensemble

Duration: c. 4½ minutes

Publication: unpublished, but handled by Novello

Premiere: unable to trace

SEE: B159

W136.   REQUIEM SEQUENCE (1971)

for soprano and piano

Text from the Latin Requiem Mass

Dedicated to the memory of two musicians to whom the composer owes "immense debts of gratitude," Alan Rawsthorne and Sir John Barbirolli

Duration: c. 12 minutes

Publication: unpublished, but handled by Novello

Premiere: London, the Wigmore Hall, 7 February 1979; Jane Manning (soprano) and Richard Rodney Bennett (piano).

Manuscript:A note says that this work was written in its original version, with piano, in 1971, though as work progressed on the music the composer became more and more convinced that an orchestral arrangement of the piano part would be equally valid.

W137.   SECHS GEDICHTE (1963)

for voice and piano

1. Über die Himmelsklugel (Gryphius) Allegro Marcato
2. Gebet (Mörike) Andantino
3. Mondnacht (Eichendorff)
4. Um Mitternacht (Mörike) Moderato
5. Das zerbrochene Ringlein (Eichendorff) Allegro

Deciso
6. Grabschrift Marianne Gryphiae (Gryphius) Lento

Dedicated to Meriel [Dickinson]

Duration: c. 13 minutes

Publication: unpublished

Premiere: London, 4, St. James's Square (Arts
          Council), 10 February 1964; Meriel
          Dickinson (mezzo-soprano) and Susan
          Bradshaw (piano).

SEE: B24, B149, B327

W138.   A SEQUENCE OF NOCTURNES (1962)

         for medium voice and piano

Source of text: unable to trace

Dedicated to Barbara Robotham

Duration: unable to trace

Publication: unpublished

Premiere: Blackpool, Parish Church of St. Thomas, 17
          September 1962, Barbara Robotham
          (contralto) and John McCabe (piano).

Notes: A review of a later performance mentions
          that these are settings of English poems
          and include a setting of Wordsworth's "A
          Slumber did my Spirit Seal".

W139.   A SUMMER GARLAND (1963)

         for soprano and flute, oboe, harp and cello

         1. Introduction   Andante
         2. Upon Roses (Herrick)   Con moto
         3. Song (Blake)   Scherzando
         4. The Old Cricketer (Arlott)   Lento
         5. Air (Anon-Elizabethan)   Allegro Grazioso
         6. Postlude   Tempo Comenciato

Duration: c. 10-11 minutes

Publication: unpublished, but handled by Novello

Premiere: Liverpool, Bluecoat School Hall, 2 October
          1963; Emily Maire (soprano), Judy Fenton
          (flute), Keith Wood (oboe), Mair Jones

(harp) and Wilfred Simenauer (cello).

SEE: B172

W140.   THREE LEIDER (1959)

for medium voice and piano

1. In der Fremde (Heine)
2. Tränen des Vaterlandes (Gryphius)
3. Auf meines Kindes Tod (Eichendorff)

Duration: unable to trace

Publication: unpublished

Premiere: Manchester, the Hall of the RMCM, 17
          November 1961; Meriel Dickinson
          (mezzo-soprano) and John McCabe (piano).

SEE: B102

W141.   THREE SONGS FROM SHAKESPEARE (1962)

for contralto (or mezzo-soprano) and viola

1. Pardon, goddess of the night   Lento
   (Much ado about nothing, Act 5, sc.3)

2. Orpheus with his lute   Giocoso
   (Henry VIII, Act 3, sc.1)

3. Lie on sinful fantasy!   Maestoso
   (Merry Wives of Windsor, Act 5, sc.5)

Duration: unable to trace

Publication: unpublished

Premiere: unable to trace

Manuscript: It is signed by the composer and dated
            24/11/62.

W142.   THREE TENOR SONGS (1962-63)

1. The Dug-Out (S. Sassoon) Lento

2. Do not weep maiden for war is kind (S. Crane)
   Andante Lamentoso

3. In time of the Breaking of Nations (T. Hardy)
   Lento moderato

Duration: unable to trace

Publication: unpublished

Premiere: unable to trace

Manuscript: No. 1 is dated 13/12/62 and the time
            indicated as 11.45pm-12.35am
            No. 2 is dated 16/12/62
            No. 3 is dated 3/63.

W143.   TIME REMEMBERED (1973)

         for soprano and instrumental ensemble

         1. Even such is Time (Walter Raleigh)
         2. In Memory (Lionel Johnson)
         3. Time that is fallen (Venantius Fortunatus)
         4. Elegy over a Tomb (Lord Herbert of Cherbury)
         5. Condemned and doomed to die (Sir Thomas Moore)

         Commissioned by Malvern Concert Club, with funds
         made available by The Arts Council of Great Britain,
         for their 70th anniversay concert

         1.0.1.0/1.1.0.0/piano/strings(1.0.0.1.0)

         Dedicated to Monica [the composer's wife]

         Duration: c. 25 minutes

         Publication: unpublished but handled by Novello

         Premiere: Malvern (Worcestershire), York Hall –
                   Malvern Girls' College, 4 October 1973;
                   Felicity Palmer (soprano) and the Nash
                   Ensemble with John McCabe (piano).

         SEE: B11, B150, B311

MUSIC FOR CHILDREN

W144.   AFTERNOONS AND AFTERWARDS (1981)

Seven pieces (Grades V and VI Associated Board)
for piano:

1. Swans at Stratford (Lento, grazioso)
2. On the beach (Moderato, piacevole)
3. Champagne Waltz (Allegretto)
4. Sports Car (Allegro gioviale)
5. A Game of Darts (Vivo)
6. Forlane (Andantino)
7. The Artful Dodger (Allegro)

Dedicated to Patti

Duration: c. 11 minutes

Publication: Novello & Co. Ltd., 1982

Premiere: unable to trace

W145.   DANCES FOR TRUMPET AND PIANO (1980)

Seven pieces (Grades V-VI Associated Board):

1. Polish Dance (Allegro deciso)
2. Ballard (Andantino soave)
3. P.B. Blues (Calmo)
4. Halling (Deciso)
5. Highland Habanera (Lento)
6. Siciliano (Grazioso)
7. Jigaudon (Allegro)

Dedicated to Michael J. Easton

Duration: c. 10 minutes

Publication: Novello & Co. Ltd., 1981

Premiere: unable to trace

W146.   THE LION, THE WITCH AND THE WARDROBE (1968)

Children's opera in four acts

CAST

The Witch	soprano
The Lion	bass-baritone
Susan	soprano (or treble)
Lucy	soprano (or treble)
Peter	alto
Edmund	alto
Beaver	baritone (or alto)

Mrs Beaver	soprano (or treble)
Tumnus, the Faun	treble
Maugrim	baritone
Leopard	baritone
Wolf	baritone
Dwarf	treble

Satyrs, Naiads, Dryads, Centaurs, Tigers, Dwarfs, Wolves etc.

The roles of Maugrim, Leopard and Wolf can be performed by one singer if necessary.

Libretto by Gerald Larner from the book by C.S. Lewis

Prologue (Andante)

ACT ONE

Scene 1: Interior of Tumnus's cave

Scene 2: The wood

ACT TWO

Scene 1: The wood in winter (Moderato)

Scene 2:   -ditto-

Scene 3:   -ditto-   (Moderato)

Scene 4: Beaver's cave (L'istesso tempo)

ACT THREE

Prelude and Scene 1: A clearing in the wood. This orchestral prelude depicts the coming of spring (Andante)

Scene 2: The Stone Table on a rise. Behind it, a back cloth shows the river estuary with the castle of Cair Paravel in the far distance.

Scene 3: A clearing in the wood

ACT FOUR

Scene 1: The Stone Table, late evening (Lento)

Scene 2: A night encampment (Andante)

Scene 3: The Stone Table, still at night (Vivo)

Scene 4: The Witch's palace

Epilogue

Commissioned by the Manchester Cathedral Arts
Festival, 1969

2.1.2.1/1.2.1.0/timp 3 perc organ piano/strings

Duration: 75 minutes:

> Prologue & Act 1 - c. 20 minutes
> Act 2 - c. 20 minutes
> Act 3 - c. 15 minutes
> Act 4 & Epilogue - c. 20 minutes

Publication: Novello & Co. Ltd., 1971

Premiere: Manchester Cathedral Church of St. Mary,
St. George and St. Denys, 29 April 1969;
Caroline Crawshaw (soprano), Patrick
McGuigan (bass baritone), pupils from
Cheetham's Hospital School singing the
remaining parts and providing choir and
orchestra, conducted by Gerald Littlewood.
Producer: Trevor Gamson.

SEE: B19, B72, B158, B160, B171

DERIVED WORK:

W146a   SUITE FOR ORCHESTRA (1971)

> from the opera

1. Prelude   (Andante)
2. Waltz   (Vivo)
3. Nocturne (Lento)
4. Finale   (Allegro)

Commissioned by Stoneyhurst College (Lancashire)

1.1.2.1/1.2.1.0/timp 2 perc piano/strings

Duration: c. 15 minutes

Publication: Novello & Co. Ltd., 1974

Premiere: Stoneyhurst College, 12 June 1971; First
Orchestra; unable to trace conductor.

W147.   PORTRAITS FOR FLUTE AND PIANO (1980)

> Seven pieces (Grades V-VI Associated Board):

1. Gymnopedie   (Andante)
2. Threes and Twos   (Allegretto)
3. Guitar Song   (Andantino)
4. Blues   (Allegro giocoso)
5. Vocalise   (Andante)
6. March of the Fool (Moderato)
7. Scherzo   (Allegro)

Dedicated to Richard Rodney Bennett

Duration: c. 10 minutes

Publication: Novello & Co. Ltd., 1981

Premiere: unable to trace

W148.   SUMMER MUSIC FOR ORCHESTRA (1963)

Allegro Maestoso - Lento - Allegro Giocoso - Allegro Maestoso

Written for Paul Ward (to whom it is dedicated) and the Stockport Youth Orchestra

2.2.2.2/4.2.2.0/2 perc/strings

Duration: 5½ minutes

Publication: unpublished

Premiere: Stockport, Offerton Secondary Girls' School, 19 July 1963; the Stockport Youth Orchestra, conducted by Paul Ward.

AN ENTERTAINMENT

W149.   THIS TOWN'S A CORPORATION FULL OF CROOKED STREETS (1969)

An entertainment for speaker, tenor, children's choir, mixed choir and instrumental ensemble

1. Liverpool 8   (Adrian Henri)   Andante
2. Domestic Life (Roger McGough)   Allegro
3. Nocturne   (Henri/McGough)   Lento
4. Dance of Death (McGough/Brian Patten) Deciso
5. Finale (Anon)   Vivo

Commissioned by Madeley College of Education

Tpt/philicorda/9   (or   more)   perc   piano/strings (1.1.1.1.1)

Dedicated to Ann and John

Duration: c. 45 minutes

Publication: unpublished, but handled by Novello

Premiere: Madeley (Staffs), College of Education, 28 April 1970; Alan Dover (speaker), Robert Williams (tenor), Children's Chorus from Madeley Secondary School, mixed choirs and Ensemble from Madeley College of Education, conducted by Mary Higgs.

INCIDENTAL MUSIC

A Little Bit of Singing and Dancing

See under ALL FOR LOVE (W150)

W150.   ALL FOR LOVE (1982)

Music for two one-hour plays in a drama series, produced for GRANADA TV:

(1) Combat – adapted from a story by Edith Reveley by Thomas Ellice.

Directed by Brian Mills

1.1.0.0/0.0.0.0/strings

First televised: 15 August 1982

(2) A Little Bit of Singing and Dancing – adapted from the play by Susan Hill by Hugh Whitemore.

Directed by Robert Knights

2.0.1.0/0.0.0.0/strings

First televised: 22 August 1982

Both produced by Roy Roberts

Publication: unpublished, but handled by Novello

Combat

see under ALL FOR LOVE (W150)

W151.   COME BACK, LITTLE SHEBA (1977)

Music for the television production of the play by William Inge.

GRANADA TV

Directed by Silvia Narizzano

Produced by Laurence Olivier

First televised: 8 January 1978

Music recorded 22 March 1977 by members of the Halle Orchestra, conducted by John McCabe (Granada Studio, Manchester).

Publication: unpublished, but handled by Novello

W152.   COUPLES (1975)

>   Music for the television series by Tony Parker
>
>   Thames TV

Directed by Ray Battersby

Produced by Verity Lambert

First televised: 14 October 1975

Music recorded by John McCabe (piano)

Publication: unpublished, but handled by Novello

DERIVED WORK:

W152a   THEME MUSIC

>   arranged for piano solo by the composer

Publication: Novello & Co. Ltd., 1976

Czech Mate

>   See under HAMMER HOUSE OF MURDER AND SUSPENSE (W156)

W153.   FEAR IN THE NIGHT (1972)

>   Music for the film (Hammer)
>   Screenplay/Directed by Jimmy Sangster

Music written for the following episodes:

Opening titles
Hand in bathroom window
Attack in bathroom
Peggy lying on bed
Walking in school
Bedroom
Peggy in the school, alone
Attack in cottage
Robert's departure
Peggy shoots Michael
Peggy running through school
Michael breaks door down
Peggy shoots Michael
Robert enters school
Robert looking at dormatory and school
Robert and Peggy in school
Robert shoots Molly
Robert ransacks school hall
Robert and Peggy run outside
Michael kills Robert
End titles

Musical director: Phillip Martell

Premiere: released June 1972

Publication: unpublished, but handled by Novello

SEE: B321

W154.   THE GOOD SOLDIER (1981)

Music for the TV dramatisation of the novel by Ford Maddox Ford, adapted by Julian Mitchell.

GRANADA TV

Directed by Kevin Billington

Produced by Peter Eckersley

1.1.1.1/1.0.0.0/strings

First televised: 15 April 1981

The score also contained arrangements of music by Mozart and Schubert

Publication: unpublished, but handled by Novello

SEE: B3, B144

Growing Pains

See under HAMMER HOUSE OF HORROR (W155)

Guardian of the Abyss

See under HAMMER HOUSE OF HORROR (W155)

W155.   HAMMER HOUSE OF HORROR (1980)

Music for the following TV films

(1)   13th Renunion – play by Jeremy Burnham.

Directed by Peter Sasdy

First televised: 20 September 1980

(2)   Growing Pains – play by Nicholas Palmer.

Directed by Frances Megahy

First televised: 4 October 1980

(3)   Guardian of the Abyss – play by David Fisher.

Directed by Don Sharp

Solo soprano (singing various chants) and synthesiser

First televised: 15 November 1980

All produced by Ray Skeggs

Musical director: Phillip Martell

Publication: unpublished, but handled by Novello

W156.   HAMMER HOUSE OF MYSTERY AND SUSPENSE (1984)

Music for the following TV films:

(1)   Czech Mate - play by Jeremy Burnham.

Directed by John Hough

First televised: 3 December 1984

(2)   The Sweet Scent of Death - play by Brian Clemens.

Directed by Peter Sasdy

1+1.1.0.0/0.0.0.0/timp perc harp/strings

Music written for the following episodes:

The hand
The brochure
In the house
In the kitchen
The dustbin
The figure
The rose
The rose again
The bird
Headless roses
The shotgun
In the woods
The marauder
The second marauder
Finale

First televised: 17 October 1984

Both produced by Roy Skeggs

Musical director: Phillip Martell

Publication: unpublished, but handled by Novello

W157.   HYPOTHETICALS (1979)

Signature tune for the series of six programmes transmitted by GRANADA Television as The State of the Nation: The Bounds of Freedom in June and July 1979

Directed by Eric Harrison

Produced by Brian Lapping

0.0.2.2/1.1.0.0/double bass

First televised: 17 June 1979

Publication: unpublished, but handled by Novello

W158.   LEEDS UNITED (1974)

Music for the television play by Colin Welland.

BBC Television

Directed by Ray Battersby

Produced by Kennith Trodd

1.1.1.1/1.0.0.0/2 perc/strings

First televised: 31 October 1974

Publication: unpublished, but handled by Novello

W159.   MADRIGAL AND ARABESQUE (1973)

Commissioned by GRANADA TV for use as background music to the TV station signal

Duration: Madrigal - 2 minutes
          Arabesque - 6 minutes

Publication: unpublished, but handled by Novello

Premiere: unable to trace

W160.   MICHELIN MX TYRES (1973)

Music for the television advertisement commissioned by Michelin & Co. Ltd.

2+1.2.1.2/4.3.3.0 timp. 2 perc. harp/strings

Duration: unable to trace, although there are two versions: one 'short', the other 'long'

Publication: unpublished, but handled by Novello

Premiere: unable to trace. According to the composer, it was used for a short time in 1983

W161.   OVERTURE AND OTHER MUSIC FOR A VICTORIAN MELODRAMA (1959)

"Christmas Eve" or "Duel in the Snow": an original domestic drama in three acts by Edward Fitzball.

Duration: unable to trace

Publication: unpublished

Premiere: Liverpool, Bluecoat School Theatre, 24 October 1959; unable to trace performer(s).

W162.   THE RIVALS (1957-8)

Incidental music for solo piano to R. B. Sheridan's play. Produced by A. Durband

Duration: unable to trace

Publication: unpublished

Premiere: Liverpool, the Institute Hall, 29 January 1958; John McCabe (piano).

DERIVED WORK:

W162a   SUITE FOR SOLO PIANO FROM THE RIVALS (after Sheridan's comedy)

1. March for Sir Anthony Absolute (Allegro Moderato)
2. Jig for Sir Lucius O'Trigger (Vivo Giocoso)
3. Galop for Bob Acres (Vivace)
4. Waltz for Lydia Languish (Andantino)
5. Waltz for Mrs Malaprop (Giocoso)
6. Tango for Jack Absolute (Allegro)

Duration: unable to trace

Publication: unpublished

Premiere: unable to trace

Notes: The composer later orchestrated this suite. Unable to trace the instrumentation.

W163.   SAM (1973)

Music for the television series

GRANADA TV

1+1.0.2.0/0.1.0.0/side drum/strings

First televised: 12 June 1973

Publication: unpublished, but handled by Novello

SEE: B56

DERIVED WORKS:

W163a   THEME MUSIC, arr. by the composer (1975)

Instrumentation: as above

Publication: unpublished, but handled by Novello

Premiere: London, Royal Albert Hall, 18 October
          1975; the Royal Philharmonic Orchestra,
          conducted by Jack Parnell.

W163b   THEME MUSIC, arr. by John Golland for brass band
         (1975)

Soprano cornet, solo B-flat cornet, 3 B-flat
cornets, flugel horn, solo E-flat horn, 2 E-flat
horns, 2 B-flat baritones, 2 B-flat trombones,
bass trombone, B-flat euphonium, E-flat and
B-flat basses and percussion

Duration: 3½ minutes

Publication: Paxton Music Ltd., 1984

Premiere: unable to trace

Sweet Scent of Death

See under HAMMER HOUSE OF MURDER AND SUSPENSE (W156)

W164.   THESE FOOLISH THINGS (1988)

Music for the television production of the play
by Elizabeth Spender

BBC Television

Directed by Charles Gormley

Produced by Andy Park

Timp 2 perc harp guitar strings

Music composed for the following episodes:

At Night – Cole Porter (arr. McCabe)
Exclusion (2MI)
In the Car (2M2)
Farewell (2M3)
Finale – Jack Strachey (arr. McCabe)
Finale B (2M4)

First televised: 28 February 1989 (The music was recorded in Glasgow, October 1988)

Publication: unpublished, but handled by Novello

Thirteenth Reunion

See under HAMMER HOUSE OF HORROR (W155)

W165.   YOUNG MUSICIANS OF THE YEAR (1982)

Theme tune for the 1982 BBC Television series

1.1.1.1/1.1.0.0/piano/strings

First televised: 13 April 1982

Publication: unpublished, but handled by Novello

MUSIC FOR BRASS, WIND, ETC.

W166.   <u>CANZONA FOR WIND AND PERCUSSION</u> (1970)

Commissioned by the Hilden Trust for the 1971 Farnham Festival

1.1.2.1/1.2.1.0/timp 2 perc/piano

Duration: c. 7 minutes

Publication: Novello & Co. Ltd., 1975

Premiere: Farnham, the Parish Church, 13 May 1971; Frensham Heights School Orchestra, conducted by Brian Northcott.

W167.   <u>CENTENNIAL FANFARE</u> (1987)

for brass and percussion

Written for the centenary of the London College of Music, 1987

4 horns in F, 3 trumpets in B-flat, 2 tenor trombones, 1 bass trombone, tuba and side drum

Duration: c. 50 seconds

Premiere: London, the Barbican, 9 March 1987; London College of Music Ensemble, conducted by John Chapman (The LCM Centennial Concert).

W168.   <u>CLOUDCATCHER FELLS</u> (1985)

for brass band

Great Gable)
Grasmoor   )   (slow)
Grisedale   )

Haystacks   )   (quick)
Catchedicam (Catstye Cam))

Angle Tarn   (slow)

Grisedale Brow   )
Striding Edge   )   (quick)
Helvellyn   )

Commissioned by Boosey & Hawkes Band Festivals (with funds provided by the Arts Council of Great Britain) as the test piece for the 1985 Finals of the National Brass Band Championship of Great Britain.

The title comes from a poem by David Wright, and the work is associated with various places in the Lake District which have particular personal significant for the composer. The emphasis is on the Patterdale area, though other parts of the Lake District are also referred to, and the work falls into a series of sections which group themselves into larger units, so that it becomes almost a four-movement work, played continuously.

E-flat soprano cornet, solo B-flat cornet, solo B-flat cornets 3/4, 3 B-flat cornets, fugel horn, solo E-flat horn, 2 E-flat horns, 2 B-flat baritones, 2 B-flat trombones, bass trombone, 2 B-flat euphoniums, 2 E-flat basses, 2 B-flat basses, timpani and percussion

Dedicated to the memory of the composer's father

Duration: 13 minutes

Publication: Novello & Co. Ltd., 1985

Premiere: London, Royal Albert Hall, 6 October 1985 when it received 18 performances from various bands.

RECORDINGS: D6

W169.   DESERT II: HORIZON (1981)

for 10 brass instruments: piccolo trumpet, 2 trumpets in C, flugelhorn, horn, trombones and tuba.

Quasi con moto – Allegro – Andante – Deciso

Commissioned by the 1981 Harrogate International Festival with funds from the Arts Council

Duration: c. 14 minutes

Publication: unpublished, but handled by Novello

Premiere: Ripon, the Cathedral Church of St Peter and St Wilfred, 4 August 1981; the Philip Jones Brass Ensemble.

First London: Queen Elizabeth Hall, 17 October 1981; the Philip Jones Brass Ensemble.

DERIVED WORK:

W169a   VERSION FOR BRASS BAND (1987)

Publication: unpublished, but handled by Novello

Premiere: London, the Royal Albert Hall, 8 October 1988; 4 bands conducted by Howard Snell.

RECORDINGS: D8

W170.   FANTASY FOR BRASS QUARTET (1965)

for 2 trumpets, horn (or tenor trombone) and tenor trombone (or horn)

Introduction (Lento) and Pastorale (Andantino)
Capriccio (Giocoso)
Chorale (Lento)
Fughetta (Allegro)

Commissioned by Novello & Co. Ltd.

Duration: c. 8-9 minutes

Publication: Novello & Co. Ltd., 1966

Premiere: Salford, the University, 1966; the Halle Brass Consort.

Manuscript: it is described as 'Opus 35'.

W171.   IMAGES (1977-78)

for brass band

Lively - Leisurely - Flowing - Lively - Decisive - Reflective - Agitated

Commissioned by Besses o' th' Barn Band, with the aid of funds provided by the Arts Council of Great Britain

Soprano cornet in E-flat, 4 solo cornets in B-flat, 3 cornets in B-flat, flugal horn in B-flat, solo and 2 tenor horns in E-flat, 2 baritones B-flat, 2 tenor and bass trombone, 2 euphoniums, E-flat and B-flat basses and percussion

Dedicated to Ifor James and Besses o'th' Barn Band

Duration: c. 14 minutes

Publication: Novello & Co. Ltd., 1982

Premiere: London, Goldsmiths Hall, 30 March 1978; Besses o'th' Barn Band, conducted by Ifor James.

DERIVED WORK:

W171a   VERSION FOR CONCERT BAND (1978)

Commissioned by the University of Redlands, California and performed there on 14 May 1978.

First U.K.: Huddersfield, St. Paul's Church, 11 February 1982; the Polytechnic Wind Band, conducted by Barrie Webb.

W172. ROUNDS FOR BRASS QUINTET (1967)

for 2 trumpets, horn, tenor trombone and bass tuba

Allegro
Andante
Allegro moderato
Lento ma movendo
Allegro moderato

Commissioned by the Halle Brass Consort

Duration: 11-12 minutes

Publication: Novello & Co. Ltd., 1968

Premiere: Salford, the University, 26 February 1968; the Halle Brass Consort.

RECORDINGS: D20

SEE: B9, B45

Sam: theme music arranged for brass band

see under SAM (W163a)

W173. SYMPHONY FOR 10 WIND INSTRUMENTS (1964)

1. Allegro: Tutti I
2. Lento : Soli I
3. Vivo   : Tutti II
4. Lento (Groups - Tutti III - Trios)
5. Vivo   : Tutti IV - Contrasts - Tutti V
6. Lento : (Soli II - Tutti VI)

Commissioned for the 10th Anniversary Concert of the Portia Ensemble

2.2.2.2/2.0.0.0

Dedicated to the Portia Ensemble

Duration: c. 19 minutes

Publication: Score and parts to be published by Novello & Co. Ltd.

Premiere: London, the Wigmore Hall, 14 December
1964; the Portia Ensemble.

SUPPLEMENTARY LIST

W174.   JANUARY SONATINA:

      for unaccompanied B-flat clarinet (1990)

      Slow - Presto possible - Fast, rhythmical

      Commissioned by Phillip Rehfeldt

      Dedicated to Barney [Childs], on his 64th

      Notes: The composer writes: This is the first in a series of sonatinas for solo wind instruments, which was written in January 1990 (hence the title) at the invitation of the American clarinetist Phillip Rehfeldt for a collection of unaccompanied clarinet works he gathered to celebrate the 64th birthday of the American composer Barney Childs, to whom the piece is dedicated. The presentation was made to the composer on 13 February 1990.

      Publication: (in the U.S.A) will be as part of a large Festschrift for Barney Childs on his 64th birthday entitled Etudes for the 21st Century Clarinetist.

Discography

This selected discography includes long playing records, cassettes and compact discs available or deleted, mono or stereo.

The "see" references, e.g. SEE: B237, identify citations in the "Bibliography" section.

McCABE AS COMPOSER

D1.   AUBADE (Study No.4) for piano (W38)

   RCA Red Seal RL 25076
   John McCabe (piano)

   SEE: 50
B124, B135

D2.   BAGATELLES for piano (W42)

   Pye Golden Guinea GSGC 14116
   John McCabe (piano)

   SEE: B165, B297

D3.   CANTO for guitar (W76)

   DGG 2530 079
   Siegfried Behrend (guitar)

   SEE: B105, B132, B140

D4.   CAPRICCIO (Study No.1) for piano (W40)

   RCA Red Seal RL 25076
   John McCabe (piano)

   SEE: B124, B135

D5.   (THE) CHAGALL WINDOWS (W5)

>   HMV ASD 3096
>   Halle Orchestra/James Loughran
>
>   SEE: B123, B295, B379
>
>   EMI Greensleeves ED291219-1   (compact disc)
>   ED291219-4   (cassette)
>
>   SEE: B290

D6.   CLOUDCATCHER FELLS (W168)

>   Chandos BBRD 1032
>   CHAN 8483   (compact disc)
>   BBTD 1032   (cassette)
>   Black Dyke Mills Band/ Peter Parkes

D7.   COVENTRY CAROL (W109)

>   Argo ZRG 5499
>   Elizabethan Singers/Simon Preston (organ)/ Louis
>   Halsey
>
>   SEE: B61
>
>   Abbey XMS 697
>   Leeds   Parish   Church   Choir/Anthony   Langford
>   (organ)/ Donald Hunt
>
>   SEE: B59

D8.   DESERT II - HORIZON (W169)

>   Polyphonic QPRL 039D .
>   CPRL 039D   (cassette)
>
>   Massed bands/Howard Snell

D9.   DESERT III - LANDSCAPE (W82)

>   Pagecoll S-1 (Australia)
>   The Australian Piano Trio

D10.   DIES RESURRECTIONIS (W64)

>   Abbey LPB 665
>   Christopher Bowers-Broadbent (organ)
>
>   SEE: B374
>
>   RCA Victrola LVLI 5019
>   Melville Cook (organ)

SEE: B373

D11.   ELEGY (W65)

Decca Eclipse ECS 626
Edward Higginbottom (organ)

SEE: B371

D12.   FANTASY ON A THEME OF LISZT for piano (W41)

RCA Red Seal RL 25076
John McCabe (piano)

SEE: B124, B135

D13.   GAUDI (Study No.3) for piano (W44)

RCA Red Seal RL 25076
John McCabe (piano)

SEE: B124, B135

D14.   MARY LAID HER CHILD (W117)

Abbey LPB 748
Norwich Cathedral Choir/Michael Nicholas

D15.   MINICONCERTO (W68)

Abbey APR 606
Gillian Weir (organ)/James Blades (percussion)/
David Willocks

D16.   MUSICA NOTTURNA (W89)

Pagecoll S-1 (Australia)
The Australian Piano Trio

D17.   NOTTURNI ED ALBA (W30)

HMV ASD 2094
Jill Gomez/City of Birmingham Symphony Orchestra
/Louis Fremaux

SEE: B173, B309

EMI Greensleeves ED 291219-1 (compact disc)
                ED 291219-4 (cassette)

SEE: B290

D18.   PARTITA for solo cello (W91)

> L'Oiseau-Lyre DSL018
> Julian Lloyd Webber (cello)
>
> SEE: B296
>
> Pagecoll S-1 (Australia)
> Janis Laurs (cello)

D19.   (LE) POISSON MAGIQUE (W71)

> Vista VPS 1025
> Graham Barber (organ)
>
> SEE: B372

D20.   ROUNDS for Brass Quintet (W172)

> Pye Golden Guinea GSGC 14114
> Halle Brass Consort
>
> SEE: B109

D21.   SOSTENUTO (Study No.2) for piano (W59)

> RCA Red Seal RL 25076
> John McCabe (piano)
>
> SEE: B124, B135

D22.   STRING TRIO (W105)

> Argo ZRG 761
> Cardiff Ensemble
>
> SEE: B49, B294

D23.   SYMPHONY (Elegy) No.1 (W33)

> Pye Virtuoso TPLS 13005
> London Philharmonic Orchestra/John Snashall
>
> SEE: B130, B291, B322

D24.   SYMPHONY No.2 (W34)

> HMV ASD 2904
> City of Birmingham Symphony Orchestra/Louis
> Fremaux
>
> SEE: B173

D25.   THREE FOLK SONGS (W133)

>   Cameo Classics GOCLP 9020
>   Sylvia Eaves (soprano)/Thea King (clarinet)/
>   Courtney Kenny (piano)

D26.   THREE PIECES FOR CLARINET AND PIANO (W106)

>   Coronet 3116
>   Brian Schweickhardt (clarinet)/ J. Cobb (piano)

D27.   TUNING (W36)

>   Alpha CAPS 367
>   National Youth Orchestra of Scotland/McCabe

D28.   UPON THE HIGH MIDNIGHT (W129)

>   Abbey LPB 787
>   Worchester Cathedral Choir/P. Trepte (organ)/
>   Donald Hunt

D29.   VARIATIONS FOR PIANO (W63)

>   RCA Red Seal RL 25076
>   John McCabe (piano)
>
>   SEE: B124, B135

D30.   VARIATIONS ON A THEME OF HARTMANN (W37)

>   HMV ASD 3096
>   Halle Orchestra/ James Loughran
>
>   SEE: B123, B379
>
>   EMI Greensleeves ED291219-1 (compact disc)
>   ED291219-4 (cassette)
>
>   SEE: B290

McCABE AS PERFORMER (arranged in composer order)

D31.   ABBOTT : Alla Caccia

>   Pye GSGC 14087
>   Ifor James (horn)
>
>   Also includes: P.R. Fricker Sonata for horn and
>   piano
>   P. Hindemith Sonata in F for
>   horn and piano

C. Nielsen   Canto serioso

SEE: B325

D32.   BAX : Piano Quartet

Chandos   ABRD 1113
          CHAN 8391 (compact disc)
          ABTD 1113 (cassette)

Members of the English String Quartet

Also includes: A.Bax Harp Quintet
                     String Quartet No.1.

SEE: B6, B128

D33.   BAX : Piano Sonata No.4. - Allegretto quasi andante

Decca Ace of Diamonds SDD 444

Also includes:
G.Holst   Nocturne; Jig; Two Folk Song Fragments
J. Ireland   Sonatina
E.J. Moeran   Bank Holiday
R. Vaughan Williams The Lake in the Mountains
                    Hymn Tune Prelude
                    Suite of Six Short Pieces
P. Warlock   Five Folk-Song Preludes

SEE: B89, B370

D34.   BERKELEY, L.: Duo for cello and piano

L'Oiseau Lyre DSLO 18
Julian Lloyd Webber (cello)

Also includes:
M. Dalby   Variations for cello and piano
P.R. Fricker Cello Sonata

D35.   BRAHMS : Four Pieces
               Three Intermezzi
               Variations and fugue on a theme of Handel

Oryx Basic Record Library BRL 78
                          BRL 78 (cassette)

D36.   BRIDGE : Elegy for cello and piano

ASV ACA 1001
ZCACA 1000 (cassette)

With Julian Lloyd Webber (cello)

Also includes:
B. Britten   Suite No.3 for solo cello
J. Ireland   Cello sonata

SEE: B8, B129

D37.   BRITTEN : Cello Sonata

Phillips 422 345 - 2PH (compact disc)

Julian Lloyd Webber (cello)

Also includes:
S. Prokofiev   Ballade for cello and piano
D. Shostakovitch   Cello sonata in D minor

SEE: B151

D38.   BRITTEN : Notturno

Pye GSGC 14116

Reissued PRT GSGC 2069
             ZOGC 2069 (cassette)

Also includes:
A. Copland   Variations
J. McCabe   Five Bagatelles
C. Nielsen   Chaconne
A. Rawsthorne   Bagetelles
A. Schoenberg   Six Little Pieces
A. von Webern   Variations

SEE: B88, B165

D39.   BRITTEN : Tema "Sacher"

ASV DCA 592
   CDDCA 592 (compact disc)
   ZCDCA 592 (cassette)

Julian Lloyd Webber (cello)

Also includes:
M. Arnold   Fantasy
J. Ireland   The Holy Boy
A. Rawsthorne   Cello Sonata
W. Walton   Passacaglia

SEE: B351

D40.   CASKEN : La Orana

Wergo WER 60096
Jane Manning (soprano)

Also includes: Firewheel

String Quartet

SEE: B298

D41.   CLEMENTI : Sonata in D

Hyperion A 66057

Also includes:
M. Clementi   Monferrinas
Sonata in F
Sonata in G minor

SEE: B60

D42.   COOKE : Rondo in B-flat

Cornucopia IJ 100
With Ifor James (horn)

Also includes:
L. Baker   Cantilena
T. Dunhill   Cornucopia
J. Eccles (arr. Eger) Sonata in G minor
Gwilt   Sonata
Stirling   Variations on a Tyrolean
theme
Trad.(arr Stirling)   Carnival of Venice
G. Vinter   Hunter's Moon

SEE: B292

D43.   ELGAR : Piano Works

Rediffusion Prelude PRS 2503

SEE: B7, B131

D44.   GOEHR : Four songs from the Japanese

Pye GSGC 14105

Re-issued Nonesuch H 71209
Marni Nixon (soprano)

Also includes:
C. Ives   songs
G. Schürmann   Chuench'i

SEE: B133, B293

D45.   GRIEG : Piano Works

        RCA GL 25329
           GK 25329 (cassette)

        SEE: B182

D46.   GRIEG : Piano works

        Oryx Basic Record Library BRL 97
                                BRL 97 (cassette)

D47.   HAYDN : Keyboard Sonatas

        HMV HQS 1301

        SEE: B110

D48.   HAYDN : Piano Works Volume 1

        Decca 1 HDN 100-2

        SEE: B90, B111, B148

D49.   HAYDN : Piano Works Volume 2

        Decca 2 HDN 103-5

        SEE: B90, B112, B147, B148, B341

D50.   HAYDN : Piano Works Volume 3

        Decca 3 HDN 106-8

        SEE: B148, B323

D51.   HAYDN : Piano Works Volume 4

        Decca 4 HDN 109-11

        SEE: B148, B324

D52.   HAYDN : Piano Works Volume 5

        Decca 5 HDN 112-115

        SEE: B113, B148, B163

D53.   JOUBERT : Piano Works

        Pearl SHE 520

        Reissued Max Sound MSCB 33 (cassette)

SEE: B41, B107, B289

D54.   MENDELSSOHN : Capriccio Brilliant (transcribed for piano/brass band)

        Pye GSGL 10510
        Besses o' th' Barn Band/Ifor James

        Also includes:
        G.F. Handel   Sonata in G minor
        J. Horovitz   Sinfonietta for Brass
        P. Sievewright Jazz Intermezzo
        P. Yorke   The Shipbuilders Suite

D55.   MOERAN : Rhapsody in F sharp minor

        Lyrita SRCS 91

        New Philharmonic Orchestra/ N. Braithwaite

        Also includes:
        F. Bridge   Phantasm

        SEE: B369

D56.   MOZART : Piano Works

        Oryx Basic Record Library BRL 27
                                     BRL 27 (cassette)

D57.   MOZART : Piano Works

        Oryx Basic Record Library BRL 28
                                       BRL 28 (cassette)

D58.   NIELSEN : Piano Works

        Decca Ace of Diamonds SDD 475-6

        SEE: B183, B306

D59.   PINTO : Piano Sonatas

        Phoenix DGS 1014

D60.   SATIE : Piano Works

        Saga 5387

        SEE: B136

D61.   SATIE : Piano Works

    Saga 5472

    SEE: B137

D62.   SCARLATTI : Keyboard Sonatas

    Hyperion A66025

    SEE: B350

D63.   SCHUMANN : Piano Works

    Oryx Basic Record Library BRL 59
                            BRL 59 (cassette)

D64.   WALTON : Piano Quartet

    Meridian CDE 84139 (compact disc)
              KE 77139 (cassette)

    Members of the English String Quartet

    Also includes:
    W. Walton   String Quartet in A minor

    SEE: B161

Bibliography

"See" references refer to individual works and particular performances of those works as described in the "Works and Performances" section (e.g., SEE: W133) and in the "Discography" (e.g., SEE: D33).

ARTICLES AND FEATURES ABOUT AND BY McCABE

B1.   Abraham, Gerald. "Ancient and Modern in Abbey Concert". The Daily Telegraph, 25 June 1968, p.19.

"The first performance of John McCabe's Concertante Music...was conducted by George Odam. It is an immediately attractive work, specially written for Newton Park.... Its central movement is a chorale-with-variations dedicated to the memory of Martin Luther King, the theme rather unimpressive in the classical tradition of variation themes, but developing with ingenuity and in one of the variations with great expressive power."

SEE: W8

B2.   Acton, Charles. "Reports: Dublin." Musical Times, 110 (March 1969), p.290.

"John McCabe's Capriccio, which he played himself, is a very enjoyable toccata-like essay in tremolando single notes with some progressions of rich romantic chords, as slight as its title but a delightful work for a final recital group."

SEE: W40

B3.   Adam, Corinna. "Television: sad stories." The Listener, 105 (16 April 1981), p. 518.

A review of The Good Soldier, Julian Mitchell's adaptation of Ford Madox Ford's favourite novel, but with no mention of McCabe's incidental music.

SEE: W154

B4.   Addison, Richard. "Listen, Look, Learn. "Music Teacher, 49 (June 1970), p. 14.

A set of questions for teachers about two of the Five Bagatelles for piano.

SEE: W42

B5.   Alps, Tim. "Orchestral." Music and Musicians, 28 (February 1980), p.60.

"John McCabe's The Shadow of Light which was given its premiere by the Royal Philharmonic Orchestra...was composed in response to the commission from the orchestra for a work to celebrate the bicentenary of the death of William Boyce....Many of Boyce's dance movements are cleverly orchestrated and the final fugue and quodlibet tie up many of the loose ends."

SEE: W31

B6.   Anderson, Robert. "British and Czech." The Musical Times, CXXVI (May 1985), p. 289.

A review of the English String Quartet's performance of Arnold Bax's chamber music on Chandos 1113. "John McCabe beautifully judges the multitudinous piano part."

SEE: D32

B7.   Anderson, Robert. "Record Reviews." The Muscial Times, 117 (December 1976), pp. 1003-4.

A review of Elgar's complete piano works on Prelude PRS 2503.

"McCabe is sympathetic throughout and once again obsessive Elgarians will be pleased."

SEE: D43

B8.   Anderson, Robert. "Record Reviews." The Musical Times, cxxii (June 1981), p. 388.

A review of the ASV ACA 1001 recording.   "John McCabe has full control of Ireland's teeming piano part and there are no balance problems...."

SEE: D36

B9.   Anon.   "Balanced Brass."   The Times (London),   27 February 1968, p.11.

"It was left to John McCabe to reach out for more truly musical expression in his Rounds for Brass Quintet.... The opening fanfare disclosed motifs which were built into complex structures in the ensuing Toccata, but it was in the slow movement that we glimpsed...the possibilities offered by brass sonorities in more profound musical expression."

SEE: W172

B10.   Anon.   "Balanced new duet sonata."   Western Daily Press, 9 July 1964, p. 7.

"...the first performance of Three Pieces for clarinet and piano by John McCabe had a warm reception.

His writing in the second piece, Improvisation sub-titled Bosonova, was a delight in balance between a subdued piano part and the slowing melodic clarinet."

SEE: W106

B11.   Anon.   "Concert Club highlight."   Malvern Gazette and Ledbury Reporter, 27 September 1973, p.12.

Details about the forthcoming first performance of Time Remembered, a chamber cantata for soprano and seven instruments.

SEE: W143

B12.   Anon.   "Concert Notes."   The Strad, 89 (April 1979), p. 1139.

A review of the first performance of Star Preludes. "This fascinating work is proof that the music reflects the age in which it is born. The main idea is based on 'stars whirling about in space' and certainly the atmosphere of astral eeriness was captured from the first few bars."

SEE: W104

B13.   Anon. "Editorial Notes." The Strad, LXXVII (July 1966), p.115.

Details about the first Violin Concerto, a "...work [which] could be described as conservative, with movements that suggest the composer is not unashamed to acknowledge the astringent melancholies of Walton, Rawsthorne and Prokofiev.

In this work he has nearly transcended these influences - already he writes for the violin with ease...and he balances his soloist against well-considered orchestral textures."

SEE:W19

B14.   Anon. "Editorial Notes." The Strad, LXXVII (August 1966), p. 147.

A review of the first performance of the First Symphony in which McCabe "...is alert and alight to sound - which is also musical sound, and if sometimes textures reminded one of masters of the immediate past such as Hindemith and perhaps Walton, one was also struck by the new sonic emphasis with which these debts were now repaid."

SEE: W33

B15.   Anon. "Guild award for John McCabe." The Times (London), 29 December 1975, p.4.

"At the Guild's [Composers' Guild] annual luncheon...the guild's award for special contribution to British music (was presented) to John McCabe, composer-performer whose programmes regularly include works by living British composers."

B16.   Anon. "John McCabe." Musical Events, 21 (July 1966), p.13.

A brief biography of McCabe, together with details of forthcoming new works.

B17.   Anon. "John McCabe." Musical Opinion, 106 (July 1983), p.319.

A note about the appointment of "John McCabe, the distinguished composer and pianist (who) has accepted the post of Director of the London College of Music...the smallest of the five main London music colleges."

B18.   Anon. "John McCabe at 50" Music and Musicians
        International, 37 (May 1989), p.41.

        A detailed schedule of 50th birthday concerts for
        the summer of 1989.

B19.   Anon. "John McCabe's first opera. "Musical Events,
        24 (January 1969), p.32.

        An announcement about The Lion, The Witch and The
        Wardrobe, an opera in "four continuous acts with
        prologue and epilogue (which) will be mounted on
        a revolving stage."

        SEE: W146

B20.   Anon. "Liverpool Institute Music Club." Liverpool
        Daily Post, 15 March 1958, p.4.

        An account of a concert at the Liverpool
        Institute Music Club.

        "Also studying at Manchester is J. McCabe,
        (a)...musical pianist of nineteen who has
        something to say in the sphere of composition as
        well. A Passacaglia for two pianos bore more
        than a hint of Ravel...."

        SEE: W54

B21.   Anon. "McCabe at 50." Music and Musicians
        International, 37 (April 1989), pp. 2-3.

        A profile of the composer's 50th birthday
        celebrations which highlighted some of the main
        events throughout the year featuring his work.

B22.   Anon. "Major Musical Event of the Week." Southport
        Visitor, 16 May 1967, p.6.

        A description of the preparations at Southport's
        Floral Hall for the premiere of the First Piano
        Concerto.

        SEE: W16

B23.   Anon. "Music strongly committed." The Times
        (London), 19 April 1966, p.14.

        An account of the Park Lane Group concert which
        included the first London performance of Alun
        Hoddinott's third piano sonata, played by John
        McCabe, "...a vigorous, accomplished
        advocate...."

B24.   Anon. "New Look or Old Habits?" <u>The Times</u>
        (London), 11 February 1964, p.13.

        "The idiom of McCabe's settings would be called
        conservatiave (deriving from Hindemith), but they
        have a sure sense of style and some real
        interpretative ideas."

        SEE: W137

B25.   Anon. "Philharmonic Choir at Church." <u>Northampton
        Chronicle and Echo</u>, 29 October 1976, p.3.

        A photograph of the composer with Graham Mayo,
        conductor of the Northampton Philharmonic Choir,
        at a reception held after the choir's performance
        of <u>Stabat Mater</u> at St. Matthew's Church.

        SEE: W125

B26.   Anon. "Sombre McCabe work cunningly varied." <u>The
        Times</u> (London), 5 July 1966, p.16.

        A review of the opening concert of the 1966
        Cheltenham Festival which included the first
        performance of John McCabe's <u>First Symphony</u>.
        "The musical material is thoroughly worked out
        and closely argued...."

        SEE: W33

B27.   Anon. "Taxing new music." <u>The Times</u> (London), 28
        February 1967, p.8.

        "Their recital...last night, which relied
        entirely on the piano playing of John McCabe,
        certainly taxed one's powers of concentration by
        including five premieres.

        John McCabe's...<u>Five Bagatelles</u>...made efficient
        and imaginative capital out of the challenge to
        produce easy serial pieces for amateurs and
        students...."

        SEE: W42

B28.   Anon. "Tribute to Composer." <u>The Messenger</u> (Sale
        and Altrincham), 6 May 1983, p.21.

        An announcement about the concert to celebrate
        the eightieth birthday of the English composer
        Thomas Pitfield, with works specially written by
        Michael Ball, John McCabe and Gordon Crosse.

        SEE: W83

B29.   Anon.   "Vivid Halle colouring." The Times, 9 July
        1966, p.13.

        "Last night it [Halle Orchestra] had sterner
        tasks to discharge, notably that of introducing
        John McCabe's Symphony No. 1, subtitled "Elegy"
        to London, just five days after its Cheltenham
        premiere. Sir John Barbirolli and his players
        brought up the orchestral colours most vividly."

        SEE: W33

B30.   Anon.   "World premiere at Kelso an exciting
        landmark." Kelso Chronicle and Jedburgh Gazette,
        11 January 1980, p.1.

        Details about the concert, which included the
        premiere of Paraphrase on Mary Queen of Scots,
        and McCabe's career.

        SEE: W53

B31.   Aprahamian, Felix. "Mozart's geisha girls." The
        Sunday Times, 13 February 1983, p.41.

        "This week also brought two native novelties of
        quality. John McCabe's Concerto for Orchestra,
        given by the LPO under Sir Georg Solti at the
        Festival Hall..., was commissioned to mark the
        orchestra's fiftieth anniversary. A large-scale
        symmetrical piece in five linked sections, it
        goes far beyond the mere display of orchestral
        colour and prowess in its complex but always
        striking working-out of a basic theme. Already
        gripping at a first hearing it will need more
        performances to be assimilated at its true
        worth."

        SEE: W15

B32.   Aprahamian, Felix. "Piano premiere of power." The
        Sunday Times, 25 November 1984, p.41.

        "Wednesday's BBC Invitation Concert by the
        Symphony Orchestra at the Maida Vale Studio
        offered the UK premiere of an exciting Piano
        Concerto by John Corigliano...which kept both the
        conductor Richard Buckley, and soloist, John
        McCabe, extremely busy.

        McCabe confirmed his prodigious keyboard mastery
        in two other movements of breath-taking
        brilliance and a fascinating scherzo in which the
        piano and orchestra combine in scoring of
        unusually interesting spacing. The slow movement

seemed more contrived and, so duller and less
distinguished...."

B33.   Aprahamian, Felix. ["Reviews."] The Sunday Times,
        9 November 1980, p.40.

        A report that "John McCabe also played a more
        concerto-like accompaniment, for Jane Manning in
        John Casken's la Orana, Gauguin, a pungent
        onamatopoeic musical dismemberment of his own
        purple poem."

B34.   B.,J. "Rich moods in new piano concerto." The
        Daily Telegraph, 20 May 1967, p.13.

        A review of the First Piano Concerto's premiere
        at Southport.

        SEE: W16

B35.   Barkla, Neil. "Bouquets for the Sandon." Liverpool
        Daily Post, 20 December 1965, p.3.

        An account of the first performance of McCabe's
        Concertante for Harpsichord and Chamber Ensemble.
        "This seems to me Mr McCabe's best work to date,
        and the attention is held for a full twenty
        minutes by the fascinating timbres he extracts
        from his chosen medium...."

        SEE: W7

B36.   Barkla, Neil. "Composer saves jinx-hit work."
        Liverpool Daily Post, 21 February 1972, p.3.

        A report about the "...misfortunes (which) have
        twice prevented the first performance of John
        McCabe's Metamorphosen for Harpsichord and
        Orchestra....

        Nor were they absent on Saturday, when it was the
        composer himself who finally played the work....

        Despite these handicaps, the performance was
        sufficient to give an impression of a significant
        and highly interesting piece which employs a
        large orchestra with strict economy to allow the
        solo instruments to show through."

        SEE: W29

B37.   Barkla, Neil. "Saying a graceful goodbye...."
        Liverpool Daily Post, 6 August 1977, p.3.

An account of Sir Charles Groves' farewell Philharmonic Concert which included the premiere of McCabe's third piano concerto.

"John McCabe's new concerto must be heard again.... The solo part was brilliantly played by Ilan Rogoff and first impressions suggest more attention to rhythm and harmony than to melody."

SEE: W18

B38.   Barkla, Neil. "What the absent missed." Liverpool Daily Post, 30 June 1958, p.8.

A report about the playing of "...Turina's Rapsodia Sinfonica for piano and strings...by John McCabe, a promising young Merseyside musician now studying at Manchester University and who has recently appeared with the Royal Liverpool Philharmonic Orchestra at a concert for schools."

B39.   Barstow, Chris. "Chamber: Delme String Quartet." The Strad, 93 (January 1983), pp. 621+23.

Concert notes about the premiere of John McCabe's Fourth String Quartet which is described as "...a 20 minute work whose straight forward alternation of slow and fast sections leaves little room for structural interest or complexity."

SEE: W97

B40.   Bawden, Rex. "The boy who became a man of music." Liverpool Daily Post, 19 April 1989, pp. 18-19.

A synopsis of McCabe's life - "...Merseyside's most successful composer" - written to mark his 50th birthday.

B41.   Birkin, Kenneth. "Joubert." The Musical Times, cxxix (February 1988), pp. 90-91.

A review of MSCB 33 on 34 containing Joubert's piano and choral music.

"On the composer's own admission, the performances of the piano works as recorded here by John McCabe are 'definitive'. McCabe's intuitive grasp of the language, his technical brilliance and interpretative control contribute to make his reading a sound document of notable authenticity and artistic significance."

SEE: D53

B42.   Blezzard, Judith.   "Reports: Liverpool."   The
        Musical Times, 118 (October 1977), p. 845.

        "A capacity audience gave Sir Charles Groves a
        well-deserved ovation at his farewell concert...

        John McCabe's Piano Concerto no. 3 was given its
        first performance by Ilan Rogoff.... It is an
        exciting, urgent and virtuso piece, deriving much
        from jazz and ostinato rhythms."

        SEE: W18

B43.   Blunn, John R.   "Last night: Halle concert."
        Manchester Evening News, 10 January 1975, p.8.

        "First impressions of The Chagall Windows,
        inspired by Marc Chagall...were of a beautifully
        scored and consistently appealing work. It is a
        pleasant, rich and colourful work which deserves
        its place in the repertory."

        SEE: W5

B44.   Blyth, Alan.   "Other recitals: music of the
        spheres." Music and Musicians, 13 (March 1965),
        pp. 41+58.

        A review of the concert when Movements for
        clarinet, violin and cello was first performed.

        "It is agreeable enough to listen to, but its
        palindronic form seems to serve little
        constructive purpose: the three outer movements
        sounded better first time round than in the
        retrograde."

        SEE: W88

B45.   Bowen, Merion.   "Contemporary."   Music and
        Musicians, 20 (June 1972), p.69.

        "John McCabe's Rounds for brass quintet was more
        substantial and better organised. Most of the
        thematic material of is five movements comes from
        the opening fanfares on muted brass, these
        fanfares recurring at various points."

        SEE: W172

B46.   Boyd, Malcolm. "Cardiff." The Musical Times, 109
        (June 1968), p.559.

        "John McCabe's Canto makes a pleasant addition to
        the guitar repertory...."

SEE: W76

B47.   Boyd, Malcolm.   "Cardiff."   The Musical Times, 112
        (July 1971), p.685.

        "By far the most accomplished and rewarding of
        the new works was John McCabe's Basse Danse for
        two pianos, played by the composer and Ian Bruce,
        to whom the work is dedicated.   McCabe has here
        adopted...the structure of some of the 'basses
        danses' in Attaingnant's collection of 1530, in
        which themes first heard in a predominantly slow
        section   reappear   in   a   faster   tempo.   The
        themes...are   McCabe's   own   -   economical,
        distinctive   and   memorable   -   and   expertly
        conceived for the two instruments."

        SEE: W39

B48.   Boyd, Malcolm.   "Festivals: Cardiff, St. David's."
        The Musical Times, 111 (May 1970), p.528.

        "Another   first   performance   was   that   of   John
        McCabe's Gaudi (Study no. 3), part of a brilliant
        piano recital by Valerie Tryon.   McCabe uses
        vividly contrasting textures and dynamics in an
        interesting if not, at first hearing, entirely
        convincing attempt to recreate in music the
        spirit   of   the   Spanish   architect's   unusual
        buildings."

        SEE: W44

B49.   Boyd,   Malcolm.   "Record   Reviews."   The   Musical
        Times, 116 (February 1975), p. 149.

        "McCabe's String Trio, completed in 1965 (on Argo
        ZRG 761)...is more eclectic and prodigal with its
        ideas...."

        SEE: D22

B50.   Boyd, Malcolm.   "RPO's McCabe commission."   Music
        and Musicians, 26 (July 1978), pp. 8+10.

        "John   McCabe's   Third   Symphony   received   its
        premiere on 11 July at the Festival Hall.   An RPO
        commission and entitled 'Hommages' it makes use
        of   material   derived   from   the   works   of   two
        composers very important to McCabe - Haydn and
        Nielsen, the former represented by the theme of
        the slow movement of his Quartet, Op. 76 no. 6,
        the latter by chords derived from the Piano
        Suite, Op. 45.   Many characteristics of McCabe's
        music are present in this symphony: the clarity,

the conciseness..., the texture interest, the
harmonic impulse and so on. It is a clear score
with much of interest...."

SEE: W35

B51.   Boyd, Malcolm. "South Wales." <u>The Musical Times</u>,
        109 (February 1968), p.160.

A report about the weekly chamber music recitals
organised by the faculty of music at University
College, Cardiff.

"Visiting artists appear from time to time, but
most   of   the   recitals   are   given   by   the
University's resident executants - at present the
Wang Quartet and John McCabe (piano). This
season will include, for the first time, two
works   specially   commissioned   for   these
concerts....
...on the whole the playing of the quartet this
term has been remarkably good, and John McCabe
has shown himself a consistently intelligent and
expressive pianist."

B52.   Boyd, Malcolm. "South Wales." <u>The Musical Times</u>,
        110 (June 1969), p. 659.

A very brief mention of the first performance of
McCabe's <u>Oboe Quartet</u> in the Reardon Smith
Lecture Theatre at University College, Cardiff.

SEE: W94

B53.   Boyd, Malcolm. "South Wales." <u>The Musical Times</u>,
        cxx (November 1979), p. 940.

"The title of the first movement of McCabe's
<u>Third String Quartet</u> ('Variants') was chosen as a
50th-birthday   tribute   to   the   composer   Alun
Hoddinott,   while   for   the   last   movement,   a
passacaglia, McCabe acknowledges the influence of
Britten;   the   first   of   the   two   Scherzos   is
supposedly inspired by Beethoven's example, and
the second one (a palindromic structure) adopts a
'phase' technique of a kind associated with Steve
Reich....the work, finely played by the Gabrieli
Quartet,   certainly   contains   enough   distinctive
and original material...."

SEE: W96

B54.   Boyd, Malcolm "Wales." <u>The Musical Times</u>, cxix
        (September 1978), p.787.

"The new work...was <u>Reflections of a Summer Night</u>.... His setting for chorus and small orchestra of five interlinked poems...evokes the atmosphere of sultry summer evenings....
...the work's blend of mainly sustained choral sound and allusive orchestral commentary is persuasively shaped, and the languid tones of muted strings, horn and English horn are effectively offset by judicious use of a harpsichord and various percussion instruments."

SEE: W123

B55.   Bradbury, Ernest. "Harrogate." <u>The Musical Times</u>, 111 (October 1970), p. 1021

"One must also mention John McCabe, a highly cultivated, sensitive, discerning composer, playing his own <u>Fantasy on a theme of Liszt</u> and the first performance of his piano study <u>Aubade</u> at a morning recital.

McCabe is a composer who grows mightily in musical stature."

SEE: W38, W41

B56.   Buckman, Peter. "Standards and stamina." <u>The Listener</u>, 94 (3 July 1975), p.22.

A review of <u>Sam</u> (Granada TV), but with no direct reference to McCabe's incidental music.

SEE: W163

B57.   C., M.R. "Indisputable merits of cellist." <u>The Daily Telegraph</u>, 7 December 1966, p.17.

"The recital brought the first performance of John McCabe's <u>Partita for solo cello</u> written for and dedicated to Mr. Gough. Approaching to the form of theme and variations, the music is fluently conceived and resourcefully exploits the expressive and virtuosic aspect of the instrument."

SEE: W91

B58.   Campbell, Margaret. "Concert notes." <u>The Strad</u>, 91 June 1980), pp. 95-96.

Notes about the first London performance of McCabe's <u>Second Violin Concerto</u> which is described as "...a compelling and beautifully

conceived work which should be allotted an
immediate place in the concerto repertory."

SEE: W20

B59.   Chislett, W.A. "Carols for 1970." <u>The Gramophone</u>,
        XLVIII (December 1970), p. 980.

        "From the same company comes a record from the
        Leeds Parish Church - Abbey XMS 697. The
        programme is a judicious mixture of the old and
        new, ranging from Byrd to recent carols by...John
        McCabe...."

        SEE: D7

B60.   Chissell, Joan. "Clementi." <u>Gramophone</u>, 60 (January
        1983), p. 845.

        A review of the recording Hyperion A 66057.
        "McCabe plays with a sense of mission and
        his...piano comes over with commendable
        truthfulness."

        SEE: D41

B61.   Chissell, Joan.   "Contemporary   carols."   <u>The
        Gramophone</u>, XLIV (December 1966), pp. 327-8.

        A review of ZRG 5499. "...the pieces by...Maw
        and McCabe are all easily enjoyable, even by the
        conservative listener."

        SEE: D7

B62.   Chissell, Joan. "Flexibility." <u>The Times</u> (London),
        18 April 1970, p.III.

        A description of the London premiere of McCabe's
        <u>Concerto for piano and wind quintet</u>.

        "...it was easy to appreciate all the fine
        craftsmanship that have gone into the music's
        making."

        SEE: W78

B63.   Chissell, Joan. "LSO: Festival Hall." <u>The Times</u>
        (London), 10 December 1971, p.11.

        An account of the London premiere of <u>Notturni ed
        Alba</u>.
        "The vocal line is shapely...and many nice
        details of imagery are picked up by the orchestra

- not least "desire for the loved one" by languishing violins."

SEE: W30

B64.   Chissell, Joan. "LSO/Previn." The Times (London), 18 April 1977, p.6.

"...Princess Alice, Duchess of Gloucester, was there to listen to a programme starting with a new curtain-raiser by John McCabe called Jubilee Prelude.

'Prelude' was apt. So brief a piece could scarcely have been called an overture. Yet is is more than a fanfare although growing from fanfare-like motifs, which are taken over from brass and percussion by full orchestra in what McCabe calls its 'second verse'. The brass scoring is ear-catching."

SEE: W28

B65.   Chissell, Joan. "McCabe/Troup." The Times (London), 5 April 1971, p.8.

"McCabe's Basse Danse for two pianos might be described as post-Debussyian, at any rate its slower sections. But alike in textural and rhythmic ingenuity (the latter most noticeably in faster tempo) it reveals a much more exploratory McCabe than we sometimes meet."

SEE: W39

B66.   Clarke, Mary. "Mary Queen of Scots." Dancing Times, LXVI (April 1976, pp. 354-55.

A description of McCabe's two act ballet Mary Queen of Scots after its premiere in Glasgow by the Scottish Ballet.

SEE: W2

B67.   Clements, Andrew. "BBC Philharmonic." Financial Times, 18 August 1989, p. 13.

"The work new to London was John McCabe's Fire at Durilgai...a 15-minute evocation of conflagaration and the desert landscape of Australia.... It is a strange, centre-less piece...though the ending is fierce and emphatic. The writing is expert and involving from moment to moment, but it never gathers momentum or leaves a lasting trace."

SEE: W26

B68.   Clements, Andrew. "King's Singers/Elizabeth Hall."
        Financial Times, 2 February 1988, p. 15.

        "The McCabe, Scenes from America Deserta, was
        written for the King's Singers in 1986; this was
        its first performance in London. It is the most
        recent of a series of works in which McCabe has
        explored aspects of desert landscape; in this
        case it is the American desert seen through the
        eyes of Reyner Banham."

        SEE: W124

B69.   Cole, Hugo. "John McCabe's 'Movements' at the Arts
        Council." The Guardian, 26 January 1965, p.11.

        "Movements is a well sounding and vigorous piece
        of music. The terms, not striking in their own
        right but apt to the situations in which they
        appear, the clear texture of the music, and the
        general high but not over-insistent level of
        dissonance are all of a piece.

        But there was still plenty to enjoy and be
        grateful for in the agreeable and consistent tone
        of voice and the ease of movement of this music."

        SEE: W88

B70.   Cole, Hugo. "John McCabe's Partita for Cello at the
        Wigmore Hall." The Guardian, 7 December 1966,
        p.7.

        "The work is a theme and seven variations,
        continuity is effected by the simple device of
        ending each immediate section with a musical
        question mark. McCabe never explores the cello's
        character in great depth, but his music belongs
        to and is shaped by the instrument."

        SEE: W91

B71.   Cole, Hugo. "Lone Ranger." The Guardian, 8 October
        1971, p. 10.

        An appreciation and detailed survey of McCabe's
        life and music.

B72.   Cole Hugo.   "McCabe."   The Musical Times,   113
        (January 1982), p. 64.

"John McCabe was the soloist in the first London performance of his Second Piano Concerto.... The subtitle (Sinfonia Concertante) could refer both to the pianist's fairly modest, unvirtuosic role, and to the use of a group of nine solo instruments within the chamber orchestra. It is a particularly well-sounding work, with dissonances so knowingly spaced that they never muddy the clear water. McCabe's acute feeling for the precise layout of a score allows him to create original and individual music without ever resorting to extreme measures."

SEE: W17

B73.   Cole, Hugo.   "Manchester Cathedral: The Lion, the Witch and the Wardrobe." The Guardian, 30 April 1969, p. 10.

"Libretto, production, and above all the music of the new work have generally a professional expertise. McCabe gives each singer opportunities according to his capacities, orchestrates with rare imagination and discretion, allowing the full fury of Cheetham's Hospital orchestra...to be unleashed grandly at moments of violent action."

SEE: W146

B74.   Cole, Hugo.   "The new Cantata Orchestra at the QEH." The Guardian, 6 July 1968, p.6.

"John McCabe's Concerto for Chamber Orchestra, written in 1962 but first performed last night, was an uncomplicated, robust and attractive piece, admirably confident in its refusal to overload straight forward themes with more significance than they can take...."

SEE: W11a

B75.   Coombs, Sara.   "Ripon Cathedral: Guildhall String Ensemble." Harrogate Advertiser, 7 August 1987, p. 13.

"The oddity in Monday evening's programme was the world premiere of Rainforest II for trumpet and 11 strings.... This modern piece was thoroughly electric. It featured humming and buzzing strings pieced by the clear tones of the trumpet, only occasionally falling into true discord.

It was full of surprises and flashes of lightening and certainly got the adrenalin going. It went down extremely well with soloist Hakan

Hardenberger and composer John McCabe receiving thunderous applause."

SEE: W101

B76.   Craddock, Peter. "Bartok: Orchestral Music by John McCabe." _Music in Education_, 39 (1975), p. 167.

A review of the BBC Music Guide. "John McCabe explores Bartok's orchestral output with a depth of understanding and sympathy that can only come from a fellow composer, tracing the development of style from the early Straussian pieces through the middle period of folk synthesis to the works of the last decade which McCabe unfashionably but refreshingly   regards   as   Bartok's   greatest achievement."

B77.   Crankshaw, Geoffrey. "Festival Hall: Suite or symphony?" _Music and Musicians_, 15 (September 1966), p. 48.

"First heard at the recent Cheltenham Festival, John McCabe's _Symphony No. 1_ received its London premiere at Festival Hall on 8 July. Sir John Barbirolli and the Halle Orchestra had obviously taken great pains to present this sombre but thoughtful work to its best advantage. The three movements...are well constructed...."

SEE: W33

B78.   Crichton, Ronald. "Aeolian Singers." _The Musical Times_, 108 (August 1967), p. 722.

"McCabe's text [for _Aspects of Whiteness_] is a splendidly florid piece of poetic prose from Melville's _Moby Dick_ which would provide enough imagery to support a large choral symphony. McCabe goes straight through it using mainly a form of rhythmic chanting, almost at the rate of speech. It is efficiently carried out, there are effective moments (the opening is one of them) and the composers sensitive feeling for the rhythms of the prose is obvious...."

SEE: W107

B79.   Crichton, Ronald. "Bach Cantatas." _Financial Times_, 27 November 1963, p. 24.

"...Simon Preston gave the first London performance of _Dies Resurrectionis_, an organ work by the young Liverpool composer, John McCabe....Dies Resurrectionis consists of three

sections of Messiaen-like intensity but of a
brevity untypical of the French composer, [and
consists of] short, sudden and often impressive
bursts of sound lasting just long enough to whet
one's appetite...."

SEE: W64

B80.   Crichton, Ronald. John McCabe." The Musical Times,
        116 (May 1975), p. 446.

        "The composer-pianist John McCabe, engaged in the
        recording of the complete keyboard sonatas of
        Haydn, played three of them in his recital at the
        Purcell Room on 18 March. There was a sparse
        audience, confirming the general and saddening
        impression that in large doses, and apart from
        the big oratorios, Haydn is among the least
        popular of very great composers. His own Fantasy
        on a Theme of Liszt is an effective bravura piece
        on the 12-note theme from the Faust Symphony's
        first movement, a tribute not only to Liszt but
        to Chopin and (the composer assures us) to
        Schumann as well."

        SEE: W41

B81.   Crichton, Ronald. "Orchestral." The Musical Times,
        109 (December 1968), p. 1131.

        "John McCabe's Variations on a theme of Hartmann
        received their first London performance at this
        concert. There is some attractive music both
        among the four short opening variations and the
        longer   Sarabande-Chaconne   and   concluding
        fugue...."

        SEE: W37

B82.   Cross, Anthony. "Birmingham." The Musical Times,
        cxxi (August 1980), p. 515.

        "John McCabe's Second Violin Concerto (first
        performed by Erich Gruenberg and the CBSO on 20
        March) is firmly in the Romantic concerto
        tradition in its reliance on thoroughly
        conventional writing for the soloist -
        protagonist, who dominates almost throughout.
        But the emphasis is on lyricism rather than
        virtuosity. This and the richness of orchestral
        sound...no doubt explains the warm reception for
        an ambitious, extended score...."

        SEE: W20

B83.   Cross, Anthony.   "Festivals: Birmingham."   The
        Musical Times, 112 (November 1971), p. 1090.

        "Among several new works, the Feeney commission
        was McCabe's Second Symphony, played with evident
        relish by its dedicatees, Fremaux and the
        CBSO....The new work might...be more
        appropriately called Concerto; the brilliantly
        effective instrumental writing, the emphasis on
        fragmentary material and ostinato-like
        repetition, inevitably focused attention on the
        ideas themselves rather than on the form as a
        whole."

        SEE: W34

B84.   Cross, Anthony. "Liverpool." The Musical Times 107
        (February 1966), p. 138.

        "The Sandon Studios Music Group, a mixed
        professional and amateur organisation which
        devotes much of its efforts to propagating
        contemporary music, celebrated its 60th birthday
        in 1965. To mark the occasion John McCabe wrote
        his Concertante for harpsichord and chamber
        ensemble....

        ...McCabe might have been influenced by the
        avant-garde, though in the event the work,
        maintaining a total language, proved to be in the
        good old British tradition of compromise with
        more radical continental procedures...."

        SEE: W7

B85.   Cross, Anthony.   "Liverpool."   The Musical Times,
        108 (January 1967), p. 58.

        "McCabe's Movements for clarinet, violin and
        cello, consisting of several short bagatelles
        grouped in palindromic form round a central
        Adagio, proved to be a work of considerable
        fluency...."

        SEE: W88a

B86.   Cross, Anthony. "Reports: Birmingham." The Musical
        Times, 111 (April 1970), p. 411.

        "In commissioning John McCabe's Concerto for
        piano and wind quintet..., the Birmingham Chamber
        Music Society, whose attitude to new music is not
        the most adventurous, no doubt expected an
        effective piece written in a basically
        traditional language. In this they were not
        disappointed. The work's element of display –

not confined to the pianist – its great variety
of character, its rhythmic vitality, made an
immediate impact."

SEE: W78

B87.   Crutchfield, Will. "Chamber: Rainforest by McCabe."
        The New York Times, 2 December 1984, p. 80.

An account of the first performance of Rainforest
I in New York which is described as strong and
involved. "There is a good deal of colourful
instrumental writing, and the harmonic language
is softly, lushly dissonant."

SEE: W100

B88.   Dawes, Frank. "Record Reviews." The Musical Times,
        110 (November 1969), p. 1150.

A review of Pye GSGC 14116. "Without impinging
on   extremist   fringes,   McCabe   gives   us   a
conspectus of much that is most vital in the
piano music of this century, and yet presents a
programme that is varied enough...to hold the
interest   through   nearly   an   hours   highly
concentrated music. The playing is notable for
its great fidelity to the printed scores."

SEE: D38

B89.   Dawes, Frank. "Record Reviews." The Musical Times,
        116 (June 1975), p. 543.

A review of Decca SDD 444. "...some worthwhile
music   resulted,   and   McCabe's   representative
selection presents some of the best of it in
first-rate performances."

SEE: D33

B90.   Dawes, Frank. "Record Reviews." The Musical Times,
        117 (November 1976), p. 914.

A review of volumes 1 and 2 of the Haydn Piano
Sonatas on Decca HDN 100-02 and 103-5.

"McCabe is a well-nigh ideal interpreter of this
music. He plays clearly, unfussily, and with a
quick response to dramatic and poetic qualities."

SEE: D48; D49

B91.   Dennis, Brian. "Unadventurous Partita." Music and
        Musicians, 15 (February 1967), p. 66.

        A review of the premiere of Partita for solo
        cello, "...competently played by its dedicatee,
        Christopher Gough."

        SEE: W91

B92.   Dewhirst, Paul. "Premiere night for Nocturnal."
        The Daily Telegraph, 9 October 1970, p. 14.

        "Although it was receiving its first
        performance...John McCabe's Nocturnal for Piano
        Quintet was written in 1966, in response to a
        commission from the Park Lane Group.

        Despite an intelligent performance by the
        Lancaster Ensemble...this 13-minute work did not,
        as a whole, convince."

        SEE: W90

B93.   Dewhirst, Paul. "Weekend of McCabe music." The
        Daily Telegraph, 22 March 1976, p. 6.

        "The new work, Sonata on a Motet, draws its
        initial inspiration from Tallis's great 40-part
        motet, 'Spem in Alium'. There are a number of
        direct quotations which are varied when they
        recur during the five contrasted sections of
        this...piece.

        Throughout McCabe creates pleasing and varied
        string sonorities which seemed to be admirably
        realised by the Camerata...."

        SEE: W32

B94.   Dickinson, Peter. "John McCabe." The Musical
        Times, 106 (August 1965), pp. 596-598.

        A detailed appreciation of McCabe's life and
        music, with musical examples and a list of works.

B95.   Dommett, Kenneth. "Three Choirs." Music and
        Musicians, 19 (November 1970), pp. 30+79.

        An account of the 1970 3-Choirs Festival in
        Hereford, and particular mention of "...the last
        and most substantial of the few special
        commissions, John McCabe's Notturni ed Alba.

        The resultant score displays a command of
        orchestral textures unparalleled in anything else

I have heard from this composer and a sensibility
that surpassed by a long way anything heard
during the week."

SEE: W30

B96.   Driver, Paul. "Lessons in Bach that put his
        brilliance in the shade." The Sunday Times, 20
        August 1989, p. C9.

        "Downes's programme began with the London
        premiere of a work written for the orchestra to a
        BBC commission by John McCabe.

        He convincingly captures the sinuous glint of
        preliminary sparks, the crackle of kindled
        timber, the vigorous spread of flame and eventual
        roaring blaze.

        ...the easy confidence of his gestures and
        mercurial effectiveness of his formal plan were
        definitely impressive."

        SEE: W26

B97.   East, Leslie. "Modern Piano." Music and Musicians,
        19 (June 1971), p. 69.

        A mention of the London premiere of McCabe's
        Basse danse for two pianos, "...a brilliant,
        diamond-cut piece, with faint Stravinskian
        echoes, full of strong dynamic contrasts and
        generating genuine rhythmic excitement."

        SEE: W39

B98.   East, Leslie. "Orchestras." Music and Musicians,
        20 (March 1972), p. 74.

        Reviews of the London premieres of Notturni ed
        Alba and the Second Piano Concerto.

        The former is described as "...achieving a
        striking evocation of its subject without
        demonstrating overt allegience to anyone else."

        The latter is described as "...novel and
        refreshing (and) worth hearing again...."

        SEE: W17, W30

B99.   East, Leslie. "Premieres." Music and Musicians, 20
        (July 1972), p. 64.

"It was the film itself rather than the soundtrack of Sam Peckinpah's The Wild Bunch, that, according to the composer, provided the main impulse behind John McCabe's Symphony No. 2, given its first London performance by the CBSO....

The five meticulously and fluently scored sections achieve diversity through mood, pace and texture and coherence through the 'remembrance' of themes.

...it deserves wider adoption: it is the sort of work, given loving care in preparation, that could win quite a few converts to modern music."

SEE: W34

B100.   Elliot, J.H. "Manchester composers." The Guardian, 10 June 1960, p. 5.

"The largest work, John McCabe's Partita for String Quartet, seemed to me...the most fully integrated. The work reveals an estimable capacity for sustained musical thinking, unfolded with point and economy, but not oppressed by the theoretical necessity."

SEE: W92

B101.   Elliot, J.H. "Midday concert at the Houldsworth Hall, Manchester." The Guardian, 25 March 1964, p. 11.

"The programme ended with a work specially written for the occasion by Mr McCabe, Musica Notturna - not ...a wholly languorous piece alien to the midday hour. On the contrary, this trio tends to turn night into day during some extremely wakeful phases.

Mr McCabe composes with fluency, concealing his artifice as an artist should. This is a good work...."

SEE: W89

B102.   Elliot, J.H. "Modern music in Manchester." The Guardian, 18 November 1961, p.5.

"Mr McCabe...accompanied Meriel Dickinson in his own settings of German poems, devised in the Lieder style as conceived by a contemporary - an experiment which has more originality...."

SEE: W140

B103.   Elliot, J.H.   "Music in Manchester."   The Guardian,
         6 March 1963, p. 7.

         "The public orchestral rehearsal...was devoted
         mainly to a new work by a young composer who
         gives every indication of a bright future. His
         present achievement is impressive. John McCabe's
         Sinfonia   Concertante   for   Violin   and
         Orchestra...(has) positive qualities and (is)
         laden with 'still fairer hopes'.

         There are some splendid ideas, both musical and
         purely orchestral, in many phases of the work."

         SEE: W19

B104.   Elliot, J.H.   "New Organ Triptych."   The Guardian, 2
         March 1963, p. 5.

         "The programme was given special interest by the
         first performance of a triptych, merger into one
         continuous movement, by John McCabe. This is a
         short   but   well-shaped   work.   This   Dies
         Resurrectionis   obviously   has   its   religious
         connotations, and the three sections have their
         own emotional atmosphere. The new work seems to
         mark a phase in the development of a personal
         style by this gifted young composer."

         SEE: W64

B105.   F., S.   "Recitals and miscellany."   High Fidelity
         Magazine, August 1971, pp. 96+8.

         An American review of the DGG recording, 2530
         079, featuring English Guitar Music and including
         McCabe's Canto.   "It is a strong, adventurous,
         individual piece, full of subtle colors and
         delicate tone effects, and I found it engrossing
         throughout its five movements."

         SEE: D3

B106.   Falding, John.   "McCabe - man of music."   The
         Birmingham Post, 22 September 1973, p.6.

         An interview with McCabe "...about the remarkable
         success of his double-edged career."

B107.   Fanning, David J.   "Joubert."   Gramophone,   66
         (November 1988), p. 816.

         A review of Max Sound/Harmonia Mundi MSCB 33.

"John McCabe's mellow, undemonstrative playing
seems well adapted to the music."

SEE: D53

B108.   Fawkes, Richard. "A Concerto with Tunes." Music
and Musicians, 28 (March 1980), pp. 14-15.

An interview with McCabe and Erich Gruenberg who
gave the premiere of the 2nd Violin Concerto in
Birmingham, with a repeat performance in London
the following day.

SEE: W20

B109.   Fiske, Roger.   "Halle Brass Consort."   The
Gramophone, XLVI (December 1968), p. 859.

A review of Pye Golden Guinea GSGC 14114. "The
McCabe is in every sense the most modern and also
the most considerable work....

...the music is lucid and compelling and stamped
with individual thinking."

SEE: D20

B110.   Fiske, Roger.   "Haydn."   The Gramophone,   51
(December 1973), p. 1222.

A review of the Haydn keyboard sonatas on HMV HQS
1301.

"...John McCabe's loving performances are a model
for all....

These are intensely musical performances, finely
phrased and full of understanding...."

SEE: D47

B111.   Fiske, Roger. "Haydn: Piano Works." Gramophone, 53
(October 1975), pp. 657-8.

A review of volume one of the set, on Decca 1 HDN
100-2.

"Many great pianists cannot be bothered with
these sonatas.   But McCabe, as you quickly
realise, plays them not to fill a gap in the
catalogue but because he loves them. He puts the
music first, virtuoso flamboyance nowhere."

SEE: D48

B112.   Fiske, Roger.   "Instrumental: Haydn."   Gramophone,
          53 (May 1976), pp. 1782+87.

          A review of the second volume of Haydn Piano
          Sonatas, recorded on Decca HDN 103-5.

          SEE: D49

B113.   Fiske, Roger.   "Instrumental: Haydn."   Gramophone,
          55 (October 1977), pp. 661-2.

          A review of the fifth and final volume of Haydn
          Piano Sonatas, recorded on Decca 5 HDN 112-5.

          SEE: D52

B114.   Genower, Peter (ed).   "McCabe through the looking
          glass."   T V Times, 12-18 July 1975, pp. 15-16.

          An introduction to the documentary, The Jerusalem
          Windows, directed by Peter Potter of GRANADA TV
          "...who has succeeded in making an understated
          insight into the chronology of composing,
          McCabe-style."

          SEE: W5

B115.   Gilardino, Angelo.   "La Musica Contemporanea per
          chitarra in Gran Bretagna."   Fronimo, 1 (October
          1973), pp. 8-14.

          An article, in Italian, discussing modern English
          works for the guitar against the background of
          performances by English guitar virtuosos, with
          mention of McCabe's Canto.

          SEE: W76

B116.   Goodwin, Noel.   "Dance Macabre: Music."   Dance and
          Dancers, 19 (May 1968), pp. 19-20.

          An appreciation of John McCabe's first symphony
          and the way the music is used in Peter Wright's
          ballet, Dance Macabre.

          SEE: W33a

B117.   Goodwin, Noel.   "Literary Sources."   Dance and
          Dancers 29 (August 1978), pp. 20-23.

          An account of Shadow-Reach, a ballet using music
          from McCabe's second symphony and Hartmann
          Variations, and based on Henry James's book 'The
          Turn of the Screw.'

SEE: W34a

B118.   Grayson, Barrie. "A concerto of delights." The
         Birmingham Post, 15 March 1980, p. 6.

         An interview with the composer and Erich
         Gruenberg about the 2nd Violin Concerto.

         SEE: W20

B119.   Green, Charles. "Composer's kiss ends solo." The
         News (Portsmouth), 27 April 1972, p.2.

         An account of the premiere of McCabe's Concerto
         for oboe d'amore and chamber orchestra, a work
         commissioned for the 1972 Portsmouth Festival.

         SEE: W14

B120.   Greenfield, Edward. "Playing with fire, from the
         fells to Dirilgai." The Guardian, 21 April 1969,
         p. 29.

         An examination of McCabe's career, both as a
         composer and as a pianist.

B121.   Griffiths, Paul. "Bartok." The Musical Times, 116
         (April 1975), p. 342.

         A review of McCabe's book on Bartok which is
         described as a "worthy addition."

B122.   Griffiths, Paul. "John McCabe's night." The Times
         (London), 12 July 1978, p. 11.

         A review of McCabe's third symphony, performed by
         the RPO under Charles Dutoit at the Royal
         Festival Hall.

         SEE: W35

B123.   Griffiths, Paul. "McCabe: The Chagall Windows,
         etc." The Musical Times, 117 (February 1976), p.
         143.

         A review of the EMI recording: ASD 3096. "The
         Chagall Windows is an intense and richly coloured
         orchestral piece...."

         The Hartmann Variation...give an impression of
         brilliant youthful talent, bursting with
         enthusiasm and influences."

SEE: D5; D30

B124.   Griffiths, Paul. "McCabe: Variations, etc." The
         Musical Times, 118 (November 1977), pp. 923-4.

         A review of the RCA RL 25076 recording containing
         solo piano music by McCabe which is described as
         "...abounding in energy and colour...."

         SEE: D1; D4; D12; D13; D21; D29

B125.   Griffiths, Paul. "New music." The Musical Times,
         cxxi (February 1980), pp. 121-2.

         "Between those works McCabe's orchestral fantasy
         [The Shadow of Light] appeared as colourful as a
         bird of paradise. It was the result of a very
         curious commission for a piece to mark the
         bicentenary of the death of Boyce, from which
         circumstance McCabe drew the idea of a somnolent
         nocturne into which might be woven dream episodes
         picturing 18th-century life with the aid of
         themes from Boyce."

         SEE: W31

B126.   H., M. "Rawsthorne the highlight." The Times
         (London), 19 June 1969, p.11.

         "More positive was Mr McCabe's own Fantasy on a
         Theme of Liszt, for solo piano. In spite of
         strongly contrasting episodes and some
         effectively virtuosic writing, this appeared to
         be an unduly static piece, its thought trapped on
         one level of intensity."

         SEE: W41

B127.   Harris, Richard L. "Contemporary piano music."
         Music Teacher, 66 (September 1987), p. 27.

         Part two in a series aimed at encouraging
         teachers to explore less familiar piano pieces
         from the contemporary repertoire, with a
         paragraph on John McCabe's Five Bagatelles
         (1964).

         SEE: W42

B128.   Harrison, Max. "Bax: Piano Quartet (1922)...."
         Gramophone, 62 (February 1985), p. 987.

         A review of the Chandos digital recording ABRD
         1113. "The performances are highly sympathetic,

something that until comparatively recently could not be counted on in Bax's long unfashionable music."

SEE: D32

B129.   Harrison, Max. "Bridge: Elegy for cello and piano." Gramophone, 58 (May 1981), p. 1486.

A review of the ASV recording: ACA 1001 in which Julian Lloyd-Webber's and John McCabe's performances are described as "fine".

SEE: D36

B130.   Harrison, Max. "Cruft: Divertimento for strings." Audio Record Review, 8 (December 1967), p. 45.

A review of the Pye Virtuoso recording TPLS 13005 which includes McCabe's first symphony. "McCabe's use of orchestral colour is uncommonly restrained but, because of his pungent harmonic vocabulary and concise musical thinking, a strong emotional impact is registered."

SEE: D23

B131.   Harrison, Max. "Elgar, Piano Works." Gramophone, 54 (October 1976), p. 627.

A review of the Rediffusion Prelude recording PRS 2503.

SEE: D43

B132.   Harrison, Max. "English Guitar Music." The Gramophone, XLIX (September 1971), pp. 473-4.

A review of the DGG recording 2530 079 which includes a performance of Canto for guitar. It is described as illustrating "...the modern exploration of the instrument's further potential and has many intriguing moments...."

SEE: D3

B133.   Harrison, Max. "Goehr: Four songs from the Japanese." Audio Record Review, 8 (December 1967), p. 47.

A review of the Pye recording GGC 4105. "These five song performances are most welcome...."

SEE: D44

B134.   Harrison, Max.   "John McCabe."   The Times (London),
         19 March 1975, p. 14.

         An account of a recital given by McCabe at the
         Purcell Room which included two of Haydn's piano
         sonatas.

B135.   Harrison, Max.   "McCabe: Fantasy on a theme of
         Liszt."   Gramophone, 55 (June 1977), p. 75.

         A review of RCA Red Seal RL 25076, a recording of
         McCabe's solo piano music which "...represents a
         considerable achievement, for each of these
         scores has real originality, and leads one to
         hope, he will write more for the instrument.
         Although none of the pieces on this record is in
         any sense exhibitionistic, they could only have
         been written by a composer with a virtuoso's
         understanding of the piano, and McCabe plays them
         with an immediacy that surely reflects the
         vividness of his aural imagination."

         SEE: D1; D4; D12; D13; D21; D29

B136.   Harrison, Max.   "Satie: Piano Works."   Gramophone,
         52 (December 1974), p. 1182.

         A review of the Saga 5387 recording.

         SEE: D60

B137.   Harrison, Max.   "Satie: Piano Works."   Gramophone,
         58 (June 1980), p. 54.

         A review of John McCabe's second recital of Satie
         on the Saga label - 5472 - which "...like its
         predecessor...boasts an excellent programme."

         SEE: D61

B138.   Healy, John.   "English Music in a Modern Vein."   The
         Journal (Newcastle), 19 February 1964, p. 3.

         "Mr McCabe's piece is not cast in the usual
         variation form. There is no recognisable theme
         announced at the outset - only a series of chords
         and twiddlings at the extremities of the
         keyboard.

         Nevertheless it has much effective writing and
         the three well contrasted sections seemed to
         present a good deal of thoughtful invention."

         SEE: W63

B139.   Helm, Everett.   "Cardiff: Festival der Musik..."
        Neue Z.F.M., 131 (June 1970), pp. 289-290.

        A survey (in German) of the 1970 Cardiff Festival
        with mention of the first performance of Gaudi.

        SEE: W44

B140.   Henahan, Donal. "Recordings: Segovia's 60-year Love
        Affair." The New York Times, 4 April 1971, p.
        D25.

        A review of the Behrend disc from DGG of English
        Guitar music, with a brief mention of "...John
        McCabe's more complex Canto for Guitar...."

        SEE: D3

B141.   Heslop, Caroline. "John McCabe." Music Teacher, 66
        (October 1987), pp. 25-27.

        A detailed interview with the composer about his
        life and music.

B142.   Hollander, Hans. "Aldeburgh und Cheltenham." Neue
        Z.F.M., 127 (September 1966), pp. 350-352.

        An   article   (in   German)   describing   the
        performances of new English music, with a
        paragraph on the first symphony which is
        described as "...romantic (and) skilfully
        developed from a simple, clearly symbolically
        melodic basis."

        SEE: W33

B143.   Hughes, Eric and Day, Timothy. "Discographies of
        British Composers: no. 16 - John McCabe.
        Recorded Sound, no. 82 (July 1982), pp. 77-85.

        A discography listing all known commercial discs,
        together with BBC Transcription discs held at the
        National Sound Archive in London.

B144.   Ivory, James.   "Constancy, that's the virtue!"
        Sight and Sound, 50 (Summer 1981), p. 207.

        A review of The Good Soldier, but with no mention
        of McCabe's musical score.

        SEE: W154

B145.   J.,   A.G.   "Recital   of   modern   music."
        Gloucestershire Echo, 9 July 1964, P. 6.

        "...Three Pieces for Clarinet and Piano, did
        not...bear   any   stylistic   affinity   to   the
        offerings of the so-called Manchester school...;
        rather it showed a closeness to neo-classicism.
        Affording ample scope to two good players, it is
        the work's second piece, sub-titled bossa nova,
        which   seems   to   contain   the   most   original
        ideas....The three pieces were obviously enjoyed
        by the audience who accorded the composer a warm
        reception."

        SEE: W106

B146.   J., G. "Superb playing by Halle opens Festival."
        Gloucestershire Echo, 5 July 1966, p. 7.

        A review of the First Symphony' premiere at the
        Cheltenham Festival.

        "It has undoubtedly been written by a master of
        the orchestra. Moreover in general the work is
        extremely impressive at first hearing."

        SEE: W33

B147.   Jacobson, Bernard. "Haydn's Piano Sonatas." Stereo
        Review (USA), September 1978, p. 108.

        A review comparing the various recordings of
        Haydn's piano sonatas including volume two of the
        McCabe series. He is described as "...a far more
        perceptive   and   sympathetic   interpreter...(who)
        offers an attractive and unusually convincing
        view of the music."

        SEE: D49

B148.   Jacobson, Bernard. "Haydn's Piano Sonatas." Stereo
        Review (USA), 41 (September 1981), p.108.

        A review of discs of Haydn's piano sonatas
        including three recorded by John McCabe who is
        described as "...a far more perceptive and
        sympathetic interpreter."

        SEE: D48-D52

B149.   Jacobson, Bernard. "Musicianly mezzo." Music and
        Musicians, 12 (April 1964), p. 41.

"The same two artists gave the first performance of _Sechs Gedichte_, composed last year by John McCabe.   McCabe   really   has   tackled   the song-composer's problem of extracting the kernel of the poem's meaning, and in most cases he has expressed it musically in memorable form.   Far the best of the six songs was an unerring evocation of Mörike's midnight scene, the streams singing in a piano accompaniment that was both picturesque as tone-painting and a haunting melody in its own right."

SEE: W137

B150.   Jenkins,   Lyndon.   "The   Nash   Ensemble."   _The Birmingham Post_, 6 October 1973, p. 2.

"Interest at this concert centred chiefly around John   McCabe's   new   work,   _Time   Remembered_, commissioned by the Malvern Concert Club for its 70th anniversary....

To my ear the scoring throughout is fascinating in its variety, often spare but equally often round and full, with many passages which sit well upon the different instruments.

What McCabe has written...is a work at once attractive, easily grasped at a first hearing, and which one would gladly hear again soon."

SEE: W143

B151.   Johnson,   Stephen.   "Chamber: Britten   −   Cello Sonata."   _Gramophone_,   67   (October   1989),   pp. 682+684.

A review of the Philips recording 422 345-2PH, which includes the Britten and Shostakovich cello sonatas.

SEE: D37

B152.   Joseph, Jeffrey.   "John McCabe and the LCM."   _Music Teacher_, 64 (September 1985), pp. 12-13.

A potted history of the London College of Music and its present director, John McCabe.

Also mentioned are several specific features of tuition which demonstrate "Mr McCabe's special methodology,   innovatory   flair   and/or   musical philosophy."

B153.   K., M. "First performance at Floral Hall."
        Southport Visitor, 20 May 1967, p. 1.

        An account of the First Piano Concerto's premiere
        which is described as "...dramatic in
        concept...modern...and a challenge to the
        orchestra...."

        SEE: W16

B154.   Kelly, Seamus. "Irish Ballet Company at the Abbey."
        The Irish Times, 20 June 1978, p. 8.

        "Domy Reiter-Soffer's...interpretation of 'The
        Turn of the Screw' (his title is Shadow Reach) is
        as dramatically gripping as the Britten opera,
        while John McCabe's score is immensely effective
        for the dance idiom in Patrick Murray's eerily
        spooky setting."

        SEE: W34a

B155.   Kennedy, Michael. "A fanfare for the brass band."
        The Daily Telegraph, 30 March 1988, p. 19.

        A brief history of the brass band movement, "...a
        great tradition of music-making...with...John
        McCabe, already director of the London College of
        Music, the brass band is...assured of serious and
        authoritative study...."

B156.   Kennedy, Michael. "McCabe's vision of the outback."
        The Daily Telegraph, 16 January 1989, p. 12.

        A review of the first performance of Fire at
        Durilgai.

        "With his customary mastery of modern orchestral
        resources, McCabe paints a vivid, almost
        cinematic soundpicture of the outback...following
        it with a scherzo section in which the themes
        flicker and blaze with the unpredictability of
        spreading fire.

        It is an example of skilled compositional
        craftsmanship...."

        SEE: W26

B157.   Kennedy, Michael. "Manchester." The Musical Times,
        107 (February 1966), pp. 138-9.

        "On Nov 24 Maurice Handford...conducted an
        assured first performance of the Variations on a
        Theme by Hartmann by...John McCabe.

This 20-minute piece is of great brilliance and shows McCabe in full command of orchestral virtuosity. In McCabe we have a composer in the Britten and Williamson school - not bound by any theories, but capable of laying hands on whatever is apposite to his individual mode of expression."

SEE: W37

B158.   Kennedy, Michael. "Manchester." The Musical Times, 110 (June 1969), p. 656.

A review of The Lion, the Witch and the Wardrobe in which "McCabe's brilliant score, eclectic, allusive and also inventively original, admirably fuses the comedy and magic of the fairy-tale with the nobler religious elements. In doing so he has avoided sanctimoniousness and has contrived to write a children's opera which could also be performed by adults, for this is a 'big' work and an important landmark in its composer's career. His melodic gifts have never been more pronounced nor has he previously excelled the skill with which his sheer professionalism has been concealed by the apparent spontaneity of the writing."

SEE: W146

B159.   Kennedy, Michael. "Manchester: Mellers and McCabe." The Musical Times, 108 (March 1967), p. 243.

"...both singers were heard to better advantage in John McCabe's Rain Songs, three short but attractive settings of translations of Chinese poems.

...there was a marked originality in the use of the antique medium which...these modern composers had chosen."

SEE: W135

B160.   Kennedy, Michael. "Moving eloquence of McCabe's opera." The Daily Telegraph, 30 April 1969, p. 21.

Further impressions of McCabe's The Lion, the Witch and the Wardrobe.

"It is an eclectic book and the musical setting is eclectic too, in a justifiable and by no means derogatory way and in the sense that Elgar meant when he spoke of music being in the air around us. McCabe is a man of his time and he has pressed into his service the influences which have made him a composer of individuality."

SEE: W146

B161.   Kennedy, Michael. "Walton, Piano Quartet." _Gramophone_, 65 (October 1987), pp. 598+602.

A review of the Meridian recording KE 77139/CDE 84139.

"This new recording by the English Quartet has the inestimable advantage of John McCabe's piano playing, full of subtleties and delicate flecks of tone-colour and of a composer's fellow-feeling for those passages where the 'joins show'."

SEE: D64

B162.   Kerner, Leighton. "In for a Penny..." _Village Voice_, 26 (23 December 1981), p. 80.

A review of the Pittsburgh Symphony Orchestra's British Festival which included the American premiere of McCabe's Hartmann Variations. It is described as "...totally charming in its splendidly pleasing orchestration...."

SEE: W37

B163.   Kipnis, Igor. "Hadyn's riches." _Stereo Review_, October 1979, pp. 132-33.

Comparison of several recordings including volume five "...of John McCabe's mammoth project of recording the complete Haydn keyboard sonatas...."

"The forty-year-old British pianist, known equally well in his country as a composer (and also as a writer and critic) has an unusually sympathetic feel for this music."

SEE: D52

B164.   Larner, Gerald. "Bath." _The Musical Times_, 109 (August 1968), p. 746.

"The other was John McCabe's _Concertante Music_, given by Newton Park College of Education in the Abbey on 24 June.

The McCabe proved to be a successful exercise in making the most of the special qualities and

instrumental forces which student teachers have
to offer....

...the most attractive aspect of the work is the
use of the two percussion groups....McCabe uses
them   imaginatively,   producing   interesting
textures   in   combination   with   the   conventional
orchestral instruments....The most memorable of
the four movements is the third, a chorale with
variations written in memory of Martin Luther
King."

SEE: W8

B165.   Larner, Gerald.   "Instrumental: Webern-Variations."
         Records and Recordings, Vol 12 (August 1969), p.
         64.

         A recording (Pye Golden Guinea GSGC 14116) of a
         McCabe   recital   which   includes   his   own   Five
         Bagatelles.   "... he is outstandingly good in
         Schoenberg, Britten and Rawsthorne, superb in
         Copland and Nielsen, incomparable in McCabe."

         SEE: D2; D38

B166.   Larner, Gerald.   "John McCabe piano concerto."   The
         Guardian, 20 May 1967, p. 5.

         A   review   of   the   piano   concerto's   first
         performance at Southport.   It is described as
         "...a highly attractive work and one of the most
         skilful in this form written in this country in
         recent years.   Its point is mainly its piano
         writing, poetic, lucid and colourful in itself
         and even more imaginative in blend and contrast
         with the orchestral instruments.   ...the effect
         of the concerto is fresh and original."

         SEE: W16

B167.   Larner, Gerald.   "John McCabe Recital at Marple."
         The Guardian, 6 March 1964, p. 11.

         An account of a McCabe recital which featured
         Haydn, Beethoven, Schubert and his own Variations
         for piano.

         SEE: W63

B168.   Larner, Gerald. "John McCabe's 'Concertante' at the
         Bluecoat   Hall,   Liverpool."   The   Guardian,   20
         December 1965, p. 7.

"It was interesting to hear another new McCabe work so soon after his Hartmann Variations at a Halle concert...and, although the Concertante was written a year after the other piece, they have much in common.

The writing for the harpsichord is characteristic in its rapidly articulated brilliance, and there is an interesting exploration of the possible combination of its tone with the wind quintet and strings...."

SEE: W7

B169.   Larner, Gerald.   "John McCabe's First Symphony." The Guardian, 5 July 1966, p. 9.

"The symphony...has a strong sense of purpose, and the purpose is boldly persued....

Sir John Barbirolli conducted the Halle Orchestra in a powerful, convinced performance...."

SEE: W33

B170.   Larner, Gerald.   "John McCabe's Sonata for clarinet, cello and piano." The Guardian, 23 May 1969, p. 8.

"Another new work commissioned for the Arts Festival...was given its first performance in Macclesfield last night. This was John McCabe's Sonata for clarinet, cello and piano, which was commissioned by Brocklehurst Whiston Ltd for the De Peyer Trio's Concert in the King's School. The De Peyer Trio...played the work with, it seemed, complete conviction and, certainly with considerable accomplishment."

SEE: W103

B171.   Larner, Gerald.   "The Lion, the Witch and the Wardrobe." The Musical Times, 110 (April 1969), p. 372.

A detailed synopsis of and an introduction to The Lion, the Witch and the Wardrobe, written by the librettist.

SEE: W146

B172.   Larner, Gerald.   "Liverpool Concert at Bluecoat Chambers." The Guardian, 3 October 1963, p. 7.

"The centrepiece of John McCabe's A Summer
Garland...is a setting of a poem by John Arlott
called 'The Old Cricketer'.

...Mr McCabe displays a sensitivity in the
setting of words, and in the reflection of their
atmosphere...."

SEE: W139

B173.   Larner, Gerald. "McCabe: Notturni ed Alba." The
         Musical Times, 115 (February 1974), pp. 138-9.

         A review of HMV ASD 2094 which contains Notturni
         ed Alba and Symphony no. 2.

         "The CBSO makes the most of McCabe's skilfully
         contrived scoring in both works, with particular
         distinction in the percussion and the woodwind,
         and Jill Gomez songs beautifully in the medieval
         Latin lyrics of Notturni ed Alba."

         SEE: D17; D24

B174.   Larner, Gerald. "McCabe's Concertante at Bath
         Festival." The Guardian, 25 June 1968, p. 6.

         A review of the first performance in Bath Abbey,
         the music being described as having "...echoes of
         Messiaen here and there, but there is more to the
         scoring than that, above all in the intriguing
         and mysteriously shifting textures of the
         extended slow movement...."

         SEE: W8

B175.   Larner, Gerald. "Manchester." The Musical Times,
         116 (June 1975), p. 559.

         "On 9 January James Loughran and the Halle
         Orchestra gave the first performance of John
         McCabe's The Chagall Windows....

         It is a likeable and communicative work, full of
         ideas...not devoid of influence from Messiaen and
         Ives, welcome for the lack of structural
         inhibition even if it does seem less well
         disciplined than McCabe's music
         characteristically is."

         SEE: W5

B176.   Larner, Gerald. "Manchester: BBC PO/Downes." The
         Guardian, 16 January 1989, p. 38.

"John McCabe set himself a difficult task when, in response to a commission from the BBC, he chose to draw on the bush fire in Patrick White's The Tree of Man for his inspiration. The problem was not to imitate the sound of fire - which was not his intention anyway - but to supply the creative oxygen which would keep his music crackling for close on twenty minutes.

...he has succeeded...in creating a score which is brilliant in its clarity, vivid in its colouring and consistently taut in its rhythms."

SEE: W26

B177.   Larner, Gerald.   "Manchester: John McCabe."   The Guardian, 22 March 1976, p. 8.

"McCabe was represented..by the first performance of his Sonata on a Motet, commissioned by the Camerata....It is a single movement work in five sections derived from Tallis's forty-part motet Spem in Alium - which, as the composer remarked in an admirably lucid talk afterwards, he might have called Fantasia on a theme by Thomas Tallis if someone else had not used the title already."

SEE: W32

B178.   Larner, Gerald.   "New work by John McCabe at the Free Trade Hall."   The Guardian, 25 November 1965, p. 7.

"The new work was the Variations on a Theme of Hartmann which John McCabe wrote last year. The Variations is an entertaining and lyrical work and, while it has no pretentions to greatness or significant statements, it was not put to shame by its immediate neighbours in the programme...."

SEE: W37

B179.   Larner, Gerald.   "New works at the Manchester Festival." The Guardian, 4 June 1973, p. 8.

"...a commission for a ballet score should not have caused McCabe undue problems. The evidence of one of the Northern Dance Theatre performances of his The Teachings of Don Juan...suggests that he took it very naturally.   For much of its length it is genuine ballet music, rhythmically inventive,   vivid   in   characterisation, resourcefully scored for its small ensemble. It is distinguished, moreover, by a baritone part so well written as to inspire a superb performance from Patrick McGuigan...."

SEE: W3

B180.   Larner, Gerald. "Northern Consort Recital." The Guardian, 21 January 1965, p. 9.

Observations on the first public performance of John McCabe's English Songs.

SEE: W110

B181.   Larner, Gerald. "Southport." The Musical Times, 108 (August 1967), p. 731.

An account of the piano concerto and its first performance. "The most pleasing impression made by the ...concerto is of an abundance of melodic and texture ideas and of subtlety in its form. The piano writing...is fresh and effective and strikes one by its orginality....

This is one of the most skilful of recent works in the form by British composers...."

SEE: W16

B182.   Layton   Robert.   "Grieg: Slatter,   Op.   72." Gramophone, 59 (August 1981), p. 295.

A review of the RCA Gold Seal GL 25329 recording.

"John McCabe score full marks for enterprise and common sense....McCabe plays all these with great spirit and intelligence...."

SEE: D45

B183.   Layton,   Robert.   "Nielsen: Piano   Works." Gramophone, 53 (January 1976), p. 1218.

A review of the Decca Ace of Diamonds recording SDD 475-6.

"John McCabe...plays the early pieces with unfailing,   instinct   and   musicianship. ...McCabe's playing is splendidly alive and sensitive."

SEE: D58

B184.   Leslie,   Ann.   "John   Ogdon   discovers   a perfectionist." Daily Express, 10 December 1964, p. 14.

An article describing the careers of Ogdon and McCabe with contribution from each. Ogdon says of McCabe: "He's really brilliant. One of a whole group of Northern musicians I admire tremendously at the moment - probably he's the least well-known."

B185.   Levi, Erik. "John McCabe's Second Symphony." The Guardian, 27 September 1971, p. 10.

A review of the Second Symphony's first performance noting that "...McCabe has an ability to write inventive, often memorable material...."

SEE: W34

B186.   Lindsay, Maurice. "Music that made me proud of Scotland." The Glasgow Herald, 28 June 1978, p. 8.

Mention of the Clarinet Concerto which is described as "...both imaginative and well-written for the instrument....Miss Hilton gave this rewarding addition to the repertoire of her instrument an enthusiastic and compelling first performance."

SEE: W12

B187.   Loveland Kenneth. "Best of McCabe's music." The Times (London), 27 August 1970, p. 9.

"In much of the recent music of John McCabe there has been a growing response to imagery and the picturesque coupled with a corresponding maturing technical expertise to add control and direction. All these gifts are brought to a high state of fusion in Notturni Ed Alba....

This is clearly the most significant work the composer has written. The large orchestra is used not for dynamic power, but for sheer beauty of sound and in elaboration of the poetry's inner vision.

An important success for McCabe...."

SEE: W30

B188.   Loveland, Kenneth. "Cardiff." Music and Musicians, 19 (April 1971), p. 74.

"Basse danse...is a stimulating piece, percussive and emphatic....

With plenty of terse, truculent phrases and
chances for display, it is a useful addition to
the two-piano repertory."

SEE: W39

B189.   Loveland, Kenneth. "Exciting things in new McCabe."
         The Times (London), 31 August 1972, p. 6.

"Voyage is about the legendary search of St.
Brendan for the promised land, a seven-year
journey which makes him a kind of coracle-borne
flying Irishman. Monica Smith's libretto reduces
the story to manageable lengths, but retains the
Celtic romanticism, twilight fancies and rather
endearing belief in the unbelieveable.

McCabe translated all this into a similarly
evocative score, generously endowed with
glittering percussion sounds...appropriately
permeated with the touch of the visionary....The
choral writing is richly varied with some moments
of...whispering and speech in the manner of
Penderecki. One hopes that he has a return
ticket; there is much in Voyage that is exciting
and deserving of an early repeat performance."

SEE: W130

B190.   Loveland, Kenneth. "Farewell to Menuhin." Music
         and Musicians, 17 (September 1968), pp. 35+62.

"John McCabe's Concertante Music...was carefully
tailored to their demands, making exciting
antiphonal use of lots of percussion distributed
on either side of the main body of players and
including an elegy in memory of Martin Luther
King which was founded on a nobly thought brass
chorale...."

SEE: W8

B191.   Loveland, Kenneth. "Festivals: Three Choirs." The
         Musical Times, 116 (November 1975), p. 995.

"John McCabe's Goddess Trilogy...is a flamboyant
work, exploring all the known range of the horn,
and a few unlikely corners as well, full of
variety and interest."

SEE: W84

B192.   Loveland, Kenneth. "John McCabe at 50." Musical
         Opinion, 112 (April 1989), p. 120.

An appreciation of John McCabe and his music
which is described as "...arresting, but
communicative, strong on vitality but serious and
self-examining where necessary, often
characterised by glittering instrumetal colours
and picturesque, evocative timbres, marked by a
practicality behind which a practising musician
evidently stands (he is, of course, an
outstandingly fine pianist), the product of
someone who would not be in the least ashamed to
be dubbed a romantic."

B193.   Loveland, Kenneth.   "John McCabe's tribute to the
summer of '76."   The Times   (London), 28 July
1978, p. 9.

"In Reflections of a Summer Night the music
is...more contemplative and the tempi drift
lazily. The choral writing...is concentrated and
might profitably have explored a wider harmonic
range. Yet it does not convey the image implicit
in the title, and the surrender to an idea. Both
as a spinner of atmosphere and as an explorer of
words, McCabe appears skilfully in control of his
intentions and the work has a logical unity."

SEE: W123

B194.   Loveland, Kenneth.   "McCabe: Philharmonic Hall,
Liverpool."   The Times   (London), 21 February
1972, p. 9.

"At the third time of asking, John McCabe's
Metamorphosen for harpsichord and orchestra got
off the ground at the Royal Liverpool
Philharmonic Orchestra's concert on Saturday, but
it was a close-run thing. The scheduled first
performance in April 1969 was cancelled because
of circumstances involving the soloist, Rafael
Puyana who then damaged a finger before the
postponed premiere in August 1970. After
rehearsing on Friday Mr Puyana was taken off, and
on Saturday a distress call to London brought the
composer...to give the first performance and
collect the kind of welcome British audiences
always reserve for those who rise above
adversity. ...of far more interest is the
success with which McCabe has solved the problem
of creating the kind of textural picture which
enables the harpsichord to retain an audible, and
at times even sturdy, identity."

See: W29

B195.   Loveland, Kenneth.   "Music in Cardiff."   Music and
Musicians, 18 (June 1970), pp. 32-3.

"There was new piano music in both festivals.
John McCabe's <u>Gaudi</u>, played by Valerie
Tryon...reproduces the impact on a sensitive mind
of the challenging elements of Antonin Gaudi's
architecture through powerfully static chords and
shimmering decorations."

SEE: W44

B196.   Loveland, Kenneth. "New oboe quartet." <u>Music and
Musicians</u>, 17 (April 1969), p. 79.

"McCabe's writing is fluent, a gift which means
that the natural progression from fragmentary
introductory material through tension to release
is effectively achieved, and his work bears the
stamp of a composer who spends a fair proportion
of his time actually playing – it is practical."

SEE: W94

B197.   Loveland, Kenneth. "Ogdon in Cardiff." <u>Music and
Musicians</u>, 16 (July 1968), p. 35.

Mention of <u>Canto</u> for guitar and its first
performance by William Gomez.

"There is a suggestion of traditional colouring
and mood in this piece – distant echoes, haunting
nostalgia – but the wide range of the colour and
effective harmonies are entirely his own."

SEE: W76

B198.   Loveland, Kenneth. "Premiere of McCabe quartet."
<u>The Times</u> (London), 12 February 1969, p. 8.

("John McCabe's <u>Quartet for Oboe and String
Trio</u>)... is a fascinating piece which holds the
attention less by the strength of its content
than by the originally with which it is
expressed. The one movement form which the
composer favours is handled expertly....

All of this is confidently written and it sounds
quite effective in performance."

SEE: W94

B199.   Loveland, Kenneth. "Three Choirs." <u>The Musical
Times</u>, 111 (October 1970), pp. 1021-2.

"...John McCabe's <u>Notturni ed Alba</u> (is) easily
his most assured and imaginative piece so far.
McCabe's success is two-fold. His orchestral

writing...creates a luxuriant sound. His second
success is that in all this profusion the voice
is never covered...."

SEE: W30

B200.   Loveland, Kenneth.   "Three Choirs."   The Musical
         Times, 113 (November 1972), pp. 1108-9.

         "John McCabe's Voyage was the biggest new work, a
         45-minute setting of Monica Smith's text based
         on the legend of St. Brendan....   It is more
         successful in detail than in total....But Voyage
         illustrates how confidently McCabe now gets to
         grips with a subject, and with what assurance he
         handles large forces. The choral and orchestral
         textures are varied and imaginatively allied to
         situations, and the score benefitted from the
         care with which Christopher Robinson brought all
         the ideas into a well-focused musical picture,
         and from usually reliable solo singing."

         SEE: W130

B201.   Loveland, Kenneth.   "Three   Choirs   Festival:
         Worcester." The Times (London), 27 August 1975,
         p. 5.

         "John McCabe's Goddess Trilogy for horn and
         piano...is based on the goddess sisters of Celtic
         mythology, whose several significances and forms
         give the composer much scope for strikingly
         varied writing, with fascinating switches of
         timbre and colour and passages of quite wild
         acrobatics...."

         SEE: W84

B202.   Loveland,   Kenneth.   "(A)   throw-back   composer
         returns." Wales on Sunday, 19 March 1989, p. 16.

         An appreciation of McCabe's career with mention
         of the Fishguard Music Festival.

         "It is a time for welcoming back old friends, and
         prominent among them will be John McCabe, among
         the   most   communicative   of   living   British
         composers and himself the subject of widespread
         celebration this year."

B203.   M., D.A.W. "Wigmore Hall: John McCabe." The Daily
         Telegraph, 1 February 1979, p. 15.

         "John McCabe, well known on the concert platform
         as pianist and composer, gave a rewarding account

of Schubert's Sonata in D last night. This work
demands of the performer an exceptional sense of
structure, particularly in the lengthy finale
Rondo. There was also a perfectly judged rubato
in the slow movement. What made the performance
so complete was the combination of an innate
musical simplicity with a true underlying
virtuosity."

B204.   McCabe, John.   "Ad Solem Ensemble at Manchester
         University."   The Guardian, 6 November 1965, p.
         6.

         A review of a concert at the Faculty of Music,
         Manchester University which included the String
         Quartet by Haydn and Debussy, together with the
         Brahms Piano Quartet.

B205.   McCabe, John.   "Alan Rawsthorne."   The Musical
         Times, 112 (October 1971), pp. 952-954.

         An appreciation of the music of Rawsthorne, "...a
         composer   of   the   highest   integrity...a
         craftsman...a poet of the human spirit...."

B206.   McCabe, John.   "Avant   garde."   Records   and
         Recordings, 12 (December 1968), pp. 22-24.

         An article prompted by the apprearance of six
         records of avant-garde music: DGG 104988-93.
         "The performances are all authoritative and
         mostly full of conviction, the recordings
         magnificently clear and spacious."

B207.   McCabe, John.   "Avant   garde."   Records   and
         Recordings, 13 (January 1970), pp. 24-26.

         A description of some avant-garde items appearing
         in the DGG recording 643541-46.

B208.   McCabe, John.   "Avant-garde from Wergo."   Records
         and Recordings, 13 (February 1970), pp. 26-28.

         Several new recordings from the Heliodor/Wergo
         Catalogue which are described as "...mixed as
         these collections usually are...there are many
         good things in them."

B209.   McCabe, John.   "(The) avant-garde - then and now:
         Letter"   Composer,   no. 60 (Spring 1977), pp.
         37-8.

A letter in answer to a stimulating conversation between Denis Aplvor and Francis Routh who made "...a number of interesting and valid points, and some that are more contentious."

B210.   McCabe, John.   "Bartok: Orchestral Music." BBC (BBC Music Guide), 1974, 64 pp.

An examination of Bartok's orchestral works (excluding the concertos), with music examples.

B211.   McCabe, John.   "Beethoven's Ninth in Manchester and Moshe Atzmon at Liverpool." The Guardian, 9 May 1966, p. 9.

A review of a performance of Beethoven's Choral Symphony by the Halle Orchestra, and a concert given by the RLPO under Moshe Atzmon.

B212.   McCabe, John, et al. "Bernard Haitink - a new tradition at the Concertgebouw." Records and Recordings, 14 (March 1971), pp. 38-41.

Reviews of new Philips recordings (including Takemitsu's November Steps and Messiaens's Et exspecto resurrectionem) by John McCabe.

B213.   McCabe, John, "Bernstein on the beat." Records and Recordings, 16 (April 1973), pp. 36-7.

Leonard Bernstein's latest recordings - including one of Stravinsky's La Sacre du Printemps - are reviewed by McCabe, Heinitz and Markson, and confirm his status as a conductor of the first rank.

B214.   McCabe, John.   "Best of Britain." Records and Recordings, 16 (September 1973), pp. 42-43.

E.J. Moeran's Symphony was the first recording to be sponsored by the British Council. John McCabe reviews the new HMV recording and assesses the achievement of the British Council in the field of recorded music.

B215.   McCabe,   John.   "(The) Birds."   Records and Recordings, 14 (July 1971), pp. 42-3.

A review of the new Erato recording of Messiaen's Catalogue d'Oiseaux.

B216.   McCabe, John. "Birmingham Symphony Orchestra." The
         Guardian, 21 March 1967, p. 7.

         A review of a concert given by the CBSO at the
         Festival of Twentieth century Music in Cardiff.

B217.   McCabe,   John.   "Book   Reviews."   Records   and
         Recordings, 14 (February 1971), p. 116.

         A review of Soviet Composers by Stanley D. Krebs
         (Allen and Unwin, 1970) which is described as
         "...well worth reading...."

B218.   McCabe,   John.   "Book   Reviews."   Records   and
         Recordings, 15 (November 1971), p. 29.

         A review of To Speak for Ourselves, edited by
         Alan Smyth (William Kimber 1971), which describes
         life in the London Symphony Orchestra.

B219.   McCabe,   John.   "Book   Review."   Records   and
         Recordings, 15 (February 1972), pp. 8+10.

         A review of Barbirolli, Conductor Laureate by
         Michael Kennedy (MacGibbon and Kee 1971) which is
         described   as   "...simply   one   of   the   best
         biographies I have read...."

B220.   McCabe,   John.   "Book   Reviews."   Records   and
         Recordings, 16 (April 1973), p. 9.

         A review of two books about Bartok: Bela Bartok
         letters, edited by J. Demeny (Faber 1973) and

         Bela Bartok by J. Ujfalussy (Corvina Press 1973)
         which the reviewer says "...neither is completely
         satisfying."

B221.   McCabe,   John.   "Book   Reviews."   Records   and
         Recordings, 16 (May 1973), p. 8.

         A review of Delius by Eric Fenby (Faber 1973)
         which   is   described   as   "an   outstanding
         contribution to this valuable series."

B222.   McCabe,   John.   "Book   Reviews."   Records   and
         Recordings, 17 (May 1974), p. 9.

         A review of "Memos" by Charles E. Ives, edited by
         John   Kirkpatrick   (Calder   and   Boyars   1974),
         "a...book crammed with humour and good sense."

B223.   McCabe, John. "Brilliant Baptism." New Statesman,
         71 (18 February 1966), p. 236.

         An account of Richard Rodney Bennett's Symphony
         and its first performance at the Royal Festival
         Hall by the LSO under Istvan Kertesz.

B224.   McCabe, John. "Busoni's Doktor Faust." Records and
         Recordings 13 (September 1970), pp. 26-27.

         An appreciation of Busoni's Doktor Faust,
         prompted by the appearance of the DGG recording
         featuring Fischer-Dieskau.

B225.   McCabe, John. "Cadillac." Records and Recordings,
         13 (March 1970), pp. 28-9.

         A review of the new DGG recording of Paul
         Hindemith's masterpeice, with Fischer-Dieskau in
         the title role.

B226.   McCabe, John. "Composer at the keyboard." Records
         and Recordings, 14 (February 1971), pp. 32-34.

         An appreciation of Rachmaninov's career and
         review of a recording of the four piano
         concertos.

B227.   McCabe, John. "Composer to the defence." Music and
         Musicians, 15 (December 1966), pp. 64+66.

         A reply to points raised in two articles by Noel
         Goodwin.   "Having restrained myself from
         commenting in writing on Mr Goodwin's first
         outburst, I feel that there are one or two fairly
         obvious points in both his articles that need
         reply."

B228.   McCabe, John. "Concertante Music." Music in
         Education, 32 (September/October 1968), pp.
         246-7.

         An account of Concertante Music, commissioned for
         the 1968 Bath Festival, together with a
         postscript written George Odam who conducted the
         new work.

         SEE: W8

B229.   McCabe, John.   "Congress in Retrospect:
         Composers-in-residence." Organist's Review, 59
         (no. 236), 1974 p. 16.

Views on the 1974 IAO Congress which "...chose a most contrasted set of 'resident composers' and it was for me a most valuable experience to be one of these."

B230.   McCabe, John.   "Cost of conductors."   The Times (London), 4 May 1976, p. 13.

A letter to the Times about the cost of conductors.

"The conductor's fee, large or small, is merely one among many costs involved in concert-going...."

B231.   McCabe, John.   "Critic's choice 1969."   Records and Recordings, 13 (December 1969), p. 19.

"In many ways this has been a very good year for out-of-the-way pieces; not all the records have been of really outstanding quality in every department...but my choice of ten best records have been issues that have not only proved immensely rewarding to me personally but have deserved a high place of importance on any record collector's list."

B232.   McCabe, John.   "Dedicated to Delius."   Records and Recordings, 14 (March 1971), pp. 44-50.

Reviews of the new HMV recording of Appalachia and Brigg Fair by Sir John Barbiroli, and the CBS reissue of Sir Thomas Beecham's famous recordings of Sea Drift and Hassan.

B233.   McCabe, John.   "Egon Wellesz and Hans Gal Concert in Manchester."   The Guardian, 23 October 1965, p. 6.

Review of a concert celebrating the 75th birthday of Dr Hans Gal and the 80th birthday of Dr Egon Wellesz.

B234.   McCabe, John.   "English music in Lyrita."   Records and Recordings, 14 (June 1971), pp. 50-53.

A review of some recent orchestral issues including pieces by Holst, Bliss, Walton and Bax.

B235.   McCabe, John.   "Festival of Twentieth Century Music."   The Guardian, 20 March 1967, p. 5.

A review of a concert of music for two pianos, given by John Ogdon and Brenda Lucas as part of the 1967 Cardiff Festival.

B236.   McCabe, John.   "Filmharmonic '70."   Records and Recordings, 5 (December 1971), p. 51.

A review of the two-disc Polydor album of excerpts from the first of the Filmharmonic concerts.

B237.   McCabe, John.   "Gerhard: creator in exile."   Records and Recordings, 15 (February 1972), pp. 44-5.

A discussion about the influences on Roberto Gerhard and a review of the recording of his Violin Concerto and Fourth Symphony.

B238.   McCabe, John.   "Halle Prom at the Free Trade Hall." The Guardian, 17 June 1966, p. 11.

Notes on a concert given by the Halle which includes pieces by Copland, da Falla and Tchaikovsky.

B239.   McCabe, John.   "Hannikainen and the Halle."   The Guardian, 28 October 1965, p. 9.

A review of a Halle concert which included the first British performance of Opus Sonorum by the 44-year old Kokkonen, one of Finland's leading contemporaries.

B240.   McCabe, John.   "Haydn: Piano Sonatas."   BBC (BBC Music Guide) 1986, 90 pp.

A book describing Haydn's sonatas which were composed throughout his career from the earliest days until his second visit to London in 1794/95, when he was 62.   "...although they do not represent the music of his last decade they do show his enormous development as a composer up to that period."

B241.   McCabe, John.   "In front of the Microphone." Records and Recordings, February 1982, pp. 7-8.

Veiws by McCabe on being recorded.   "...recording acts as a supreme challenge to the artist's powers of concentration and imagination and...I personally find it such a fascinating and worthwhile endeavour."

B242.   McCabe, John.   "International competition."   <u>Records
         and Recordings</u>, 13 (December 1969), pp. 32-33.

         "Musical competitions of one sort or another are
         in a way quite an industry these days, and they
         have both great advantages and draw backs.   The
         new Qualiton record prompts one to conclude
         these things...."

B243.   McCabe, John.   "Janice Williams."   <u>The Guardian</u>, 3
         December 1965, p. 11.

         A review of a concert given by Janice Williams in
         the Whitworth Art Gallery, Manchester.

B244.   McCabe, John.   "The Knot Garden."   <u>Record and
         Recordings</u>, 17 (April 1974), pp. 24-27.

         A review of the recording of <u>The Knot Garden</u>,
         "...in some ways the most fascinating of all
         (Tippett's operas)."

B245.   McCabe, John.   "Last night of the Halle Proms."   <u>The
         Guardian</u>, 20 June 1966, p. 7.

         An account of the last night of the Proms in the
         Free Trade Hall, Manchester.

B246.   McCabe, John.   "Latter-day Romantic."   <u>Records and
         Recordings</u>, 16 (October 1972), p. 44.

         An appreciation of the life and music of William
         Alwyn, prompted by the release of a recording of
         <u>Symphony No. 3</u> and <u>The Magic Island</u>.

B247.   McCabe, John.   "Liszt - Colossus of the Keyboard."
         <u>Records and Recordings</u>, 14 (April 1971), pp.
         46-9.

         Reviews of new recordings of Liszt's piano and
         organ works by Danice Chorzempa, Louis Kentner,
         Thomas McIntosh and Ronald Smith.

B248.   McCabe, John.   "Liverpool Concert."   <u>The Guardian</u>,
         13 April 1966, p. 9.

         Views on a RLPO concert conducted by Charles
         Groves.

B249.   McCabe, John.   "Loussier and Bach."   <u>Records and
         Recordings</u>, 14 (Decca 1970), pp. 52-3.

Review of the five-volume Decca release of
Jacques Loussier's Play Bach series.

B250.   McCabe, John. "Manchester Concert." _The Guardian_,
        28 January 1966, p. 11.

        A review of a piano recital given in Manchester
        by Anne-Marie Weydahl.

B251.   McCabe, John. "Manchester Midday Concert at the
        Houldsworth Hall." _The Guardian_, 6 April 1966,
        p. 9.

        Review of a recital by John Lill which includes
        Haydn's two-movement Sonata in G minor.

B252.   McCabe, John. "Maurice Fueri Recital." _The
        Guardian_, 30 October 1965, p. 6.

        A review of a "...complete concert of extended
        works for unaccompanied violin (which may) not be
        to everybody's taste...."

B253.   McCabe, John. "Midsummer Magic." _Records and
        Recordings_, 14 (May 1971), pp. 50-53.

        A review of the new Philips recording, made last
        year concurrently with the performances at the
        Royal Opera House, of Michael Tippett's _The
        Midsummer Marriage_.

B254.   McCabe, John. "Music of the Sixties." _The
        Guardian_, 7 February 1966, p. 7.

        Views of a concert in the Reardon Smith Theatre,
        Cardiff given by soloists from the Paris Music
        Centre, conducted by Keith Humble.

B255.   McCabe, John. "Nielsen Concert." _The Guardian_, 22
        November 1965, p. 7.

        Highlights of the Nielsen centenary concert,
        given in the Town Hall, Chester, are described.

B256.   McCabe, John. "The Philadelphia Heritage." _Records
        and Recordings_, 13 (June 1970), pp. 28-31.

        An appreciation of the Philadelphia Orchestra,
        prompted by a visit of the Orchestra to London
        and the release of several recordings.

B257.   McCabe, John.   "Prokofiev's Cinderella."   <u>Records and Recordings</u>, 12 (November 1968), pp. 30-1.

An account of <u>Cinderella</u> and its score, "...a remarkable tribute to his ability to sustain his inspiration freshly through the composition of many other works and considerable temporal difficulties".

B258.   McCabe, John.   "Question mark over orchestral visit."   <u>The Times</u> (London), 20 April 1982, p. 15.

A letter to The Times about the proposed visit to London in 1983 of the Los Angeles Philharmonic.

B259.   McCabe, John.   "Rachmaninov."   Novello (Novello Short Biographies), 1974, 32 pp.

A survey of Rachmaninov's life and music, together with a list of main compositions.

B260.   McCabe, John.   "Record Survey of British Music released in 1972."   <u>Composer</u>, no. 49 (Autumn 1973), pp. 23-5.

An article describing 1972 as a "...quite spectacular year for releases of British music on record."

B261.   McCabe, John.   "Record Survey of British Music released in 1972 - Part 2.   <u>Composer</u>, no. 50 (Winter 1973-4), pp. 27-30.

A continuation of the previous article, together with a discography of British Music 1972.

B262.   McCabe, John.   "Review: Don Pasquale in Cardiff."   <u>The Guardian</u>, 15 May 1967, p. 5.

A review of the Welsh National Opera Company's production of <u>Don Pasquale</u> with Geraint Evans in the title role.

B263.   McCabe, John.   "Reviews of three new Abbado discs."   <u>Records and Recordings</u>, 15 (April 1972), pp. 26-27.

A survey and examination of Abbado's recordings, together with reviews of three new ones of music by Berg, Scriabin and Tchaikovsky.

B264.   McCabe, John.   "Rosslyn Tureck Recital."   The Guardian, 29 March 1967, p. 7.

A review of a piano recital given by Rosalyn Tureck in the Free Trade Hall, Manchester.

B265.   McCabe, John.   "Royal Liverpool Philharmonic Orchestra."   The Guardian, 24 November 1966, p. 7.

A review of a RLPO concert at the Brangwyn Hall, Swansea.

B266.   McCabe, John.   "Russian Double Bill."   Records and Recordings, 11 (July 1968), pp. 16-17.

A review of Russian recordings of music by Rachmaninov and Tchaikovsky.

B267.   McCabe, John.   "Russian Revolutions."   Records and Recordings, 13 (August 1970), pp. 16-19.

A review of some recordings of music devoted to the propagation of Communist ideals.

B268.   McCabe, John.   "St. Matthew Passion."   The Guardian, 25 April 1966, p. 7.

A review of a performance of Bach's St. Matthew Passion in Liverpool.

B269.   McCabe, John.   "The Second Viennese School." Records and Recordings, 15 (November 1971), pp. 58-61.

Reviews of the DGG set of Schoenberg, Berg and Webern String Quartets, and Fisher-Dieskau's disc of the same composers' songs.

B270.   McCabe, John.   "Serenade Concert."   The Guardian, 18 March 1967, p. 5.

A review of a Serenade Concert given in Cardiff Castle as part of the city's Festival of Twentieth-century music.

B271.   McCabe, John.   "Shared honour."   The Sunday Times, 24 April 1983, p. 24.

A letter about female conductors including Jane Glover and Iris Lemare.

B272.   McCabe, John. "Sounds all round." <u>Records and Recordings</u>, 16 (February 1973), pp. 38+90.

An article about the first quadradiscs and the discrete system of quadraphonic recording.

B273.   McCabe, John. "Spectrum '69." <u>Records and Recordings</u>, 13 (October 1969), pp. 39-41.

A review of three new recordings devoted to American music.

B274.   McCabe, John. "Symphony No. 1 (Elegy)." <u>Musical Events</u>, 21 (July 1966), p. 14.

An account of the composer's first symphony, movement by movement.

SEE: W33

B275.   McCabe, John. "Symphony No. 2." <u>Musical Events</u>, 27 (March 1972), pp. 24-25+32.

An essay about McCabe's <u>Symphony No. 2</u>, including useful background information about it.

SEE: W34

B276.   McCabe, John. "Symphonies and Suites." <u>Records and Recordings</u>, 15 (October 1971), pp. 52-55.

A detailed review of the Philips boxed set of Tchaikovsky's Symphonies and Suites.

B277.   McCabe, John. "(The) Tchaikovsky Ballets." <u>Records and Recordings</u>, 14 (November 1970), pp. 48-50.

Useful background to add details of the Tchaikovsky ballets, prompted by the release of new recordings.

B278.   McCabe, John. "(The) Tchaikovsky Operas." <u>Records and Recordings</u>, 14 (October 1970), pp. 56-59.

A survey of Tchaikovsky's operas and a review of <u>Eugene Onegin</u>, a recording conducted by Mstislav Rostropovich.

B279.   McCabe, John. "(The) third avant-garde." <u>Records and Recordings</u>, 14 (January 1971), pp. 50-53.

A review of a DGG album of avant-garde discs, the
third such collection from this source.

B280.   McCabe, John.   "(The) 13 symphonies."   Records and
Recordings, 12 (May 1969), pp. 24-27.

A discussion about the recordings available of
Schostakovitch's complete symphonic literature,
and reviews of the HMV recording of the Eighth
Symphony, with Kiril Kondrashim and the Moscow
Philharmonic Symphony Orchestra.

B281.   McCabe, John.   "(The) Trendsetters."   Records and
Recordings, 14 (September 1971), pp. 52-3.

A review of Henze's El Cimaron and Stockhausen's
Stimmung, both recordings issued on the DGG
label.

B282.   McCabe, John.   "Turntable."   Records and Recordings,
13 (September 1970), pp. 32-3.

An appreciation of the careers of Sir John
Barbirolli and George Szell, both of whom died
during the same week.

B283.   McCabe, John.   "(The) Twentieth century."   Records
and Recordings, 15 (June 1972), pp. 28-31.

A review of records of piano music by Janacek,
Rachmaninov, Prokofiev, Ives and Boulez.

B284.   McCabe,   John.   "Twentieth-Century   Melodist."
Records and Recordings, 13 (April 1970), pp.
18-19.

Useful background information to Walton's three
concertos for string instruments which give
"...something of a conspectus of his career to
date, for they represent quite distinctly the
three phases of his work."

B285.   McCabe, John.   "Twenty Glances at the Child Jesus."
Records and Recordings, 12 (August 1969), pp.
23-25.

A review of Messiaen's work for piano, recorded
by Thomas Rajna, recorded on the Psyche label.

B286.   McCabe,   John.   "Village   Romeo."   Records   and
Recordings, 16 (February 1973), pp. 36-37.

A review of the first recording of Delius's masterpiece, A Village Romeo and Juliet.

B287.   McCabe, John. "Well composed at 70." Records and Recordings, 15 (May 1972), pp. 32-36.

An essay on the music of William Walton, together with reviews of two new recordings of Facade.

B288.   McCabe, John. "Xenakis the Greek." Records and Recordings, 12 (January 1969), pp. 18-19.

An appreciation of Xenakis's music, prompted by the appearance of two recordings on the HMV and Nonesuch labels.

B289.   MacDonald, Malcolm. "Joubert: Piano Works." Gramophone, 53 (December 1975), p. 1082.

A review of the Pearl SHE 520 recording of John Joubert's piano music. "McCabe has the measure of this music everywhere, and has also written the perceptive sleeve-note. He and Joubert make a formidable combination...."

SEE: D53

B290.   MacDonald, Malcolm. "McCabe: The Chagall Windows." Gramophone, 65 (November 1987), p. 740.

A review of the EMI Greensleeves re-issue (ED 291219-1) of The Chagall Windows, Hartman Variations and Notturni ed Alba.

"John McCabe has perhaps not had the general acceptance, as a composer, that I think his music deserves. It is strong, or gentle, as the occasion demands; it is often of great beauty, with many ravishing sounds produced by means of exceedingly accomplished scoring; its harmonic idiom is generally a development of tradition, seldom a contradiction of it; and emotionally the music tends to concentrate on what is right with the human race, not on what is wrong with it."

SEE: D5; D17; D30

B291.   MacDonald, Malcolm. "McCabe: Symphony...." The Gramophone, XLV (January 1968), p. 376.

A review of the Pye Virtuoso (TPLS 13005) recording which includes the first symphony. "...as it stands a serious symphonic impression

is certainly made: this is a most worthwhile work
to add to the recorded repertory."

SEE: D23

B292.   MacDonald, Malcolm.   "Pot-Pourri."   Gramophone,   58
        (October 1980), p 517.

        A review of the Cornucopia IJ 100 recording which
        introduced John McCabe as accompanist for some of
        the items.

        SEE: D42

B293.   Mann,   William.   "Goehr: Four   Songs   for   the
        Japanese."   The Gramophone, XLV (January 1968),
        pp. 390-91.

        A review of the Pye Golden Guinea (GSGC 14105)
        recording.

        "...John McCabe is an able composer in his own
        right, and plays like someone from whom no
        musical secrets are hid."

        SEE: D44

B294.   Mann, William.   "Hoddinott: Piano Sonata No. 6."
        Gramophone, 51 (March 1974), p. 1711.

        A review of a recording (Argo ZRG 761) which
        includes McCabe's String Trio.

        "McCabe...writes capably for the difficult medium
        of string trio and provides active music that can
        be overheard with pleasure but does not force you
        to give him all your attention."

        SEE: D22

B295.   Mann,   William.   "McCabe: The   Chagall   Windows."
        Gramophone, 53 (October 1975), p. 621.

        A review of the HMV ASD 3096 recording.   "John
        McCabe's   music...is   admirable   background
        material, beautifully scored, thoroughly varied."

        SEE: D5

B296.   Mann, William.   "Modern Cello Works."   Gramophone,
        54 (April 1977), pp. 1569-70.

        A review of the L'Oiseau-Lyre recording DSL 018
        which includes McCabe's Partita for solo cello.

It is described as "...vivid and full of musical sap, individual but creatively indebted to J.S. Bach and sometimes Bartok...."

SEE: D18

B297.   Mann, William.   "Twentieth-Century Piano Music." The Gramophone, XLVII (October 1969), p. 584.

A review of the Pye Golden Guinea recording GSGC 14116, which includes McCabe's 5 Bagatelles.

"McCabe's own Bagatelles...include some well imagined piano sonorities and some bursts of exuberance...."

SEE: D2

B298.   Marks, Anthony.   "20th century." The Musical Times, cxxvii (May 1986), p. 281.

"Jane Manning also appears on The Moving Fires of Evening (Wergo WER 60096), a recording of works by John Casken. She brings great conviction to la orana, Gauguin, also accompanied by John McCabe."

SEE: D40

B299.   Marsh, Robert C. "CSO finds heart of fire new work." Chicago Sun-Times, 4 May 1984, p. 55.

"Georg Solti does not conduct a great deal of new music with the Chicago Symphony, but when he decides to play a contemporary work, he gives it everything he has. Such was the case last night when beginning his final programs for the season he introduced John McCabe's Concerto for Orchestra....

McCabe, respected in Britain as both a composer and pianist, has written a big, bold piece of music that cannot be fully assimilated with one hearing but gives the distinct impression of being important work. McCabe's concerto was unusually well received, the strength of the writing and the force of the performance were both apparent."

SEE: W15

B300.   Maycock, Robert. "Fifty not out." Classical Music, no.374 (8 April 1989), p.37.

An interview with the composer on the eve of his 50th birthday, with mention of his career and its important landmarks. The title of the article alludes to cricket, another of McCabe's passions.

B301.   Maycock, Robert. "John McCabe." in "John McCabe" (Novello & Co), 1989, pp.20-21.

An appreciation of John McCabe's compositions and musicianship, written in celebration of the composer's 50th birthday.

B302.   Maycock, Robert. "Rachmaninov the progressive?" Music and Musicians, 23 (January 1975), p.32.

A review of McCabe's booklet on Rachmaninov and his music. "... it is... gratifying that no less a composer than John McCabe has produced an account of the music that takes its composer's stature almost for granted and finds much to enthuse about in practically every work.

... McCabe... draws attention to less obvious beauties, and leads on from there to valuable comments on the underlying strengths of the music."

B303.   Maycock, Robert. "Speed and light." The Independent (London), 17 August 1989, p.10.

" ... began with the London premiere of Fire at Durilgai by John McCabe. This is a composer that orchestras like to play....

It is another big single movement... but... congently shaped and sounding well: McCabe casts widely for his sonorities... and arranges them into a confident, individual pattern of orchestral colour.

... the players clearly know the piece thoroughly, and delivered it with panache, not least the percussionists, who earned their early interval...."

SEE: W26

B304.   Maycock, Robert. "Variations on a form: John McCabe's string quartets. The Musical Times, cxxx (July 1989), pp.386-388.

An appreciation of McCabe's five string quartets, the latest receiving its first performance at the Fishguard Festival in July 1989.

SEE: W92; W95; W96; W97; W98

B305.   Morley, Christopher.   "Birmingham."   <u>Music and
         Musicians</u>, 28(May 1980), pp.64+66.

         "(John McCabe's <u>Violin Concerto No.2.</u>) ... is one
         of   undoubted   personality,   performed   with
         assurance and devotion by its dedicatee....

         It is also an exploration of the predominantly
         lyrical charcter of the violin, sometimes pitting
         the sole instrument against hostile, anti-lyrical
         elements in the orchestra.

         ... one is left with the impression of McCabe's
         usual gift of imaginative use of instrumental
         colour, impressively recreated by Gruenberg and a
         top-form CBSO."

         SEE: W20

B306.   Morrison, Bryce. "Nielsen piano music." <u>Music and
         Musicians</u>, 25(December 1976), pp. 43+44.

         A review of two recordings of Neilsen's piano
         music, both by John McCabe, on SDD 475 and SDD
         476.

         "John McCabe's performance are capable.... McCabe
         is more convincing in the miniatures, and is
         particularly sensitive to the way that <u>The
         Spinning Top</u> circles within an ever-decreasing
         radius until the whip sets it moving again."

         SEE: D58

B307.   Morrison, Richard. "King's Singers."   <u>The Times</u>
         (London), 1 January 1988, p.14.

         "And there were two commissioned pieces. John
         McCabe <u>Scenes in America Deserta</u> was a further
         exploration of this composers fruitful obsession
         with desert imaginery.

         It was rich in subtle colouristic effects that
         were brilliantly executed."

         SEE: W124

B308.   Morrison, Richard. "Playing with fire." <u>The Times</u>
         (London), 17 August 1989, p.14.

         "To call John McCabe an unsung hero is not
         literally accurate, since his atmospheric music
         is sung and played a great deal. Nevertheless he

is one of those unglamorous figures upon whom a
country's musical life, at many levels from youth
orchestras   upwards,   ultimately   depends:
composers, performers and administrators (McCabe
is all three) who, while they may never create an
artistic   statement   as   significant   as   Peter
Grimes, pursue an honest craft with sustained
imagination. The music (of Fire at Durilgai)
develops in... unexpected ways, albeit in a
fairly conventional harmonic idiom.   Its slow
introduction is pictorial enough.... There are
ominous tuba notes, and a colourful build-up
towards much which makes much play with scurrying
woodwind   ideas.   But   the   music,   never
one-directional for more than a few seconds, soon
becomes   a   masterly   kaleidoscope   of   changing
instrumentation."

SEE: W26

B309.   Murray,   David.   "McCabe.   Symphony   No.2."   The
        Gramophone, 51 (November 1973), p.928.

        A review of the HMV ASD 2904 recording which also
        includes Notturni ed Alba. "His textures are
        always   lucid,   his   orchestration   impersonally
        skilful."

        SEE: D17

B310.   N., B. "Fascinating Work." Liverpool Echo, 20
        December 1965, p.2.

        A review of McCabe's Concertante for harpsichord
        and chamber orchestra and it first performance.

        SEE: W7

B311.   N., M.V. "Premiere of McCabe cantata." Malvern
        Gazette, 11 October 1973, p.12.

        "Malvern Concert Club's 70th anniversary was
        marked by a new work by John McCabe, commissioned
        for the occasion and conducted by the composer.

        Entitled Time Remembered, the cantata is a
        setting of poems in English and Latin on the
        theme of morality."

        SEE: W143

B312.   Nagley,   Judith.   "McCabe."   The   Musical   Times,
        cxxi(May 1980), p.331.

A review of the Second Violin Concerto's first London performance.

"A large scale work..., it makes no concession to the current fashion for terse, concentrated statement but unfolds inexorably over four substantial movements, involving vast orchestral resources that include two harps, a celesta and a battery of percussion, tuned and untuned."

SEE: W20

B313.   Nagley, Judith. "Orchestral, Choral." The Musical Times, cxxiv (April 1983), p.247.

"On the eve of a European tour with the LPO, Sir Georg Solti celebrated his last London appearance as the orchestra's principal conductor with John McCabe's Concerto for Orchestra....

Sir Georg clearly relished the excitment of this large-scale display piece, while the players too were, on their mettle and at their most responsive."

SEE: W15

B314.   Neeson, Geraldine. "Tension time at Festival." Cork Examiner, 10 May 1980, p.22.

"The William Byrd Singers from Manchester... gave the first public performance of the part-song specially commissioned for John McCabe. It is a setting of the poem Siberia by James Clarence Mangan.

Atmospheric music, it is a child of the 20th century, bleak, rugged, harsh, but there is room in the complex rhythmic plan for the emotions, and the heart beats underneath."

SEE: W116

B315.   Norris, Geofrey. "Two guides." The Musical Times, 116 (June 1975), p.541.

A review of two books on Rachmaninov. "John McCabe's booklet provides a model for the Novello Short Biographies....

In little more than 25 pages of text he breaks no new ground in biographical information, but the salient points are there, neatly integrated with a clear account of Rachmaninov's musical development."

B316.   Nott, Carolyn. "Dublin Festival of Twentieth Century
        Music." Musical Opinion 92 (February 1969),
        pp.234-5.

        "An adventurous lunch-time concert was given by
        ... the British pianist and composer, John McCabe
        ... (who) gave the first performance of his own
        Capriccio for piano, a rhapsodic work, gratefully
        pianistic, full of sensitive atmosphere and
        immediately attractive harmonics."

        SEE: W40

B317.   Odam, George. "Blow the reactionaries, let's have
        more" Bath Evening Chronicle, 26 June 1969, p.11.

        A report of a McCabe recital at the 1969 Bath.
        Festival which included a performance of "... his
        new piece Sostenuto, a study in sustaining an
        harmonic effect...."

        SEE: W59

B318.   Orledge, Robert "Liverpool". The Musical Times,
        113(May 1972), pp.482-3.

        "John McCabe's Metamorphosen ... had its
        much-postponed premiere..., the composer acting
        as last-minute soloist....

        ...McCabe seemed completely at home with the
        harpsichord, playing skilfully and sensitively
        ...."

        SEE: W29

B319.   Payne, Anthony. "Chamber Orchestral." The Musical
        Times, 109 (August 1968), p.738.

        "Another premiere was John McCabe's Concerto for
        Chamber Orchestra. The work is in five
        movements, in a single span... and shows a
        remarkable fluency in musical syntax and form."

        SEE: W11

B320.   Pettitt, Stephen. "LPO/Solti" The Times (London),
        11 February 1983, p.10.

        A report of the LPO concert when McCabe's
        Concerto for Orchestra was given its first
        performance. "With this new work ... the music
        is in a sense sparer, McCabe's predilection for
        thick textures remains, here but the formal
        outlines are more jagged, the language more
        condensed than before."

SEE: W15

B321.   Pirie, David. "Fear in the Night" <u>Monthly Film Bulletin</u>, 39(August 1972), pp.160-161.

Details about the Hammer film <u>Fear in the Night</u>, with music by John McCabe.

SEE: W153

B322.   Pirie, Peter J. "McCabe: Symphony (Elegy) 1965." <u>The Musical Times</u>, 109(April 1968), pp.347-8.

A review of the Pye recording TPLS 13005. "It is north British and even Scandinavian in feeling, magnificently and tautly constructed economically but pungently scored, and gripping."

SEE: D23

B323.   Plaistow, Stephen. "Haydn: Piano Sonatas." <u>Gramophone</u>, 54(September 1976), p.444.

A review of volume 3 on Decca 3 HDN 106-8. "John McCabe is admirable for the freshness with which he makes the ideas speak and for the unhurried ease in which he sustains an appropriate context for them."

SEE: D50

B324.   Plaistow, Stephen. "Haydn: Piano Sonatas." <u>Gramophone</u>, 54(April 1977), p.1573.

A review of volume 4 on Decca 4 HDN 109-11 with one or two criticisms "...here and there...."

SEE: D51

B325.   Plaistow, Stephen. "Ifor James : Horn Recital." <u>The Gramophone</u>, XLVI (January 1969), p.1025.

A review of the Pye Golden Guinea recording GSGC 14087, with John McCabe as accompanist.

"John McCabe's playing has splendid vitality and projection...."

SEE: D31

B326.   Pooley, A. Morley. "Abbey rises to the bangs and the bells." <u>Bath Evening Chronicle</u>, 25 June 1968, p.5.

A review of McCabe's <u>Concertante Music</u> (1968). "McCabe is extremely versatile in his use of the orchestra.... He is a five craftsman...."

SEE: W8

B327.   Porter, Andrew. "Park Lane Group." <u>The Financial Times</u>, 11 February 1964, p.20.

"Mr McCabe's <u>Sechs Gedichte</u> (1963), though drawn from three different poets and not linked in subject matter, are apparently intended as a musical whole. Their tonality centres on B flat and it seemed motivic transformations and harmonic colours linked one song to the next.

The songs are nicely written but not memorable. One carries away little more than some effective Britten-like figuration from the first of them, the oddly ejaculatory handling of <u>Das zerbrochene Ringlein</u>, and a certain doubt whether Mr. McCabe's harmonic control is always secure."

SEE: W137

B328.   Radcliffe, Philip. "Manchester." <u>The Sunday Times</u>, 12 January 1975, p.33.

"McCabe's... <u>The Chagall Windows</u>, commissioned by the Halle, (was given) its first performance this week....

McCabe has a clarity of vision and knows how to exploit orchestral colour.

<u>The Chagall Windows</u> is not a stunning work... but is is thoroughly worthwhile, because McCabe is an extremely sensitive craftsman, a composer who commands respect and admiration, always reliable, never trivial."

SEE: W5

B329.   Ramsey, Basil. "Book Review." <u>Musical Opinion</u>, 98 (May 1975), p.405.

A review of John McCabe's music guide on the orchestral works of Bela Bartok. "McCabe offers a skilful assessment of the orchestral works within the context of other music of importance...."

B330.   Reavley, Edwin. "Filling the air was my own sound
        of music." Bath and Wilts Evening Chronicle, 24
        June 1969, p.2.

        A personal view of the music at the 1969 Bath
        Festival, including   details   of   McCabe's
        Concertante Music.

        SEE: W8

B331.   Redman, Reginald. "Not all this gold glitters."
        Evening Post (Bristol), 4 March 1971, p.30.

        A mention of McCabe's Concertante Variations on a
        theme of Nicholas Maw which "... contained much
        of real interest, many of the effects being
        unusual and intriguing."

        SEE: W9

B332.   Rees, A.J. Heward. "North Wales." The Musical Times,
        cxxii (January 1981), p.45.

        A report of a McCabe recital which included the
        firt performance of "his new and evocative
        concert study Mosaic, influenced by Middle
        Eastern art...."

        SEE: W50

B333.   Rhein, John von. "Symphony serves up a beefy slice
        from the music of Solti's England." Chicago
        Tribune, 4 May 1984 (Section 2), p.9.

        A review of the first US performance of Concerto
        for Orchestra - "... an exhilaratory score, full
        of inventive detail and colourful, open
        scoring....McCabe's entry has a robust confidence
        borne of strong ideas, expertly argued."

        SEE: W15

B334.   Richards, Denby. "The Contemporary Scene." Musical
        Opinion, 98(May 1975), pp.399-400.

        "...The Chagall Windows makes very stimulating
        and thoroughly enjoyable musical listening. It
        was beauty, drama and that indescribable element
        called genius."

        SEE: W5

B335.   Richards, Denby. "Corno da camera." Music and
        Musicians, 16(February 1968), pp.51-2.

Details about <u>Dance Movement</u>, "... a rather
rambling, yet curiously evocative piece, with a
most interesting opening movement and what at
first hearing appeared to be an over-repetitive
finale.   Yet   the   scoring   showed   a   fine
appreciation of the problem of writing for horn,
violin and piano."

SEE: W79

B336.   Richards, Denby. "Difficult theme to spot." <u>Music
and Musicians</u>, 17 (January 1969), p.50.

"John McCabe's <u>Variations and theme of Hartmann</u>,
which received its first London performance... is
an   extremely   enjoyable   piece   of   orchestral
craftsmanship by a pianist of distinction, whose
compositions have already covered a wide field."

SEE: W37

B337.   Richards, Denby. "Liverpool." <u>Music and Musicians</u>,
20(May 1972), pp.65-6.

A   review   of   <u>Metamorphosen</u>   and   its   first
performance at Liverpool in February 1972.

SEE: W29

B338.   Richards, Denby, "Liverpool." <u>Music and Musicians</u>,
26(October 1977), p.51.

Concerning the first performance of the <u>Third
Piano concerto</u>, commissioned by the soloist Ilan
Rogoff, to whom it is dedicated. "In character
the new work leans more towards the lyricism of
Chagall   Windows   than   to   either   of   its
predecessors in the <u>genre</u>. In form it falls into
the traditional 3-movement structure, although
the Andante flessible central movement is linked
by an imaginative percussion passage to a lively
neo-romantic Allegro moderato."

SEE: W18

B339.   Richards, Denby. "Recitals." <u>Music and Musicians</u>,
20(July 1972), p.73.

Details about the first performance of McCabe's
<u>Concerto for oboe d'amore</u>, "... a commission from
the enterprising Portsmouth Festival...."

SEE: W14

B340.   Robertson, W.D.D. "Middlesbrough, England." Opera
         News (USA), 39(November 1974), p.57.

         An appreciation of Mother Courage and its first
         performance in Middlesbrough.

         "The music is delightful, and McCabe, a
         distinguished pianist, is quite possibly going to
         carve out a stage career and prove to unbelievers
         that opera is not dead."

         SEE: W1

B341.   Rockwell, John, "Classics of the Keyboard on Disks."
         The New York Times, 23 April 1978, pp.D20+D24.

         A brief mention of the second volume of Haydn
         piano sonatas, recorded by McCabe.

         SEE: D49

B342.   S., W.R. "Effective New Quintet." Daily Telegraph
         and Morning Post, 6 November 1962, p.11.

         "A string quintet by a young Northern composer of
         rare talent, John McCabe, received its first
         performance.... It has seven movements in
         unbroken sequence, but, with one exception, of
         ever-increasing duration, and in which material
         from the initial Prefazione is developed and
         dovetailed in a manner immediately effective and
         enjoyable."

         SEE: W99

B343.   Sabor, Rudolf. "Music Survey." Musical Events,
         21(August 1966), pp.27-8.

         Brief details about the First Symphony and its
         first performance.

         SEE: W33

B344.   Sadie, Stanley. "Concerts." The Musical Times,
         106(March 1965), pp.201-2.

         Concerning the first performance of Movements for
         clarinet, violin and cello which is described as
         "... a slight but neat work with little meaty
         content."

         SEE: W88

B345.   Sadie, Stanley. "John McCabe ; Purcell Room." The
         Times(London), 1 October 1975, p.9.

An account of a McCabe recital which contained
three Haydn piano sonatas, and a performance of
his own <u>Aubade</u>.

SEE: W38

B346.   Sadie, Stanley. "London Music." <u>The Musical Times</u>,
         105 (January 1964), p.38.

         Concerning the first London performance of <u>Dies
         Resurrectionis</u>, played by Simon Preston at a
         London Bach Society concert at St. Bartholomew-
         the-Great.

         "Harmonically,   texturally   and   rhythmically
         Messiaen's influence dominated the piece."

         SEE: W64

B347.   Sadie, Stanley. "Northern Sinfonia." <u>The Times</u>
         (London), 29 November 1971, p.8.

         "... Sinfonia Concertante, alias <u>Piano Concerto
         No.2</u>, which reaches London on Friday ... is full
         of echoes.
         ... it is neither old hat, nor derivative, but a
         bright, crisp piece, on its own terms well and
         resourcefully   composed,   artfully   integrated,
         pleasant to listen to."

         SEE: W17

B348.   Sadie, Stanley. "Variations have quirky streak." <u>The
         Times Saturday Review</u>, 2 November 1968, p.19.

         "The novelty was John McCabe's <u>Variations on a
         theme of Hartmann</u> which the Halle have often
         played in the North.   McCabe's style has now
         grown   more   personal.   This   piece   s   very
         Bartokian."

         SEE: W37

B349.   Sadie, Stanely. "Words which defy music." <u>The Times</u>
         (London), 22 June 1967, p.8.

         A review of <u>Aspects of Whiteness</u> and its first
         performance at the QEH.

         SEE: W107

B350.   Salter, Lionel. "D. Scarlatti : Keyboard Sonatas."
         <u>Gramophone</u>, 59 (January 1982), p.1034.

A review of the recording Hyperion A66025.

SEE: D62

B351.   Sanders, Alan. "British Cello Music." Gramophone, 65(January 1988, p.1102.

A review of the ASV digital recording DCA 592 which includes McCabe as accompanist to Julian Lloyd-Webber in two of the pieces.

SEE: D39

B352.   Schiffer, Brigitte. "Boulez will das Londoner Konzetleben ummodeln." Melos, 39 (1972), pp.53-55.

A review, in German, of the first London performance of Notturni ed Alba.

SEE: W30

B353.   Shaw, A.T. "Brilliant brass stirs memories." Worcester Evening News, 26 August 1975, p.3.

Details and review of the first complete performance of McCabe's Goddess Trilogy for horn and piano.

SEE: W84

B354.   Shaw, A.T. "No danger in dropping Dream of Gerontius." Berrow's Worcester Journal, 7 September 1972, p.15.

"John McCabe's Voyage was this year's big festival commission. The performance was applauded through cheers and the success of the work was gratifying to the composer, Christopher Robinson, and to the chorus who had worked hard to prepare it."

SEE: W130

B355.   Shaw, A.T. "Shouts of 'Bravo' in long ovation." Berrows Worcester Journal, 31 August 1972, p.4.

"McCabe's Voyage ... was received with acclamation....

It is a piece in which frequent use is more of the speaking voice as a vehicle of expression and in which dissonance, even cacophony has its appropriate place in a modern conception of orchestral colour."

SEE: W130

B356.   Shepherd, John. "Manchester." Music and Musicians,
         24 (July 1976), p.57.

         "In a more conservative vein ... was the first
         performance of John McCabe's Sonata on a
         Motet....

         (It) is ... clearly constructed and sinuous,
         which, was brough home by the Camerta's committed
         and well shaped performance."

         SEE: W32

B357.   Simmons. David. "London Music." Musical Opinion, 92
         (December 1968), pp.119-121.

         Mention of the first London performance of the
         Hartmann Variations which is called "... both an
         advance and a retreat on his first symphony...."

         SEE: W37

B358.   Simmons, David. "London Music." Musical Opinion,
         95(May 1972), pp.398-9.

         A personal view about the Second Symphony in
         which "... McCabe's excellent ear provide(s)
         vivid and more the workman-like orchestration."

         SEE: W34

B359.   Smith, Monica. "Macclesfield in Retrospect." Music
         in Education, 37 (July/August 1973), pp.193-4.

         Recollections of the 1973 Macclesfield festival
         which featured McCabe's music.

B360.   Stadlen, Peter. "John McCabe's new Concerto." The
         Daily Telegraph, 12 February 1983, p.13.

         "Some of the best music composed for some time by
         anyone occurs in John McCabe's Concerto for
         Orchestra.

         McCabe succeeds first of all in what is the most
         notoriously problematic dimension of contemporary
         music. Time and again one gets involved in the
         composer's harmonic inventiveness, one is amazed
         by the interest that emanates from the character
         of his chords or from the novel way the
         re-iteration of a brief motif are welded
         together, for example at the very start."

SEE: W15

B361.   Stadlen, Peter. "New McCabe concerto."   The Daily
         Telegraph, 24 March 1980, p.13.

         "The care and ingenuity that have gone into the
         making of John McCabe's Second Violin Concerto is
         unmistakeably as one studies the score.   There
         was no doubt ... as regards the composer's rich
         colouristic imagination.   His flair for putting
         the best apparatus ... to even-varying use
         provided a chief source of interest; another was
         his skill in offering scope for the formidable
         soloist while never allowing a single note tobe
         obscured by the multitudes."

         SEE: W20

B362.   Stringer, Robin. "John McCabe."   Gramophone,   55
         (October 1977), p.603.

         Review of an interview with John McCabe about his
         recording and concert activities.

B363.   T., J.F.   "Last concert of the season."   Surrey
         Daily Advertiser, 5-6 May 1975, p. 4.

         A review of a concert, given by the Guildford
         Philharmonic Orchestra, which included the
         premiere of Basse Danse in its orchestral form.
         "The work can be called contemporary medieval,
         with the stress on the former."

         SEE: W39a

B364.   Thomas, Anne. "The majestic Mother Courage." North
         Eastern Evening Gazette, 4 October 1974, p.4.

         A review of the Play of Mother Courage "...the
         kind of theatrical tour de force which leaves one
         gasping for superlatives.   John McCabe's music is
         rich in subtle rhythmic changes and it relies on
         a change of mood rather than any strong melodic
         line which would be totally out of place in such
         work.   It is matched by the warmth and humanity
         of Monica Smith's libretto."

         SEE: W1

B365.   Truscott, Harold.   "Two Traditionalists: Kenneth
         Leighton and John McCabe."
         in Foreman, Lewis (ed.)   "British Music Now."
         Paul Elek (London, 1975), pp. 145-154.

A survey of McCabe's music, together with a discography on p. 230.

B366.   W., R.W.   "School Choir's Messiah."   The Liverpool Echo and Evening Express, 19 December 1961, p.2.

A report about Christmas music, performer by the Liverpool Institute Choral Society, which included the first performance of McCabe's triptych Puer Natus in Bethlehem, "...its centre piece a highly personal setting of the Coventry Carol, with a solo part for boy soprano...."

SEE: W122

B367.   Walker, Robert Matthew.   "The London College of Music."   Music and Musicians International,   36 (January 1988), pp. 9-10.

A centenary assessment of the LCM with mention of its present director, John McCabe, and William Lloyd-Webber his predecessor.

B368.   Walsh, Stephen.   "Cheltenham Festival - McCabe and Wellesz."   The Musical Times, 107 (September 1966), pp. 791-2.

A review of the First Symphony's first performance at the 1966 Cheltenham Festival.

SEE: W33

B369.   Warrack, John.   "Bridge-Phantasm..."   Gramophone, 54 (April 1977), p. 1542.

A review of the Lyrita recording SRCS 91 which includes John McCabe playing the Rhapsody for piano and orchestra by E.J. Moeran. It is described as "...extremely well and sympatheticlly played...."

SEE: D55

B370.   Warrack, John.   "English piano works."   Gramophone, 52 (December 1974), p. 1187.

A review of the Decca Ace of Diamonds recording: SDD 444, in which McCabe is called an "...admirable advocate of them, neither enervatingly indulgent nor destructively crisp."

SEE: D33

B371.   Webb,   Stanley.   "Organ   Recital: Edward
        Higginbottom." The Gramophone, XLIX (February
        1972), p. 1401.

        A review of the Decca Eclipse recording ECS 626,
        recorded in Corpus Christi College, Cambridge
        which includes McCabe's Elegy (1965).

        SEE: D11

B372.   Webb, Stanley. "Organ Recital: Graham Barber."
        Gramophone, 53 (January 1976, p. 1221.

        A review of the Vista recording VPS 1025 which
        includes McCabe's Le Poisson Magique.

        "...John McCabe, always strongly susceptible to
        pictorial images, tranlates Paul Klee's painting
        into the novel sounds of fish darting about in
        still water."

        SEE: D19

B373.   Webb, Stanley. "Organ Recital: Melville Cook."
        Gramophone, 52 (September 1974), p. 557.

        A review of the RCA Victrola LVLI 5019 recording
        which includes McCabe's Dies Resurrectionis,
        "...a threefold vision moving from death by way
        of the tomb to the day of glory."

        SEE: D10

B374.   Webb, Stanley. "St. Albans International Organ
        Festival, 1969." The Gramophone, XLVII (December
        1970,) p. 1017.

        A review of the Abbey LPB 665 recording which
        includes McCabe's Dies Resurrectionis.

        SEE: D10

B375.   Webster,   E.M.   "Cheltenham: Say   not   the
        Struggle...." Musical Opinion, 89 (September
        1966), p. 727.

        A review of the first performance of the First
        Symphony which opened the 1966 Cheltenham
        Festival.

        SEE: W33

B376.   Webster, E.M. "Eloquent playing by John McCabe."
        The Gloucestershire Echo, 21 July 1967, p. 7.

A review of a midday concert by McCabe at the
Cheltenham Festival which included his own
Fantasy on a theme of Liszt.

SEE: W41

B377.   Webster, E.M. "The Three Choirs...." Musical
Opinion, 94 (October 1970), p.10.

View about the first performance of Notturni Ed
Alba which "... was by far the most interesting
and of far the greatest stature."

SEE: W30

B378.   Webster, E.M. "The Three Choirs Festival..."
Musical Opinion, 96(October 1972), p.13+15.

A review of Voyage which "... skilfully manages
to adhere to this tradition, while breaking some
fairly interesting new ground."

SEE: W130

B379.   Whittall, Arnold. "McCabe and Crosse." Music and
Musicians, 24(July 1976), p.37.

A review of the HMV recording ASD 3096, which
includes performances of The Chagall Windows and
the Hartman Variations.

SEE: D5; D30

B380.   Widdicombe, Gillian. "Early Concerto." The Times
Saturday Review, 6 July 1968, p.19.

Details about the first performance of McCabe's
Concerto for Chamber Orchestra (revised version)
by the New Cantata Orchestra at the Q.E.H.

SEE: W11a

B381.   Widdicombe, Gillian, "Farnham." The Musical Times,
110 (July 1969), p.764.

A review of the Farnham Festival, including a
performance of McCabe's Concertino for piano duet
and orchestra.

SEE: W10

B382.   Widdicombe, Gillian. "Hackney Arts Festival."   The
         Musical Times, 108 (June 1967), p.550.

         A brief mention of Johannis Partita and its first
         London performance.

         SEE: W67

B383.   Williams, Peter. "Mary, Queen of Scots."   Dance and
         Dancers, 27 (May 1976), pp.14-18.

         Details and review of Mary, Queen of Scots, with
         some views on the music which is described as
         "... admirable in many ways, and musically the
         many interludes... are beautiful."

         SEE: W2

B384.   Wimbush, Roger. "Here and there: John McCabe."   The
         Gramophone, XIV(August 1967), p.103.

         Brief biographical details with mention of the
         recording of the First Symphony, conducted by
         John Snashall.

         SEE: W33

B385.   Wimbush, Roger. "John McCabe."   Gramophone,   52
         (February 1975), p.1469.

         Details of McCabe compositions on record, and
         mention of the Haydn sonatas and their
         recordings.

GRAMOPHONE RECORD REVIEWS BY McCABE

B386.   Alkan, etc. Unicorn UNS 206
         Records and Recordings, 13(August 1970) p.50.

B387.   Alkan, etc. HMV HQS 1247
         Records and Recordings, 14 (September 1971) p.98.

B388.   Alwyn. Lyrita SRCS 61
         Records and Recordings, 15 (May 1972) pp. 89-90.

B389.   Alwyn, etc. Unicorn UNS 241
         Records   and   Recordings,   15   (August   1972)
         pp.67-68.

B390.   Amy. Erato STU 70593

Records and Recordings, 14 (July 1971) pp.50+52.

B391.   Andriessen. Donemus DAVS 7003
         Records and Recordings, 14(June 1971) pp.70-71.

B392.   Andriessen, etc. Donemus DAVS 7172/3
         Records and Recordings, 15 (August 1972), p.46.

B393.   Arensky, etc. HMV ASD 2607
         Records and Recording, 13 (September 1970),
         pp.43+46.

B394.   Arnold, etc. RCA Victor SB 6786
         Records and Recordings, 12 (January 1969), p.42.

B395.   Arnold, etc. HMV ASD 2612
         Records and Recordings, 14 (October 1970),
         pp.74+79.

B396.   Bach, etc. Debut 2555003
         Records and Recordings, 16 (October 1972), p.95.

B397.   Badings, etc. Donemus DAVS 7172/2
         Records and Recordings 15 (April 1972), pp.49-50.

B398.   Badings, etc. Ace of Diamonds SDD 316
         Records and Recordings, 15 (June 1972), pp.66-67.

B399.   Baines. Lyrita SRCS 60
         Records and Recordings, 15 (May 1972), p.75.

B400.   Balakirev. HMV 1259
         Records and Recordings, 15(July 1972), pp.70+74.

B401.   Ballif. Barclay 995003
         Records and Recordings, 14 (June 1971), p.91.

B402.   Barber. RCA Victor SB 6799
         Records and Recordings, 12 (August 1969), p.32.

B403.   Bartok, etc. Decca LXT 6357, SXL 6357
         Records and Recordings, 12 (October 1968), p.76.

B404.   Bartok. Philips SAZ 3670

Records   and   Recordings,   12   (October   1968),
pp.37-8.

B405.   Bartok. Qualiton SLPX 11335
          Records   and   Recordings,   12   (September   1969),
          p.86.

B406.   Bartok. Qualiton SLPX 11394-95
          Records and Recordings, 14 (May 1971), p.100.

B407.   Bartok. Qualiton SLPX 11405-7
          Records and Recordings, 14 (May 1971), p.100.

B408.   Bartok. Hungaroton SHLX 90024
          Records   and   Recordings,   14   (September   1971),
          pp.62-63.

B409.   Bartok, etc. HMV ASD 2744
          Records   and   Recordings,   15   (October   1971),
          pp.71-72.

B410.   Bartok. Erato STU 70642
          Records and Recordings, 15 (October 1971), p.103.

B411.   Bartok. Universo 6580036
          Records and Recordings, 15 (November 1971), pp.
          76-77.

B412.   Bartok. Classics for Pleasure CFP 176
          Records   and   Recordings,   15   (December   1971),
          pp.68+70.

B413.   Bartok. HMV ASD 2670, NYO 2
          Records   and   Recordings,   15   (March   1972),
          pp.54+56.

B414.   Bax. RCA Red Seal SB 6806
          Records and Recordings, 13(October 1969), p.62.

B415.   Bax. Lyrita SRCS 53
          Records and Recordings, 14 (August 1971), p.46.

B416.   Bax, etc. Revolution RCF 009
          Records   and   Recordings,   15   (October   1971),
          pp.103-104.

B417.   Bax. Lyrita SRCS 58
        Records and Recordings, 15 (May 1972), p.50.

B418.   Bax, etc. ECS 647
        Records and Recordings, 15 (September 1972),
        p.49.

B419.   Bax. Lyrita SRCS 62
        Records and Recordings, 16 (October 1972),
        pp.58-59.

B420.   Benjamin, etc. Lyrita SRCS 53
        Records and Recordings, 14 (August 1971), p.50.

B421.   Bentzon. Turnabout TV 34374S
        Records and Recordings, 16 (October 1972),
        pp.59-60.

B422.   Berg, etc. DGG 2530033
        Records and Recordings, 14 (May 1971), pp.65-66.

B423.   Berg. DGG 2530283
        Records and Recordings, 17 (April 1974), p.56.

B424.   Bergsma, etc. Turnabout TV 34428S
        Records and Recordings, 16 (February 1973),
        pp.51-52.

B425.   Berio. CBS Classics 61079
        Records and Recordings, 13 (December 1969),
        pp.88-89.

B426.   Berio. RCA Red Seal 6846
        Records and Recordings, 14 (June 1971), pp.72+77.

B427.   Berio. RCA Red Seal SB 6848
        Records and Recordings, 15 (October 1971), p.121.

B428.   Berio. RCA Red Seal SB 6850
        Records and Recordings, 15 (February 1972), p.96.

B429.   Bernstein. CBS Classics 61096
        Records and Recordings, 12 (September 1969),
        p.47.

B430.   Bernstein. Phase Four PFS 4211

Records and Recordings, 14 (March 1971), p.66.

B431.   Bernstein. etc. DGG 2530309
         Records and Recordings, 16 (April 1973), p.50.

B432.   Berwald. Decca LXT 6374, SXL 6374
         Records and Recordings, 12 (November 1968),
         pp.48-9.

B433.   Berwald, etc. Decca SXL 6462
         Records and Recordings, 13(July 1970), pp.52-53.

B434.   Blacher, etc. Helidor/Wergo 2549007
         Records and Recordings, 13(June 1970), pp.74-75.

B435.   Bliss. Lyrita SRCS 55
         Records and Recordings, 14(August 1971),
         pp.52+54.

B436.   Bloch. Everest SDBR 4252
         Records and Recordings, 15 (July 1972), pp.66-67.

B437.   Blomdahl, etc. RCA Victrola VIC 1319, VICS 1319
         Records and Recordings, 12 (November 1968),
         pp.49-50.

B438.   Blomdahl, etc. Turnabout TV 34138S
         Records and Recordings, 15 (February 1972),
         pp.55+58.

B439.   Blomdahl. Caprice LP 6
         Records and Recordings, 17 (April 1974),
         pp.73-74.

B440.   Borodin, etc. Decca LXT 6352, SXL 6352
         Records and Recordings, 11 (July 1968), p.39.

B441.   Borodin, etc. HMV XLP 30107
         Records and Recordings, 11 (August 1968),
         pp.27-8.

B442.   Borodin, etc. HMV ASD 2408
         Records and Recordings, 12 (October 1968), p.32.

B443.   Borodin, etc. Decca SXL 6414
         Records and Recordings, 13 (March 1970), p.62.

B444.   Borodin. Eclipse ECS 576
        Records and Recordings, 14 (March 1971), p.66.

B445.   Borodin. HMV ASD 2689
        Records and Recordings, 14 (May 1971), p.66.

B446.   Borodin, etc. HMV ASD 2700
        Records and Recordings, 14 (June 1971), p.77.

B447.   Borodin. Oryx EXP 50
        Records and Recordings, 14 (June 1971), pp.92+94.

B448.   Borodin, etc. Privilege 135149
        Records and Recordings, 14 (July 1971), p.54.

B449.   Borodin, etc. Music for Pleasure MFP 6037
        Records and Recordings, 15 (October 1971), p.72.

B450.   Borodin, etc. Pearl SHE 502.
        Records and Recordings, 15 (October 1971), p.108.

B451.   Borodin, etc. Studio Two TWO 395
        Records and Recordings, 16(June 1973), pp.46-47.

B452.   Borodin. Decca SPA 281
        Records and Recordings, 16(September 1973), p.61.

B453.   Boulez, etc. DGG 2530050
        Records and Recordings, 14 (March 1971), p.98.

B454.   Boulez, etc. Vox STGBY 641
        Records and Recordings, 14 (September 1971),
        pp.102-103.

B455.   Boulez. RCA Red Seal SB 6849
        Records and Recordings, 15 (November 1971), p.78.

B456.   Bozay. Qualiton SLPX 11412
        Records and Recordings, 14(December 1970), p.93.

B457.   Britten. Decca SXL 6512
        Records and Recordings, 14 (August 1971), p.54.

B458.   Britten, etc. HMV Concert Classics SXLP 30157
        Records and Recordings, 17 (November 1973), p.34.

B459.   Bruci. Philips SAL 3668
         Records and Recordings, 11 (September 1968),
         p.48.

B460.   Butterworth, etc. HMV CSD 3696
         Records and Recordings, 15 (December 1971), p.77.

B461.   Cage, etc. Nonesuch H 71202
         Records and Recordings, 12 (January 1969),
         pp.49-50.

B462.   Carter, etc. DGG 2530104
         Records and Recordings, 14 (June 1971), p.94.

B463.   Carter, etc. Vox STGBY 644
         Records and Recordings, 14 (July 1971), p.66.

B464.   Carter. Nonesuch H 71249
         Records and Recordings, 15 (February 1972),
         pp.75-76.

B465.   Carter. Nonesuch H 71234
         Records and Recordings, 16 (December 1972),
         pp.69-70.

B466.   Carter, etc. CBS 73198
         Records and Recordings, 16 (August 1973),
         pp.39-40.

B467.   Casals, etc. HMV SLS 796
         Records and Recordings, 14 (November 1970),
         pp.80+87.

B468.   Cassado, etc. Supraphon SUAST 50919
         Records and Recordings, 12 (September 1969),
         pp.80-81.

B469.   Chinese Classical Music. BBC Radio Enterprises REGL
         IM
         Records and Recordings, 12 (December 1968),
         pp.89-90.

B470.   Chopin, etc. HMV ASD 2925
         Records and Recordings, 17 (December 1973), p.64.

B471.   Copland, etc. Everest SDBR 3002

Records and Recordings, 11(May 1968), p.36.

B472.   Copland, etc. CBS 72643
        Records and Recordings,   12   (October   1968),
        pp.43+46.

B473.   Copland. CBS 72809
        Records and Recordings, 13(June 1970), p.48.

B474.   Copland. RCA Victrola VICS 1488
        Records and Recordings, 14 (October 1970), p.81.

B475.   Copland. CBS 72888
        Records and Recordings,   14   (February   1971),
        pp.63-64.

B476.   Copland. RCA Red Seal LSB 4018
        Records and Recordings, 14(July 1971), pp.54-55.

B477.   Copland. CBS 72872
        Records and Recordings, 15 (June 1972), p.44.

B478.   Copland, etc. Everest SDBR 3129
        Records and Recordings, 15 (June 1972), p.78.

B479.   Copland. CBS 73116
        Record and Recordings, 16 (May 1973), pp.49+52.

B480.   Copland. Classics for Pleasure CFP 40060
        Records and Recordings, 17(April 1974), p.38.

B481.   Davies. Unicorn RHS 307
        Records and Recordings, 14(July 1971), p.68.

B482.   Davies. Unicorn RHS 308
        Records and Recordings,   15   (November   1971),
        pp.123-124.

B483.   Debussy, etc. RCA Victrola Sovereign VICS 1514
        Records and Recordings,   14(October   1970),
        pp.81-82.

B484.   Delius, etc. Argo ZRG 727
        Records and Recordings,   16(January   1973),
        pp.62-63.

B485.   Delius. CBS Classics 61354
         Records and Recordings, 16(May 1973), p.53.

B486.   Desforges, etc. Qualiton SLPX 11413
         Records and Recordings, 14(December 1970), p.93.

B487.   Dessau. Philips SAL 3684
         Records and Recordings, 12 (February 1969),
         pp.49-50.

B488.   D'Indy, etc. Musidisc RC 742
         Records and Recordings, 14(December 1970), p.104.

B489.   Donizetti, etc. Turnabout TV 34352 DS
         Records and Recordings, 14(January 1971), p.100.

B490.   Downes. Philips SBL 7922
         Records and Recordings, 13(May 1970), pp.49-50.

B491.   Dvorak, etc. RCA Victrola VICS 1035
         Records and Recordings, 12(July 1969), p.58.

B492.   Elgar, etc. Pye Golden Guinea Collector Series GSGC
         14137
         Records and Recordings, 14(October 1970), p.82.

B493.   Erkel. Qualiton SLPX 11376-78
         Records and Recordings, 14(November 1970),
         pp.68-69.

B494.   Escher, etc. Donemus DAVS 7071/4
         Records and Recordings, 15(October 1971),
         pp.104-105.

B495.   Foerster. Suprahone SUAST 1100617
         Records and Recordings, 15(March 1972), p.65.

B496.   Gershwin. Viva VV101
         Records and Recordings, 10(August 1967), p.40.

B497.   Gershwin. Philips 6500290
         Records and Recordings, 16(February 1973), p.58.

B498.   Gershwin. Nonesuch H 71284
         Records and Recording, 17(October 1973),
         pp.98-99.

B499.   Ginastera etc. Musica Rara MUS 45
         Records and Recordings, 11(December 1967), p.72.

B500.   Ginastera, etc. RCA Victor SB 6784
         Records   and   Recordings,   12(January   1969),
         pp.53-4.

B501.   Glazunov. HMV ASD 2522
         Records and Recordings, 13(February 1970), p.47.

B502.   Glazunov. HMV ASD 2717
         Records   and   Recordings,   14(August   1971),
         pp.56-57.

B503.   Glazunov, etc. Eclipse ECS 642
         Records and Recordings, 15(May 1972), p.56.

B504.   Glazunov, etc. RCA Red Seal LSB 4061
         Records and Recordings, 15(June 1972), p.46.

B505.   Glazunov. HMV SLS 826
         Records   and   Recordings,   15(August   1972),
         pp.53-54.

B506.   Glazunov. etc HMV ASD 2858
         Records and Recordings, 16(March 1973), pp.46-47.

B507.   Glazunov. HMV ASD 2900
         Records and Recordings, 16(June 1973), p.49.

B508.   Gliere, etc. Decca SXL 6406
         Records and Recordings, 13(January 1970), p.48.

B509.   Gliere. RCA Red Seal SB 6859
         Records and Recordings, 15(June 1972), pp.46+50.

B510.   Glinka, etc. Vanguard VSL 11079
         Records   and   Recordings,   13(November   1969),
         pp.96-97.

B511.   Glinka, etc. HMV ASD 2664
         Records and Recordings, 14(February 1971), p.64.

B512.   Glinka, etc. HMV ASD 2688
         Records and Recordings, 14(July 1971), p.46.

B513.   Goehr. Argo ZRG 748
         Records and Recordings, 17(November 1973), p.60.

B514.   Gold, etc. RCA Red Seal LSB 4017
         Records and Recordings, 14(June 1971), p.78.

B515.   Gottschalk. Vanguard SRV 275
         Records and Recordings, 15(April 1972), p.56.

B516.   Gottschalk. Turnabout TV 37034S
         Records and Recordings, 16(July 1973), pp.48-49.

B517.   Gottschalk. Turnabout TV 37035S
         Records and Recordings, 16(September 1973), p.71.

B518.   Grofe, etc. CBS Classics 61266
         Records and Recordings, 15(January 1972), p.56.

B519.   Halffter, etc. Decca SXL 6467
         Records   and   Recordings,   14(November   1970),
         pp.109-110.

B520.   Halffter, etc. RCA Victrola VICS 1542
         Records and Recordings, 14(December 1970), p.76.

B521.   Hamilton. CRI SD 280
         Records   and   Recordings,   16(February   1973),
         pp.81-82.

B522.   Hamilton, etc. HMV ASD 2810
         Records   and   Recordings,   16(February   1973),
         pp.58-59.

B523.   Henkemans, etc. Donemus DAVS 7002.
         Records and Recordings, 14(July 1971), pp.56-57.

B524.   Henze, etc. CBS Classics 61133
         Records and Recordings, 13(June 1970), pp.65-66.

B525.   Henze. DGG 2530056
         Records and Recordings, 14(June 1971), pp.79-80.

B526.   Henze. DGG 2530261
         Records   and   Recordings,   16(November   1972),
         pp.50-51.

B527.   Heppener. Donemus DAVS 7172/4
         Records and Recordings, 16(November 1972), p.98.

B528.   Hewitt, etc. Nonesuch H 71200
         Records and Recordings, 16(April 1973), p.73.

B529.   Hindemith. Musica Rara MUS 23
         Records and Recordings, 10(September 1967), p.65.

B530.   Hindemith. RCA Victor SB6770
         Records and Recordings, 12(November 1968), p.75.

B531.   Hindemith, etc. RCA Victor SB 6789
         Records and Recordings, 12(March 1969), pp.69+72.

B532.   Hindemith. Oryx ORYX 1923
         Records and Recordings, 12(April 1969), p.85.

B533.   Hindemith. Cathedral CRMS 850
         Records and Recordings, 13(August 1970), p.58.

B534.   Hindemith, etc. Decca SXL 6445
         Records   and   Recordings,   14(November   1970),
         pp.91+94.

B535.   Hindemith. Argo ZRG 663
         Records and Recordings, 14(February 1971), p.93.

B536.   Hindemith. Everest SDBR 3008
         Records and Recordings, 14(March 1971), pp.76-77.

B537.   Hindemith, etc. Everest SDBR 3040
         Records and Recordings, 14(March 1971), p.77.

B538.   Hindemith. Everest SDBR 3226
         Records and Recordings, 14(March 1971), pp.75-76.

B539.   Hindemith, etc. Everest SDBR 4225
         Records   and   Recordings,   15(January   1972),
         pp.72-77.

B540.   Hindemith. Telefunken SLT 43110-12
         Records   and   Recordings,   15(September   1972),
         pp.76-77.

B541.   Hindemith. Turnabout TV 34276S
         Records and Recordings, 15(September 1972), p.58.

B542.   Hindemith. DGG 2530246
         Records   and   Recordings,   16(November   1972),
         pp.50-51.

B543.   Hindemith. Telefunken SAT 22527
         Records   and   Recordings,   16(November   1972),
         pp.73-74.

B544.   Hindemith, etc. Erato STU 70718
         Records   and   Recordings,   16(December   1972),
         pp.77-78.

B545.   Hindemith. Vox STGBY 662
         Records and Recordings, 16(March 1973), p.48.

B546.   Hindemith. Telefunken SAT 22539
         Records and Recordings, 16(May 1973), pp.75-76.

B547.   Hindemith. HMV ASD 2912
         Records   and   Recordings,   16(August   1973),
         pp.44-45.

B548.   Hindemith, etc. Unicorn RHS 312
         Records   and   Recordings,   16(August   1973),
         pp.45-46.

B549.   Hindemith. Telefunken SAT 22544
         Records   and   Recordings,   17(December   1973),
         pp.65-66.

B550.   Hindemith. Telefunken KT 11036/1-2
         Records and Recordings, 17(April 1974), p.43.

B551.   Hindemith. Hungaroton SLPX 11587
         Records and Recordings, 17(May 1974), p.34.

B552.   Holliger. DGG 2530318
         Records and Recordings, 16(August 1973), p.72.

B553.   Holmboe, etc. Turnabout TV 34168S
         Records and Recordings, 12(August 1969), p.42.

B554.   Holst. Lyrita SRCS 56

Records and Recordings, 15(May 1972), pp.56+58.

B555.   Holst. HMV ASD 2831
        Records and Recordings, 16(March 1973), p.48.

B556.   Honegger, etc. Suprahon 1100604
        Records and Recordings, 13(August 1970), p.37.

B557.   Honegger, etc. Ace of Diamonds GOS 602-3
        Records and Recordings, 14(May 1971), pp.103-104.

B558.   Honegger. Erato STU 70667-68
        Records and Recordings, 15(December 1971), p.108.

B559.   Honegger, etc. Vanguard VSD 2117-18
        Records and Recordings, 15(April 1972), p.97.

B560.   Honegger. Turnabout TV 34377S
        Records and Recordings, 16(February 1973), p.77.

B561.   Hovhanes. Unicorn UNS 243
        Records and Recordings, 15(April 1972), pp.58-59.

B562.   Ibert, etc. Supraphon SUAST 50877
        Records and Recordings, 12(November 1968),
        pp.55+58.

B563.   Ippolitov-Ivanov, etc. Turnabout TV 34218S
        Records and Recordings, 12(August 1969),
        pp.42-43.

B564.   Ippolitov-Ivanov. HMV ASD 2640
        Records and Recordings, 14(January 1971),
        pp.72-73.

B565.   Ireland. Lyrita SRCS 59
        Records and Recordings, 15(May 1972), p.73.

B566.   Ireland. Lyrita SRCS 64
        Records and Recordings, 16(October 1972), p.100.

B567.   Isang Yun. Heliodor/Wergo 2549010
        Records and Recordings, 13(June 1970), pp.51-52.

B568.   Ives. RCA Victor RB 6709, SB 6709

Records and Recordings, 10(July 1967), p.46.

B569.   Ives. Turnabout TV 4157, TV 34157S
         Records   and   Recordings,   12(October   1968),
         pp.76-77.

B570.   Ives. etc. RCA Victor SB 6798
         Records and Recordings, 12(August 1969), p.43.

B571.   Ives, etc. Nonesuch H 71222
         Records and Recordings, 13(November 1969), p.87.

B572.   Ives, etc. DGG 2530048
         Records and Recordings, 14(April 1971), pp.66-67.

B573.   Ives, etc. Phase Four PFS 4203
         Records and Recordings, 15(April 1972), p.59.

B574.   Ives. Muscial Heritage Society MHS 1240
         Records and Recordings, 16(October 1972), p.115.

B575.   Ives. Phase Four PFS 4251
         Records and Recordings, 16(November 1972), p.52.

B576.   Janacek. Supraphon SUAST 50894
         Records   and   Recordings,   12(October   1968),
         pp.50+52.

B577.   Janacek. HMV Angel SAN 256-57
         Records   and   Recordings,   13(February   1970),
         pp.38-39.

B578.   Janacek, etc. HMV ASD 2652
         Records and Recordings, 14(April 1971), pp.67-68.

B579.   Janacek. DGG 2530075
         Records and Recordings, 14(August 1971), p.57.

B580.   Janacek. Decca SXL 6507
         Record and Recordings, 15(October 1971), p.86.

B581.   Janacek. Argo ZRG 692
         Records and Recordings, 15(November 1971), p.123.

B582.   Janacek. Supraphon 1120878

Records and Recordings, 15(May 1972), p.89.

B583.   Jolivet. World Record Club ST 1025
         Records and Recordings, 14(March 1971), pp.77-78.

B584.   Jones. HMV ASD 2855
         Records and Recordings, 16(March 1973), p.51.

B585.   Kabelac, etc. Fourfront 4FE 8505
         Records   and   Recordings,   13(October   1969),
         pp.96-7.

B586.   Kadosa. Qualiton SLPX 11456
         Records and Recordings, 14(May 1971), p.81.

B587.   Kalinnikov, etc. HMV ASD 2720
         Records and Recordings, 14(June 1971), p.80.

B588.   Kalinnikov, etc. HMV ASD 2654
         Records   and   Recordings,   15(October   1971),
         pp.86+91.

B589.   Khatchaturian. Heliodor 89783
         Records and Recordings, 12(March 1969), p.53.

B590.   Khatchaturian, etc. HMV ASD 2481
         Records and Recordings, 12(July 1969), pp.60-61.

B591.   Khatchaturian, etc. RCA Victor SB 6804
         Records and Recordings, 12(September 1969), p.54.

B592.   Khatchaturian. Musidisc RC 723
         Records and Recordings, 14(November 1970), p.94.

B593.   Khatchaturian, etc. Privilege 135011
         Records and Recordings, 15(February 1972), p.61.

B594.   Khatchaturian, etc. CBS 72981
         Records and Recordings, 15(March 1972), p.73.

B595.   Khatchaturian, etc. Eclipse ECS 641
         Records and Recordings, 15(June 1972), pp.51-52.

B596.   Khatchaturian, etc. Vanguard SRV 207SD
         Records and Recordings, 16(January 1973), p.43.

B597.   Khatchaturian, etc. Decca SXL 6599
         Records and Recordings, 16(June 1973), pp.52+53.

B598.   Kmoch. Supraphone SUAST 54993
         Records   and   Recordings,   13(January   1970),
         pp.50-51.

B599.   Kodaly, etc. WRC   T783,   ST783
         Records and Recordings, 11(September 1968), p.61.

B600.   Kodaly. Decca SXL 6497
         Records and Recordings, 14(April 1971), p.98.

B601.   Kodaly. Qualiton SLPX 11397
         Records and Recordings, 14(May 1971), p.104.

B602.   Laidor. HMV ASD 2801.
         Records and Recordings, 15(July 1972), pp.52-53.

B603.   Langlais, etc. Argo ZRG 662
         Records   and   Recordings,   14(February   1971),
         pp.101-102.

B604.   Lidholm, etc. CRD 1004
         Records and Recordings, 17(March 1974), pp.60+62.

B605.   Ligeti. Helidor/Wergo 2549011
         Records and Recordings, 13(June 1970), p.78.

B606.   Liszt. Philips SAL 3783
         Records and Recordings, 13(July 1970), pp.58+67.

B607.   Liszt. Turnabout TV 34232 DS
         Records and Recordings, 13(July 1970), p.58.

B608.   Liszt, etc. Supraphon SUAST 50897
         Records   and   Recordings,   13(August   1970),
         pp.58-59.

B609.   Liszt. Turnabout TV 34246 DS
         Records and Recordings, 14(November 1970), p.110.

B610.   Liszt. Decca SXL 6485
         Records   and   Recordings,   14(December   1970),
         pp.104-106.

B611.   Liszt. Turnabout TV 34353 DS
         Records and Recordings, 14(January 1971), p.102.

B612.   Liszt. Revolution RCB 2
         Records and Recordings, 14 (February 1971), p.95.

B613.   Liszt. Revolution RCF 5
         Records and Recordings, 14(February 1971), p.95.

B614.   Liszt. Unicorn UNS 228
         Records   and   Recordings,   14(February   1971),
         pp.94-95.

B615.   Liszt. Turnabout TV 34269 DS
         Records and Recordings, 14(May 1971), p.81.

B616.   Liszt. Turnabout TV 34310S
         Records and Recordings, 14(June 1971), p.106.

B617.   Liszt. Philips 6500046
         Records   and   Recordings,   14(August   1971),
         pp.57+60.

B618.   Liszt. Philips 6500189
         Records   and   Recordings,   15(January   1972),
         pp.58-59.

B619.   Liszt. Decca SXL 6535
         Records and Recordings, 15(April 1972), pp.59-60.

B620.   Liszt. Philips 6709005
         Records   and   Recordings,   15(September   1972),
         pp.59-60.

B621.   Lovelock, etc. RCA Red Seal LSB 4005
         Records   and   Recordings,   14(December   1970),
         pp.78-79.

B622.   Lutoslawski. Helidor/Wergo 2549014
         Records   and   Recordings,   14(October   1970),
         pp.84+86.

B623.   Lutoslawski. Vox STGBY 648
         Records and Recordings, 15(March 1972), p.74.

B624.   MacDowell, etc. Decca LXT 6336,   SXL 6336

Records and Recordings, 12(March 1969), pp.84-85.

B625.   Magnard, etc. Decca SXL 6395
         Records and Recordings,   12(September   1969),
         pp.55-56.

B626.   Martin, etc. Unicorn UNS 233
         Records and Recordings,   14(September   1971),
         pp.77-78.

B627.   Martin. Vox STGBY 661
         Records and Recordings, 16(January 1973), p.43.

B628.   Martinu. Supraphon SUA 10698   SUAST 50698
         Records and Recordings, 10(September 1967), p.61.

B629.   Martinu, etc. Musica Rara MUS 44
         Records and Recordings, 11(December 1967), p.67.

B630.   Martinu. Supraphon SUAST 50909
         Records and Recordings, 12(October 1968), p.55.

B631.   Martinu, etc. Unicorn RHS 309
         Records and Recordings, 15(October 1971), p.91.

B632.   Martinu. Supraphon 1110575
         Records and Recordings,   15(December   1971),
         pp.95-96.

B633.   Martinu. Supraphon 1101014
         Records and Recordings, 16(July 1973), p.50.

B634.   Martinu. Supraphon 1101129
         Records and Recordings, 16(August 1973), p.47.

B635.   Martinu. Supraphon 1111104
         Records and Recordings, 17(February 1974), p.48.

B636.   Martinu, etc. Supraphon SUAST 50778
         Records and Recordings,   17(February   1974),
         pp.54-55.

B637.   Maw, etc. Argo ZRG 622
         Records and Recordings, 13(October 1969), p.112.

B638.   Maw. Argo ZRG 676
         Records and Recordings, 14(July 1971), p.57.

B639.   Merrick, etc. Rare Recorded Editions SRRE 117
         Records and Recordings, 14(January 1971), p.102.

B640.   Messiaen. Supraphon SUAST 50749
         Records and Recordings, 12(December 1968),
         pp.55-6.

B641.   Messiaen, etc. Decca SXL 6378
         Records and Recordings, 12(June 1969), pp.90-91.

B642.   Messiaen. HMV ASD 2470
         Records and Recordings, 12(July 1969), pp.86-88.

B643.   Messiaen. Argo ZRG 606
         Records and Recordings, 12(September 1969),
         pp.96-97.

B644.   Messiaen. Argo ZRG 633.
         Records and Recordings, 14(October 1970), p.118.

B645.   Messiaen, etc. Everest SDBR 3192
         Records and Recordings, 14(August 1971),
         pp.61-62.

B646.   Messiaen. Erato STU 70673
         Records and Recordings, 15(January 1972),
         pp.59-60.

B647.   Messiaen. Music disc RC 719
         Records and Recordings, 15(August 1972), p.69.

B648.   Mihaly. Qualiton SLPX 11455
         Records and Recordings, 14(May 1971), pp.81-82.

B649.   Milhaud, etc. Everest SDBR 3017
         Records and Recordings, 14(April 1971), pp.68+75.

B650.   Milhaud. Everest SDBR 3176
         Records and Recordings, 14(April 1971), pp.83-84.

B651.   Milligan, Spike. BBC Records RED 98M
         Records and Recordings, 15(January 1972), p.93.

B652.   Moeran. Lyrita SRCS 42
        Records and Recordings, 16 (October 1972),
        pp.101-102.

B653.   Moscheles. Vox STGBY 636
        Records and Recordings, 14(November 1970),
        pp.94-95.

B654.   Moscheles. Revolution RCF 4
        Records and Recordings, 14(January 1971), p.102.

B655.   Moszkowski. Vox STGBY 647
        Records and Recordings, 15(November 1971), p.90.

B656.   Mussorgsky, etc. DGG 135139
        Records and Recordings, 13(November 1969), p.91.

B657.   Mussorgsky, etc. HMV ASD 2559
        Records and Recordings, 13(March 1970), pp.83-84.

B658.   Mussorgsky, etc. HMV ASD 2541
        Records and Recordings, 13(April 1970), p.42.

B659.   Mussorgsky, etc. Classics for Pleasure CFP 106
        Records and Recordings, 14(November 1970), p.97.

B660.   Mussorgsky, etc. Oryx EXP 44
        Records and Recordings, 14(December 1970), p.106.

B661.   Mussorgsky, etc. Qualiton SLPX 11430
        Records and Recordings, 14(January 1971),
        pp.102-103.

B662.   Mussorgsky, etc. Turnabout TV 34258S
        Records and Recordings, 14(February 1971), p.94.

B663.   Mussorgsky, etc. Turnabout TV 34331S
        Records and Recordings, 14(July 1971), p.84.

B664.   Mussorgsky. Erato EFM 8049
        Records and Recordings, 15(October 1971), p.93.

B665.   Mussorgsky, etc. Universo 6580053
        Records and Recordings, 15(June 1972), p.56.

B666.   Mussorgsky, etc. Decca SPA 229
        Records and Recordings, 15(September 1972), p.67.

B667.   Mussorgsky, etc. RCA Toscanini Edition AT 107
        Records and Recordings, 15 (September 1972),
        pp.67-68.

B668.   Mussorgsky. Argo ZRG 708
        Records and Recordings, 16(October 1972), p.115.

B669.   Mussorgsky. Decca SET 557
        Records and Recordings, 16(March 1973), p.38.

B670.   Mussorgsky, etc. Phase Four PFS 4255
        Records and Recordings, 16(March 1973), p.54.

B671.   Mussorgsky. Telefunken SAT 22526
        Records and Recordings, 16(April 1973), p.44.

B672.   Mussorgsky, etc. Hungaroton SLPX 11586
        Records and Recordings, 16(June 1973), pp.54-55.

B673.   Mussorgsky, etc. Decca SPA 257
        Records and Recordings, 16(July 1973), p.55.

B674.   Mussorgsky, etc. Music for Pleasure MFP 57009
        Records and Recordings, 16(August 1973), p.50.

B675.   Nielsen, etc. Turnabout TV 34182S
        Records and Recordings, 12(April 1969), pp.61-2.

B676.   Nielsen. Turnabout TV 34193S
        Records and Recordings, 12(June 1969), p.91.

B677.   Nielsen. Unicorn RHS 300
        Records and Recordings, 12(August 1969), pp.
        48-49.

B678.   Nielsen. Decca SXL 6491
        Records and Recordings, 14(March 1971), p.80.

B679.   Nielsen. CBS 72890, RCA Victrola VICS 1148
        Records and Recordings, 14(April 1971), pp.75+76.

B680.   Nono. Heliodor/Wergo 2549012

Records   and   Recordings,   14(October   1970),
pp.112+114.

B681.   Ogawa. Classic 991063
Records and Recordings, 15(January 1972), p.65.

B682.   Paderewski. RCA Red Seal SB 6843
Records and Recordings, 14(June 1971), p.84.

B683.   Parry. Lyrita SRCS 48
Records and Recordings, 14(February 1971), p.71.

B684.   Penderecki. Philips SAL 3680
Records and Recordings, 12(November 1968), p.91.

B685.   Penderecki. RCA Red Seal SB 6857
Records   and   Recordings,   15(March   1972),
pp.109-110.

B686.   Penderecki, etc. DGG 2530063
Records and Recordings, 15(August 1972), p.58.

B687.   Petrovics. Qualiton SLPX 11420
Records and Recordings, 14(January 1971), p.110.

B688.   Pettersson. Decca SXL 6538
Records and Recordings, 15(May 1972), p.62.

B689.   Piston. DGG 2536103
Records and Recordings, 14(May 1971), pp.82+84.

B690.   Poulenc. Erato STU 70637
Records and Recordings, 14(July 1971), pp.58+63.

B691.   Prokofiev. RCA Victor RB 6705, SB 6705
Records and Recordings, 10(July 1967), pp.30-31.

B692.   Prokofiev. Decca LXT 6308, SXL 6308
Records   and   Recordings,   10(September   1967),
pp.52+54.

B693.   Prokofiev. WRC T 735, ST 735
Records and Recordings, 12(November 1968), p.61.

B694.   Prokofiev. RCA Victrola VIC 1207, VICS 1207

<u>Records and Recordings</u>, 12(December 1968), p.63.

B695.   Prokofiev. Vox STGBY 609
        <u>Records   and   Recordings</u>,   12(December   1968),
        pp.93-4.

B696.   Prokofiev. Hallmark HM 537, SHM 537
        <u>Records   and   Recordings</u>,   12(January   1969),
        pp.65-66.

B697.   Prokofiev. HMV ASD 2463
        <u>Records and Recordings</u>, 12(April 1969), pp.62-3.

B698.   Prokofiev. etc. CBS Classics 61071
        <u>Records and Recordings</u>, 12(May 1969), p.75.

B699.   Prokofiev. RCA Victor SB 6794
        <u>Records and Recordings</u>, 12(July 1969), pp.62+71.

B700.   Prokofiev. Vox STGBY 617
        <u>Records and Recordings</u>, 12(September 1969), p.90.

B701.   Prokofiev. Vox STGBY 621
        <u>Records and Recordings</u>, 13(October 1969), p.107.

B702.   Prokofiev. Vox STGBY 627
        <u>Records   and   Recordings</u>,   13(November   1969),
        pp.91-92.

B703.   Prokofiev. Vox STGBY 631
        <u>Records and Recordings</u>, 13(January 1970), p.78.

B704.   Prokofiev, etc. HMV ASD 2557
        <u>Records and Recordings</u>, 13(March 1970), pp.55-56.

B705.   Prokofiev. RCA Red Seal SB 6824
        <u>Records and Recordings</u>, 13(March 1970), p.74.

B706.   Prokofiev. Decca SPA 90
        <u>Records and Recordings</u>, 13(September 1970), p.61.

B707.   Prokofiev. Decca SXL 6469
        <u>Records   and   Recordings</u>,   14(October   1970),
        pp.88-89.

B708.   Prokofiev. HMV ASD 2639

Records   and   Recordings,   14(December   1970),
pp.87-88.

B709.   Prokofiev. HMV ASD 2636
Records   and   Recordings,   14(February   1971),
pp.71-73.

B710.   Prokofiev. CBS Classic 61187
Records and Recordings, 14(March 1971), p.81.

B711.   Prokofiev. HMV ASD 2669
Records and Recordings, 14(March 1971), pp.80-81.

B712.   Prokofiev. Turnabout TV 4160
Records and Recordings, 14(April 1971), p.76.

B713.   Prokofiev. Eclipse ECS 593
Records and Recordings, 14(May 1971), pp.84-85.

B714.   Prokofiev. World Record Club ST 1020
Records and Recordings, 14(Mary 1971), p.84.

B715.   Prokofiev. Eclipse ECS 597
Records and Recordings, 14(July 1971), p.63.

B716.   Prokofiev. HMV ASD 2735-36
Records   and   Recordings,   15(November   1971),
pp.68-69.

B717.   Prokofiev. HMV ASD 2758
Records and Recordings, 15(December 1971), p.84.

B718.   Prokofiev. Philips 6500103
Records and Recordings, 15(January 1972), p.77.

B719.   Prokofiev. Classics for Pleasure CFP 189
Records and Recordings, 15(March 1972), p.77.

B720.   Prokofiev, etc. Decca SXL 6532
Records and Recordings, 15(March 1972), p.77.

B721.   Prokofiev. etc. HMV ASD 2768
Records and Recordings, 15(March 1972), pp.76-77.

B722.   Prokofiev. Supraphon SUAST 50773

<u>Records and Recordings</u>, 15(March 1972), pp.77-78.

B723.   Prokofiev. etc. HMV ASD 2765
        <u>Records and Recordings</u>, 15(April 1972), p.66.

B724.   Prokofiev. Decca SPA 226
        <u>Records and Recordings</u>, 15(July 1972), p.56.

B725.   Prokofiev. HMV ASD 2800
        <u>Records and Recordings</u>, 15(July 1972), p.86.

B726.   Prokofiev. Vanguard SRV 174SD
        <u>Records and Recordings</u>, 15(July 1972), p.56.

B727.   Prokofiev. Privilege 2538073
        <u>Records and Recordings</u>, 16(October 1972), p.71.

B728.   Prokofiev. RCA Red Seal SER 5622-24
        <u>Records   and   Recordings</u>,   16(October   1972),
        pp.70-71.

B729.   Prokofiev. Classics for Pleasure CFP 200
        <u>Records and Recordings</u>, 16(January 1973), p.48.

B730.   Prokofiev. HMV SLS 837
        <u>Records   and   Recordings</u>,   16(February   1973),
        pp.48-49.

B731.   Prokofiev. RCA Red Seal LSB 4084
        <u>Records and Recordings</u>, 16(April 1973), p.73.

B732.   Prokofiev. etc. Privilege 2538232
        <u>Records and Recordings</u>, 16(June 1973), p.55.

B733.   Prokofiev. etc. RCA AT 122
        <u>Records and Recordings</u>, 16(September 1973), p.83.

B734.   Prokofiev. etc. RCA Victrola VICS 1751
        <u>Records   and   Recordings</u>,   16(September   1973),
        pp.78+83.

B735.   Prokofiev, etc. RCA Red Seal LSB 4095
        <u>Records and Recordings</u>, 17(October 1973), p.90.

B736.   Prokofiev. Decca SXL 6620-22

Records   and   Recordings,   17(October   1973),
pp.77-78.

B737.   Prokofiev. etc. HMV SLS 860(2)
Records   and   Recordings,   17(November   1973),
pp.82+84.

B738.   Prokofiev. HMV SLS 864(3)
Records   and   Recordings,   17(December   1973),
pp.71+74.

B739.   Prokofiev. Philips 6500640
Records and Recordings, 17(March 1974), p.18.

B740.   Prokofiev. HMV ASD 2947
Records and Recordings, 17(May 1974), p.66.

B741.   Rachmaninov. CBS BRG 72571, SBRG 72571
Records and Recordings, 10(September 1967), p.54.

B742.   Rachmaninov. Heliodon 89645
Records   and   Recordings,   11(November   1967),
pp.61+64.

B743.   Rachmaninov. RCA Victrola VIC 1205, VICS 1205
Records and Recordings, 11(November 1967), p.52.

B744.   Rachmaninov. Music for Pleasure MFP2078
Records and Recordings, 11(April 1968), p.56.

B745.   Rachmaninov. Decca LXT 6342,   SXL 6342
Records and Recordings, 11(May 1968), pp.48-9.

B746.   Rachmaninov. Fontana SFL 14025
Records and Recordings, 11(June 1968), p.41.

B747.   Rachmaninov. CBS 72674
Records   and   Recordings,   11(September   1968),
pp.74+76.

B748.   Rachmaninov. Turnabout TV 4145,   TV 34145S
Records and Recordings, 11(September 1968), p.74.

B749.   Rachmaninov, etc. HMV ASD 2411
Records and Recordings, 12(March 1969), pp.54+56.

B750.   Rachmaninov, etc. Decca SXL 6399; World Record Club
        ST 858
        Records and Recordings, 12(June 1969), pp.75-76.

B751.   Rachmaninov. HMV ASD 2471
        Records and Recordings, 12(July 1969), pp.71-72.

B752.   Rachmaninov. RCA Victor SB 6793
        Records and Recordings, 12(July 1969), pp.93-94.

B753.   Rachmaninov, etc. BBC Radio Enterprises REB 27S
        Records   and   Recordings,   12(September   1969),
        p.90-91.

B754.   Rachmaninov. HMV ASD 2488
        Records   and   Recordings,   12(September   1969),
        pp.59-60.

B755.   Rachmaninov. etc. Debut 642104
        Records and Recordings, 13(November 1969), p.92.

B756.   Rachmaninov. HMV ASD 2545
        Records and Recordings, 13(May 1970), pp.57-58.

B757.   Rachmaninov. HMV ASD 2539
        Records and Recordings, 13(June 1970), pp.78-79.

B758.   Rachmaninov. Eclipse ECS 559
        Records and Recordings, 13(September 1970), p.61.

B759.   Rachmaninov, etc. HMV ASD 2587
        Records and Recordings, 14(November 1970), p.106.

B760.   Rachmaninov. CBS 72857
        Records and Recordings, 14(January 1971), p.81.

B761.   Rachmaninov. Eclipse ECS 573; HMV ASD 2646
        Records   and   Recordings,   14(January   1971),
        pp.81-82.

B762.   Rachmaninov. Rare Recorded Editions SRRE 118
        Records and Recordings, 14(January 1971), p.105.

B763.   Rachmaninov. Unicorn UNS 230-31;   Revolution RCB
        11-12
        Records and Recordings, 14(February 1971), p.96.

B764.   Rachmaninov. Eclipse ECS 594
         Records and Recordings, 14(April 1971), pp.76-77.

B765.   Rachmaninov, etc. Unicorn UNS 242
         Records and Recordings, 14(September 1971),
         pp.92+94.

B766.   Rachmaninov, etc. Argo ZRG 695
         Records and Recordings, 15(November 1971), p.108.

B767.   Rachmaninov. CBS 72940
         Records and Recordings, 15(November 1971),
         pp.117-118.

B768.   Rachmaninov. Universo 6582006
         Records and Recordings, 15(March 1972), p.78.

B769.   Rachmaninov. Decca SPA 169
         Records and Recordings, 15(May 1972), p.62.

B770.   Rachmaninov, etc. Studio Two, TWO 360
         Records and Recordings, 15(July 1972), p.58.

B771.   Rachmaninov. CBS 77345
         Records and Recordings, 15(August 1972), p.58.

B772.   Rachmaninov. Decca SXLF 6565-67
         Records and Recordings, 15(September 1972),
         pp.68-69.

B773.   Rachmaninov. CBS Classics 61310
         Records and Recordings, 16(January 1973), p.48.

B774.   Rachmaninov. Philips 6500362
         Records and Recordings, 16(January 1973),
         pp.48-49.

B775.   Rachmaninov. Eclipse ECS 668
         Records and Recordings, 16(February 1973), p.62.

B776.   Rachmaninov, etc. CBS Classics 61347
         Records and Recordings, 16(March 1973), p.56.

B777.   Rachmaninov. Decca SXL 6583
         Records and Recordings, 16(April 1973), pp.62-63.

B778.   Rachmaninov, etc. HMV ASD 2872
         Records and Recordings, 16(April 1973), p.62.

B779.   Rachmaninov, etc. RCA Red Seal LSB 4081
         Records and Recordings, 16(May 1973), p.98.

B780.   Rachmaninov. RCA Red Seal LSB 4089
         Records and Recordings, 16(May 1973), p.64.

B781.   Rachmaninov. RCA Red Seal LSB 4090
         Records and Recordings, 16(May 1973), pp.64-65.

B782.   Rachmaninov. HMV ASD 2890
         Records and Recordings, 16(June 1973), pp.43-44.

B783.   Rachmaninov. RCA Quadradisc ARDI 0031; CBS Classics
         61026
         Records and Recordings, 16(July 1973), p.56.

B784.   Rachmaninov. HMV SLS 847(5)
         Records   and   Recordings,   16(August   1973),
         pp.52-53.

B785.   Rachmaninov. HMV SLS 855(3)
         Records   and   Recordings,   16(August   1973),
         pp.51-52.

B786.   Rachmaninov. RCA Victrola VIC 6057
         Records and Recordings, 17(October 1973), p.78.

B787.   Rachmaninov. Decca SPA 310
         Records and Recordings, 17(November 1973), p.47.

B788.   Rachmaninov. Decca SXL 6623
         Records   and   Recordings,   17(November   1973),
         pp.47+50.

B789.   Rachmaninov, etc. Eclipse ECS 706
         Records and Recordings, 17(November 1973), p.72.

B790.   Rachmaninov, etc. Privilege 272 6020(2)
         Records and Recordings, 17(April 1974), pp.47-48.

B791.   Rawsthorne, etc. Pye Golden Guinea GSGC 14107
         Records   and   Recordings,   12(August   1969),
         pp.61-62.

B792.   Reger. Musica Rara MUS 29
         Records and Recordings, 10(September 1967), p.66.

B793.   Respighi, etc. Everest SDBR 3004
         Records and Recordings, 11(December 1967), p.52.

B794.   Rimsky-Korsakov, etc. RCA Victor SB 6783
         Records and Recordings, 12(January 1969), p.67.

B795.   Rimsky-Korsakov, etc. HMV ASD 2475
         Records   and   Recordings,   13(November   1969),
         pp.50+55.

B796.   Rimsky-Korsakov, etc. HMV ASD 2521
         Records   and   Recordings,   13(February   1970),
         pp.85-86.

B797.   Rimsky-Korsakov, etc. HMV ASD 2540
         Records and Recordings, 13(June 1970), pp.53-54.

B798.   Rimsky-Korsakov, etc. Eclipse ECS 546
         Records and Recordings, 13(July 1970), p.45.

B799.   Rimsky-Korsakov, etc. Phase Four PFS 4177
         Records and Recordings, 13(August 1970), p.38.

B800.   Rimsky-Korsakov, etc. Classics for Pleasure CFP 126
         Records and Recordings, 14(November 1970), p.97.

B801.   Rimsky-Korsakov. Ace of Diamonds SDD 281
         Records and Recordings, 14(May 1971), p.85.

B802.   Rimsky-Korsakov, etc. Ace of Diamonds SDD 282
         Records and Recordings, 14(July 1971), p.63.

B803.   Rimsky-Korsakov, etc. Decca SPA 182
         Records   and   Recordings,   15(November   1971),
         pp.92+95.

B804.   Rimsky-Korsakov, etc. Vanguard Cardinal VCS 10060
         Records and Recordings, 15(November 1971), p.95.

B805.   Rimsky-Korsakov. HMV ASD 2846
         Records   and   Recordings,   16(February   1973),
         pp.62-63.

B806.   Rimsky-Korsakov. Ace of Diamonds GOS 642-45
        Records and Recordings, 17(April 1974), pp.31-32.

B807.   Rimsky-Korsakov, etc. HMV ASD 2974
        Records and Recordings, 17(May 1974), p.39.

B808.   Rivier. Barclay 995006
        Records and Recordings, 14(June 1971), p.84.

B809.   Roussel, etc. Gemini GME 1001
        Records and Recordings, 13(April 1970), p.49.

B810.   Roussel. HMV ASD 2586
        Records   and   Recordings,   13(August   1970),
        pp.38+43.

B811.   Roussel. Erato STU 70650
        Records and Recordings, 14(August 1971), p.64.

B812.   Roussel, etc. Turnabout TV 34405S
        Records and Recordings, 16(October 1972), p.74.

B813.   Rubinstein. Melodiya D011501-6
        Records and Recordings, 11(September 1968), p.36.

B814.   Rubinstein. Vox STGBY 642
        Records and Recordings, 14(May 1971), p.86.

B815.   Ruggles, etc. Turnabout TV 34398S
        Records and Recordings, 15(June 1972), pp.57-58.

B816.   Saint-Saens. RCA Victrola VICS 1508
        Records and Recordings, 14(November 1970), p.97.

B817.   Saint-Saens. Decca SXL 6482
        Records   and   Recordings,   14(January   1971),
        pp.83-84.

B818.   Saint-Saens, etc. Decca SPA 175
        Records and Recordings, 15(December 1971), p.84.

B819.   Salzedo, etc. Fourfront 4FE 8003
        Records   and   Recordings,   13(October   1969),
        pp.97-8.

B820.   Scharwenka, etc. RCA Red Seal SB 6815
         Records   and   Recordings,   13(February   1970),
         pp.58-59.

B821.   Scharwenka. Vox STGBY651
         Records   and   Recordings,   15(January   1972),
         pp.65-66.

B822.   Schoenberg. Everest SDBR 3171
         Records   and   Recordings,   14(August   1971),
         pp.72+74.

B823.   Schoenberg, etc. Qualiton SLPX 11385
         Records and Recordings, 15(November 1971), p.127.

B824.   Schuller. Turnabout TV 34412S
         Records and Recordings, 16(January 1973), p.50.

B825.   Schuman, etc. Turnabout TV 34447S
         Records and Recordings, 16(June 1973), p.56.

B826.   Scriabin, etc. Melodiya C 01351
         Records and Recordings, 11(June 1968), pp.44+49.

B827.   Scriabin, etc. Everest SDBR 3032
         Records and Recordings, 12(December 1968), p.67.

B828.   Scriabin, etc. HMV ASD 2482
         Records and Recordings, 12(July 1969), p.75.

B829.   Scriabin. HMV ASD 2523
         Records and Recordings, 13(January 1970), p.66.

B830.   Scriabin. Gemini GME 1015
         Records and Recordings, 14(May 1971), p.102.

B831.   Scriabin. RCA Red Seal SB 6854
         Records   and   Recordings,   15(November   1971),
         pp.97-98.

B832.   Scriabin. Decca SXL 6527
         Records and Recordings, 15(January 1972), p.66.

B833.   Scriabin. HMV ASD 2761
         Records and Recordings, 15(February 1972), p.71.

B834.   Scriabin. Vox STGBY 654
         Records and Recordings, 15(July 1972), p.63.

B835.   Scriabin. Vox STGBY 655
         Records and Recordings, 15(July 1972), p.63.

B836.   Scriabin. HMV SLS 835(4)
         Records   and   Recordings,   16(December   1972),
         pp.59-60.

B837.   Serocki. Heliodor/Wergo 2549015
         Records   and   Recordings,   15(October   1970),
         pp.89-90.

B838.   Shankar. HMV ASD 2752
         Records and Recordings, 15(November 1971), p.98.

B839.   Shostakovitch. Melodiya C 01109
         Records and Recordings, 11(June 1968), p.49.

B840.   Shostakovitch. Melodiya C 0123
         Records and Recordings, 11(June 1968), pp.49-50.

B841.   Shostakovitch. Melodiya C 01387
         Records and Recordings, 11(June 1968), p.50.

B842.   Shostakovitch. Melodiya C 201
         Records and Recordings, 11(July 1968), p.51.

B843.   Shostakovitch. WRC T 776-7, ST 776-7
         Records and Recordings, 11(August 1968), pp.34-5.

B844.   Shostakovitch.HMV ASD 2420
         Records   and   Recordings,   12(October   1968),
         pp.71-2.

B845.   Shostakovitch. RCA Victor RB 6755, SB 6755
         Records   and   Recordings,   12(October   1968),
         pp.70-71.

B846.   Shostakovitch,etc. RCA Victrola VIC 1298; VICS 1298
         Records   and   Recordings,   12(November   1968),
         pp.78-9.

B847.   Shostakovitch. HMV ASD 2409

Records   and   Recordings,   12(December   1968),
pp.67+74.

B848.   Shostakovitch. DGG 139020
Records   and   Recordings,   12(February   1969),
pp.65-66.

B849.   Shostakovitch. Supraphon SUAST 50958
Records and Recordings, 12(June 1969), pp.78-9.

B850.   Shostakovitch, etc. CBS 72730
Records   and   Recordings,   12(September   1969),
pp.62-63.

B851.   Shostakovitch, etc. HMV ASD 2511-12
Records   and   Recordings,   13(November   1969),
pp.79-80.

B852.   Shostakovitch. HMV ASD 2585
Records and Recordings, 13(July 1970), p.50.

B853.   Shostakovitch. RCA Victrola VICS 6038(2)
Records and Recordings, 13(July 1970), pp.47+50.

B854.   Shostakovitch. HMV ASD 2598
Records   and   Recordings,   13(August   1970),
pp.43-44.

B855.   Shostakovitch.WRC ST 995
Records and Recordings, 13(September 1970), p.62.

B856.   Shostakovitch. RCA Red Seal SB 6839
Records and Recordings, 14(October 1970), p.90.

B857.   Shostakovitch. Classics for Pleasure CFP 141
Records and Recordings, 14(November 1970), p.98.

B858.   Shostakovitch. Eclipse ECS 580
Records and Recordings, 14(February 1971), p.74.

B859.   Shostakovitch. HMV ASD 2633
Records and Recordings, 14(March 1971), pp.82-83.

B860.   Shostakovitch. HMV ASD 2668
Records and Recordings, 14(April 1971), p.77.

B861.   Shostakovitch. CBS Classics 61220
         Records and Recordings, 14(May 1971), p.87.

B862.   Shostakovitch. CBS 72886
         Records and Recordings, 14(June 1971), pp.84+89.

B863.   Shostakovitch, etc. HMV ASD 2709
         Records and Recordings, 14(July 1971), p.64.

B864.   Shostakovitch. RCA Red Seal LSB 5002
         Records   and   Recordings,   14(August   1971),
         pp.64+66.

B865.   Shostakovitch. HMV ASD 2718
         Records and Recordings, 14(September 1971), p.94.

B866.   Shostakovitch. HMV ASD 2747
         Records and Recordings, 14(September 1971), p.86.

B867.   Shostakovitch. HMV ASD 2741
         Records   and   Recordings,   15(October   1971),
         pp.94-95.

B868.   Shostakovitch, etc. Universo 6580042
         Records and Recordings, 15(December 1971), p.87.

B869.   Shostakovitch. Turnabout TV 34280S
         Records and Recordings, 15(March 1972), p.98.

B870.   Shostakovitch. Everest SDBR 4234
         Records and Recordings, 15(April 1972), p.81.

B871.   Shostakovitch. HMV ASD 2781
         Records and Recordings, 15(May 1972), p.63.

B872.   Shostakovitch, etc. HMV ASD 2805
         Records and Recordings, 15(July 1972), pp.63-64.

B873.   Shostakovitch. Universo 6580012
         Records   and   Recordings,   15(August   1972),
         pp.64-65.

B874.   Shostakovitch. HMV ASD 2857
         Records and Recordings, 16(November 1972), p.61.

B875.   Shostakovitch. Decca SKL 6563
        Records and Recordings, 16(January 1973), p.50.

B876.   Shostakovitch. RCA Quadradisc ARDI-0014
        Records and Recordings, 16(February 1973),
        pp.63-64.

B877.   Shostakovitch. HMV ASD 2893
        Records and Recordings, 16(April 1973), p.64.

B878.   Shostakovitch, etc. Universo 6585012
        Records and Recordings, 17(November 1973), p.85.

B879.   Sibelius. RCA Victrola VICS 1538
        Records and Recordings, 14(December 1970), p.107.

B880.   Simpson. Unicorn UNS 225
        Records and Recordings, 13(September 1970), p.64.

B881.   Simpson. Unicorn UNS 234
        Records and Recordings, 14(July 1971), p.70.

B882.   Sommer, etc. RCA Red Seal LSB 4029
        Records and Recordings, 14(July 1971), p.64.

B883.   Squire, etc. Rare Recorded Editions
        Records and Recordings, 14(January 1971),
        pp.105-106.

B884.   Stockhausen. DGG 139421-2
        Records and Recordings, 12(September 1969),
        pp.98-99.

B885.   Stockhausen. DGG 137012
        Records and Recordings, 14(April 1971), p.102.

B886.   Stockhausen, etc. Philips 6500101
        Records and Recordings, 14(July 1971), pp.78-80.

B887.   Strauss, R. etc. CBS 6420
        Records and Recordings, 12(February 1969),
        pp.68-9.

B888.   Stravinsky. Supraphon SUAST 50978
        Records and Recordings, 12(November 1968), p.93.

B889.   Stravinsky, etc. Fourfront 4FM 10002
         Records and Recordings, 12(December 1968), p.95.

B890.   Stravinsky. Saga Psyche PSY 30006; Nonesuch H 71212
         Records and Recordings, 12(March 1969), pp.76-77.

B891.   Stravinsky. Ace of Diamonds SDD 238
         Records and Recordings, 14(April 1971), pp.78-79.

B892.   Stravinsky. Ace of Diamonds. SDD 242
         Records and Recordings, 14(April 1971), p.78.

B893.   Stravinsky. Ace of Diamonds SDD 245
         Records and Recordings, 14(April 1971), p.100.

B894.   Stravinsky.Phase Four PFS 4207
         Records and Recordings, 14(April 1971), p.78.

B895.   Stravinsky. Fontana 6547003
         Records and Recordings, 14(May 1971), pp.88+91.

B896.   Stravinsky. Ace of Diamonds SDD 239
         Records and Recordings, 14(June 1971), pp.89-90.

B897.   Stravinsky. Everest SDBR 3009
         Records and Recordings, 14(June 1971), p.89.

B898.   Stravinsky, etc. Privilege 135155
         Records and Recordings, 14(July 1971), pp.64-65.

B899.   Stravinsky. Classics for Pleasure CFP 134
         Records and Recordings, 14(August 1971), p.67.

B900.   Stravinsky. Ace of Diamonds SDD 246
         Records and Recordings, 14(September 1971), p.86.

B901.   Stravinsky. CBS Classics 61104
         Records and Recordings, 15(November 1971), p.101.

B902.   Stravinsky. Decca SPA 152
         Records and Recordings, 15(December 1971), p.88.

B903.   Stravinsky, etc. Argo ZRG 674
         Records and Recordings, 15(February 1972), p.73.

B904.   Stravinsky. CBS 72976
         Records and Recordings, 15(May 1972), pp.66+71.

B905.   Stravinsky. Universo 6585003
         Records and Recordings, 15(May 1972), p.71.

B906.   Stravinsky. HMV ASD 2770
         Records and Recordings, 15(June 1972), pp.58+63.

B907.   Stravinsky. Nonesuch H 71212
         Records and Recordings, 15(July 1972), p.81.

B908.   Stravinsky. DGG 2530267
         Records and Recordings, 15(August 1972), p.65.

B909.   Stravinsky, etc. Privilege 2538165
         Records and Recordings, 16(October 1972), p.83.

B910.   Stravinsky. Universo 6580013; DGG 2530252
         Records and Recordings, 16(October 1972),
         pp.83-84.

B911.   Stravinsky. RCA Red Seal DPS 2039
         Records and Recordings, 16(May 1973), pp.67-68.

B912.   Stravinsky. HMV ASD 2845
         Records and Recordings, 16(June 1973), p.63.

B913.   Stravinsky. Decca SXL 6582
         Records and Recordings, 16(July 1973), pp.58-59.

B914.   Stravinsky. Supraphon 1101135
         Records and Recordings, 16(September 1973), p.84.

B915.   Stravinsky. Erato STU 70769
         Records and Recordings, 17(October 1973),
         pp.80-81.

B916.   Stravinsky. Arion ARN 37192
         Records and Recordings, 17(December 1973), p.87.

B917.   Stravinsky. Supraphon 50623
         Records and Recordings, 17(March 1974), p.64.

B918.   Stravinsky, etc. Supraphon 50509

Records and Recordings, 17(May 1974), p.39.

B919.   Stravinsky. Supraphon 50968
         Records and Recordings, 17(May 1974), p.51.

B920.   Szymanowski, etc. Golden Guinea GSGC 14123
         Records   and   Recordings,   12(December   1968),
         pp.86-7.

B921.   Takemitsu. DGG 2530088
         Records and Recordings, 15(October 1971), p.106.

B922.   Tavener. Apple SAPCOR 20
         Records   and   Recordings,   14(September   1971),
         p.107.

B923.   Tchaikovsky. Philips SAL 3673
         Records   and   Recordings,   12(October   1968),
         pp.73-4.

B924.   Tchaikovsky, etc. RCA Victor SB 67631
         Records and Recordings, 12(December 1968), p.105.

B925.   Tchaikovsky. Vanguard VSL 11046
         Records and Recordings, 12(December 1968), p.40.

B926.   Tchaikovsky, etc. HMV ASD 2464
         Records and Recordings, 12(March 1969), p.67.

B927.   Tchaikovsky. Ace of Diamond GOS 568-70
         Records and Recordings, 12(April 1969), pp.45+47.

B928.   Tchaikovsky. Argo ZRG 584
         Records and Recordings, 12(April 1969), pp.73-4.

B929.   Tchaikovsky, etc. Ace of Diamonds SDD 205
         Records and Recordings, 12(July 1969), pp.76-77.

B930.   Tchaikovsky. CBS Classics 61092
         Records and Recordings, 12(July 1969), pp.77-8.

B931.   Tchaikovsky, etc. HMV ASD 2480
         Records and Recordings, 12(July 1969), p.77.

B932.   Tchaikovsky. World Record Club ST 872

Records   and   Recordings,   12(August   1969),
pp.55-56.

B933.   Tchaikovsky. DGG 135109
         Records and Recordings, 12(September 1969), p.64.

B934.   Tchaikovsky, etc. HMV ASD 2490
         Records   and   Recordings,   12(September   1969),
         pp.64+75.

B935.   Tchaikovsky, etc. RCA Victor SB 6802
         Records   and   Recordings,   12(September   1969),
         pp.75-76.

B936.   Tchaikovsky, etc. HMV ASD 2499
         Records   and   Recordings,   13(November   1969),
         pp.81-2.

B937.   Tchaikovsky. Philips SAL 3734; Philips SAL 3725
         Records and Recordings, 13(December 1969), p.76.

B938.   Tchaikovsky. HMV ASD 2558
         Records and Recordings, 13(March 1970), pp.59-60.

B939.   Tchaikovsky. Eclipse ECM 540; ECS 540
         Records and Recordings, 13(April 1970), p.53.

B940.   Tchaikovsky. Decca SXL 6448
         Records and Recordings, 13(May 1970), p.60.

B941.   Tchaikovsky, etc. HMV ASD 2592
         Records and Recordings, 13(July 1970), p.52.

B942.   Tchaikovsky, etc. Phase Four PFS 4181
         Records and Recordings, 13(July 1970), pp.51-52.

B943.   Tchaikovsky, etc. DGG 2705004(2)
         Records   and   Recordings,   13(September   1970),
         pp.65-66.

B944.   Tchaikovsky, etc. DGG 2705006(2)
         Records and Recordings, 13(September 1970), p.66.

B945.   Tchaikovsky. Musicdisc RC 729
         Records and Recordings, 14(November 1970), p.101.

B946.   Tchaikovsky. Philips SAL 3793
         Records and Recordings, 14(November 1970), p.101.

B947.   Tchaikovsky. RCA Victrola VICS 1100
         Records   and   Recordings,   14(November   1970),
         pp.101-102.

B948.   Tchaikovsky. RCA Victrola VICS 1531
         Records   and   Recordings,   14(November   1970),
         pp.99-100.

B949.   Tchaikovsky. Supraphon 1110698
         Records and Recordings, 14(December 1970), p.95.

B950.   Tchaikovsky. CBS Classics 61205
         Records and Recordings, 14(January 1971), p.89.

B951.   Tchaikovsky, etc. Classics for Pleasure CFP 101
         Records   and   Recordings,   14(January   1971),
         pp.89-90.

B952.   Tchaikovsky. Decca SPA 108
         Records and Recordings, 14(January 1971), p.90.

B953.   Tchaikovsky, etc. HMV ASD 2617
         Records   and   Recordings,   14(January   1971),
         pp.88-89.

B954.   Tchaikovsky. HMV ASD 2645
         Records   and   Recordings,   14(January   1971),
         pp.86+88.

B955.   Tchaikovsky, etc. CBS Classics 61213
         Records and Recordings, 14(February 1971), p.81.

B956.   Tchaikovsky, etc. Classics for Pleasure CFP 108
         Records and Recordings, 14(February 1971), p.82.

B957.   Tchaikovsky. DGG 643212
         Records and Recordings, 14(February 1971), p.83.

B958.   Tchaikovsky. Philips 6500081
         Records and Recordings, 14(February 1971), p.82.

B959.   Tchaikovsky. RCA Victrola VICS 1422
         Records and Recordings, 14(February 1971), p.82.

B960.   Tchaikovsky, etc. Music for Pleasure MFP 2148
         <u>Records and Recordings</u>, 14(April 1971), p.79.

B961.   Tchaikovsky. CBS 72926
         <u>Records and Recordings</u>, 14(May 1971), pp.92+94.

B962.   Tchaikovsky. Decca SPA 142
         <u>Records and Recordings</u>, 14(May 1971), p.91.

B963.   Tchaikovsky. DGG 2530078
         <u>Records and Recordings</u>, 14(May 1971), pp.91-92.

B964.   Tchaikovsky. Eclipse ECS 575
         <u>Records and Recordings</u>, 14(May 1971), p.91.

B965.   Tchaikovsky, etc. RCA Red Seal LSB 4031
         <u>Records and Recordings</u>, 14(July 1971), p.65.

B966.   Tchaikovsky. Classics for Pleasure CFP 161
         <u>Records and Recordings</u>, 14(August 1971), p.68.

B967.   Tchaikovsky. HMV ASD 2594
         <u>Records and Recordings</u>, 14(Septmeber 1971), p.94.

B968.   Tchaikovsky. Unicorn UNS 240
         <u>Records and Recordings</u>,   14(September   1971),
         pp.94+98.

B969.   Tchaikovsky. Ace of Diamonds SDD 301-3
         <u>Records and Recordings</u>, 15(October 1971), p.96.

B970.   Tchaikovsky. CBS 72949
         <u>Records and Recordings</u>, 15(November 1971), p.102.

B971.   Tchaikovsky, etc. Decca SPA 119
         <u>Records   and   Recordings</u>,   15(November   1971),
         pp.101-102.

B972.   Tchaikovsky. HMV ASD 2738
         <u>Records and Recordings</u>, 15(November 1971), p.101.

B973.   Tchaikovsky. Contour 2870127
         <u>Records and Recordings</u>, 15(December 1971), p.92.

B974.   Tchaikovsky, etc. HMV SEOM 9

Records   and   Recordings,   15(December   1971),
pp.88-89.

B975.   Tchaikovsky. HMV Concert Classics SXLP 30127
         Records and Recordings, 15(December 1971), p.93.

B976.   Tchaikovsky. Supraphon 1100485
         Records   and   Recordings,   15(December   1971),
         pp.92-93.

B977.   Tchaikovsky, etc. Vanguard Cardinal VCS 10095
         Records and Recordings, 15(December 1971), p.92.

B978   Tchaikovsky. Classics for Pleasure CFP 133
         Records and Recordings, 15(January 1972), p.68.

B979.   Tchaikovsky. HMV ASD 2757
         Records   and   Recordings,   15(January   1972),
         pp.68-69.

B980.   Tchaikovsky. Phase Four PFS 4225
         Records and Recordings, 15(January 1972), p.68.

B981.   Tchaikovsky. Philips 6500132
         Records   and   Recordings,   15(January   1972),
         pp.77-78.

B982.   Tchaikovsky, etc. Privilege 2538142
         Records and Recordings, 15(January 1972), p.69.

B983.   Tchaikovsky. Eclipse ECS 636
         Records   and   Recordings,   15(February   1972),
         pp.73-74.

B984.   Tchaikovsky. Decca SPA 206
         Records and Recordings, 15(March 1972), p.86.

B985.   Tchaikovsky, etc. Universo 6580014
         Records and Recordings, 15(March 1972), p.86.

B986.   Tchaikovsky. HMV ASD 2775
         Records and Recordings, 15(April 1972), pp.70+75.

B987.   Tchaikovsky, etc. HMV SEOM 10
         Records and Recordings, 15(April 1972), p.75.

B988.   Tchaikovsky, etc. Decca SXL 6530
         Records and Recordings, 15(May 1972), pp.93-94.

B989.   Tchaikovsky. HMV ASD 2771
         Records and Recordings, 15(May 1972), pp.45-46.

B990.   Tchaikovsky, CBS Classics 61289
         Records and Recordings, 15(June 1972), pp.63-64.

B991.   Tchaikovsky. Argo ZRG 707
         Records   and   Recordings,   15(September   1972),
         pp.92-93.

B992.   Tchaikovsky. Philips 6703033
         Records and Recordings, 15(September 1972), p.71.

B993.   Tchaikovsky. RCA Toscanini Edition AT 104
         Records   and   Recordings,   15(September   1972),
         pp.71-72.

B994.   Tchaikovsky. Decca SPA 224
         Records and Recordings, 16(October 1972), p.85.

B995.   Tchaikovsky. Decca SXL 6562
         Records and Recordings, 16(October 1972), p.84.

B996.   Tchaikovsky. Eclipse ECS 653
         Records   and   Recordings,   16(October   1972),
         pp.84-85.

B997.   Tchaikovsky. Vox STGBY 659
         Records   and   Recordings,   16(November   1972),
         pp.64-65.

B998.   Tchaikovsky, etc. Vanguard VCS 10099
         Records and Recordings, 16(February 1973), p.64.

B999.   Tchaikovsky, etc. DGG 2530308
         Records and Recordings, 16(May 1973), pp.68+70.

B1000.   Tchaikovsky, etc. HMV SEOM 14
         Records and Recordings, 17(October 1973), p.81.

B1001.   Tcherepnin. DGG 139379
         Records   and   Recordings,   12(December   1968),
         pp.76-77.

B1002.   Tippett. Argo ZRG 680
          Records and Recordings, 15(January 1972), p.69.

B1003.   Tishchenko, etc. HMV ASD 2803
          Records and Recordings, 15(June 1972), pp.64+66.

B1004.   Traditional, etc. RCA Victrola VIC 1383
          Records   and   Recordings,   12(August   1969),
          pp.71-72.

B1005.   Vainberg. HMV ASD 2755
          Records and Recordings, 15(November 1971), p.102.

B1006.   Varese, etc. Vanguard VSL 11073
          Records   and   Recordings,   13(October   1969),
          pp.81-2.

B1007.   Varese. Vox STGBY 643
          Records and Recordings, 14(May 1971), p.99.

B1008.   Varese. Decca SXL 6550
          Records and Recordings, 15(September 1972), p.72.

B1009.   Vaughan Williams, etc. Revolution RCB 20
          Records   and   Recordings,   15(October   1971),
          pp.106-107.

B1010.   Vermeulen, etc. Donemus   7273/1
          Pijper, etc.   Donemus   7273/3
          De Leeuw   Donemus   7273/4
          Van Baaren   Donemus   7273/2
          Records   and   Recordings,   17(May   1974),
          pp.41-42+44.

B1011.   Vierne. Barclay 995002
          Records and Recordings, 14(June 1971), p.90.

B1012.   Villa-Lobos, etc. Everest SDBR 3041
          Records and Recordings, 11(December 1967), p.61.

B1013.   Villa-Lobos. Everest SDBR 3016
          Records and Recordings, 15(October 1971), p.98.

B1014.   Volkmann, etc. Turnabout TV 34370S
          Records and Recordings, 16(September 1973), p.89.

B1015. Wagenaar, etc. Donemus DAVS 7001
        Records and Recordings, 14(July 1971), p.66.

B1016. Walters, etc. Decca SXL 6468
        Records and Recordings, 14(October 1970), p.94.

B1017. Walton, etc. CBS 72677
        Records and Recordings, 12(November 1968), p.72.

B1018. Walton, etc. Music for Pleasure MFP 2129
        Records   and   Recordings,   12(August   1969),
        pp.56-57.

B1019. Walton. CBS Classics 61264
        Records and Recordings, 15(February 1972), p.94.

B1020. Walton. HMV Concert Classics SXLP 30138
        Records and Recordings, 15(April 1972), p.77.

B1021. Walton. HMV Concert Classics SXLP 30139
        Records and Recordings, , 15(May 1972), p.72.

B1022. Walton. Argo ZRG 725
        Records   and   Recordings,   16(November   1972),
        pp.103-104.

B1023. Walton, etc. Vox STGBY 658
        Records   and   Recordings,   16(November   1972),
        pp.102-103.

B1024. Walton, etc. Decca SXL 6601
        Records and Recordings, 16(May 1973), pp.71-72.

B1025. Walton, etc. Argo ZRG 711
        Records and Recordings, 17(October 1973), p.86.

B1026. Walton. RCA Red Seal LSB 4100
        Records and Recordings, 17(October 1973), p.86.

B1027. Walton, etc. HMV ASD 2990
        Records and Recordings, 17(May 1974) pp.44-45.

B1028. Walton, etc. CBS Classics 61365
        Records and Recordings, 17(August 1974), p.43.

B1029.   Warlock, etc. HMV CSD 3705
         Records and Recordings, 15(April 1972), pp.77-78.

B1030.   Webern. Philips 6500105
         Records and Recordings, 14(July 1971), pp.70-71.

B1031.   Wolf-Ferrari, etc. Classics for Pleasure CFP 158
         Records and Recordings, 14(August 1971), p.71.

B1032.   Xenakis. Erato STU 70526
         Records   and   Recordings,   15(October   1971),
         pp.98+103.

B1033.   Xenakis. Erato STU 70529
         Records and Recordings, 15(October 1971), p.103.

Alphabetical List of Compositions

The number following each title refers to the specific entry
in the "Works and Performances" section of this volume.

A little child there is y-born (W129)
Adieu, farewell earth's bliss (W132)
Afternoons and Afterwards (W144)
Air (W139)
Alba (W30)
All for Love (W150)
Arabesque (W159)
Artful Dodger, The (W144)
Aspects of Whiteness (W107)
Aubade (Study No.4) (W38)
Auf meines Kindes Tod (W140)

Bagatelles for 2 clarinets (W75)
Ballad (W145)
Basse Dance (W39)
Behold a Silly Tender Babe (W108)
Blues (W147)
Burlesque (W4)

Canto for Guitar (W76)
Canzona for Wind and Percussion (W166)
Capriccio (Study No.1) (W40)
Caravan (W77)
Castle of Arianrhod (W84)
Centennial Fanfare (W167)
Chaconne (W66a)
Chagall Windows (W5)
Chamber Concerto for Viola, Cello and Orchestra (W6)
Champagne Waltz (W144)
Cloudcatcher Fells (W168)
Combat (W150)
Come back, little Sheba (W151)
Concertante for Harpsichord and Chamber Ensemble (W7)
Concertante Music (W8)
Concertante Variations on a theme of Nicholas Maw (W9)
Concertino for Piano Duet and Orchestra (W10)
Concerto for Chamber Orchestra (W11)

Floraison (W84)
Folk Songs (W133)
Forlane (W144)

Galop for Bob Acres (W162a)
Game of Darts, A (W144)
Gaudi (Study No.3) (W44)
Gavotte (W45)
Gebet (W137)
Goddess Trilogy (W84)
Good Soldier (W154)
Grabschrift Marianne (W137)
Great Lord of Lords (W113)
Greensleeves Ground (W85)
Growing Pains (W155)
Guardian of the Abyss (W155)
Guitar Song (W147)
Gymnopidie (W147)

Hag, The (W132)
Halling (W145)
Hammer House of Horror (W155)
Hammer House of Mystery and suspense (W156)
Haydn Variations (W46)
Highland Habanera (W145)
Holiday Overture (W27)
Hour-Glass, The (W132)
Hush-a-ba-birdie, croon,croon (W133)
Hymne to God the Father (W114)
Hymnus ante sommus (W30)
Hypotheticals (W157)

Images (W171)
In Bethlehem that fair city (W122; W129)
In der Fremde (W140)
In memory (W143)
Intermezzo (W47)
In time of the Breaking of Nations (W142)

January Sonatina (W174)
Jig for St. Lucius O'Trigger (W162a)
Jigaudon (W145)
Johannis-Partita (W67)
John Peel (W133)
Johnny has gone for a soldier (W133)
Jubilee Suite (W28)

Keep indoors by the rain (W135)

Lamentation Rag (W48)
Landscape (W49)
Leeds United (W158)
Les Soirs bleus (W134)

Poisson Magique (W71)
Polish Dance (W145)
Portraits for Flute and Piano (W147)
Prelude for organ (W72)
Proud Songsters (W121)
Pueblo (W93)
Puer Natus in Bethlehem (W122)

Quartet for Oboe and Strings (W94)
Quartet No.2. for Strings (W95)
Quartet No.3. for Strings (W96)
Quartet No.4. for Strings (W97)
Quartet No.5. for Strings (W98)
Quintet for Strings (W99)

Rain (W135)
Rain in not controlled, The (W135)
Rain Songs (W135)
Rainforest I (W100)
Rainforest II (W101)
Reflections of a Summer Night (W123)
Requiem Sequence (W136)
Rivals, The (W162)
Rounds for brass quintet (W172)

Sam (W163)
SAM Variations (W102)
Scenes in America Deserta (W124)
Scherzo (W147)
Sechs Gedichte (W137)
Sequence of Nocturnes (W138)
Shadow of Light (W31)
Shadow Reach (W34a)
Shall I compare thee to a summer's day (W110)
Shape-Shifter (W84)
Siberia (W116)
Siciliano (W145)
Sinfonia for organ (W73)
Slumber did my Spirit Seal, A (W138)
Somnia (W30)
Sonata for Clarinet, Cello and Piano (W103)
Sonata for Piano (No.1.) (W56)
Sonata for Piano (No.2.) (W57)
Sonata on a Motet (W32)
Song (W139)
Sort of Fanfare (W58)
Sostenuto (Study No.2.) (W59)
Sports Car (W144)
Stabat Mater (W125)
Star Preludes (W104)
String Trio (W105)
Study in B-flat for Piano (W60)
Study in C-flat for Piano (W61)
Study in Limericks No. 1 (W126)
Summer Garland (W139)
Summer Music for Orchestra (W148)

Chronological List of Main Compositions

The number following each title refers to the specific entry in the "Works and Performances" section of this volume.

1950s   Gavotte (W45)
               Study in B-flat for Piano (W60)
               Study in C-flat for Piano (W61)
               Toccata in C (W62)

1957   Passacaglia for 2 pianos (W54)
               Sonata for Piano No. 1 (W56)
               Sonata for Piano No. 2 (W57)

1957-58   The Rivals (W162)

1958   Elegy for String Orchestra (W25)
               Holiday Overture (W27)
               Music for Piano (W51)
               Piano Variations (W55)

1958-59   Divertimento No. 1 (W22)

1959   Concerto No. 1 for Violin and Orchestra (W19)
               Divertimento No. 2 (W23)
               Fantasia for Organ (W66)
               Little Suite (W86)
               Overture and other music (Victorian melodrama)
               (W161)
               Study in Limericks No. 1 (W126)
               Three Leider (W140)

1959-60   Five Impromptus (W43)

1960   Coventry Carol (W109)
               Partita for String Quartet (W92)
               Pastorale Sostenuto (W70)

1961	Missa Meditationis (W118)
	Puer Natus in Bethlehem (W122)
	Sinfonia for Organ (W73)

1962	Concerto for Chamber Orchestra (W11)
	Concerto Funebre (W21)
	Five Elegies (W132)
	Quintet for Strings (W99)
	Sequence of Nocturnes (W138)
	Three Songs from Shakespeare (W141)

1962-63	Three Tenor Songs (W142)

1963	Dies Resurrectionis (W64)
	English Songs 1963 (W110)
	Sechs Gedichte (W137)
	Summer Garland (W139)
	Summer Music (W148)
	Te Deum (W127)
	Variations for Piano (W63)
	Wedding Music (W74)

1963/1976	Folk Songs (W133)

1964	Five Bagatelles (W42)
	Johannis-Partita (W67)
	Mary Laid her Child (W117)
	Movements (W88)
	Musica Notturna (W89)
	Nocturne (W69)
	Poisson Magique (W71)
	Prelude (W72)
	Symphony for 10 Wind Instruments (W173)
	Three Pieces for Clarinet and Piano (W106)
	Variations on a theme of Hartmann (W37)

1965	Bagatelles for 2 Clarinets (W75)
	Chamber Concerto (W6)
	Concertante (W7)
	Elegy for Organ (W65)
	Fantasy for Brass Quartet (W170)
	String Trio (W105)
	Symphony No. 1 (W33)

1966	Burlesque (W4)
	Concerto No. 1 for Piano and Orchestra (W16)
	Evening Canticles for Salisbury (W112)
	Great Lord of Lords (W113)
	Hymne to God the Father (W114)
	Miniconcerto (W68)
	Nocturnal (W90)
	Partita (W91)
	Rain Songs (W135)

1967   Aspects of Whiteness (W107)
            Dance-Movements (W79)
            Fantasy on a theme of Liszt (W41)
            Rounds for Brass Quintet (W172)

1968   Canto for Guitar (W76)
            Concertante Music (W8)
            Conterino for Piano Duet and Orchestra (W10)
            Intermezzo (W47)
            Lion, the Witch and the Wardrobe (W146)
            Metamorphosen (W29)
            Morning Watch (W119)
            Quartet for Oboe and Strings (W94)

1969   Capriccio (Study No. 1) (W40)
            Concerto for Piano and Wind Quintet (W78)
            Groundsleeves Ground (W85)
            Sonata for Clarinet, Cello and Piano (W103)
            Sostenuto (Study No. 2) (W59)
            This Town's a Corporation (W149)
            To Us in Bethlem City (W128)

1970   Aubade (Study No. 4) (W38)
            Basse Danse (W39)
            Canzona for Wind and Percussion (W166)
            Concertante Variations (W9)
            Concerto No. 2 for Piano and Orchestra (W17)
            Evening Canticles for Norwich (W111)
            Gaudi (Study No. 3) (W44)
            Notturni ed Alba (W30)

1971   Dance-Prelude (W80)
            Requiem Sequence (W136)
            Symphony No. 2 (W34)

1972   Concerto for Oboe d'amore and Chamber Orchestra
            (W14)
            Fear in the Night (W153)
            Quartet No.2 for Strings (W95)
            Voyage (W130)

1973   Das Letzte Gerichte (W131)
            Madrigal and Arabesque (W159)
            Maze Dances (W87)
            Sam (W163)
            Teachings of Don Juan (W3)
            Time Remembered (W143)
            Upon the High Midnight (W129)

1973-75   Goddess Trilogy (W84)

1974   Chagall Windows (W5)
              Leeds United (W158)
              Play of Mother Courage (W1)

1975   Behold a Silly Tender Babe (W108)
              Couples (W152)
              Mary, Queen of Scots (W2)

1976   Concerto No.3 for Piano and Orchestra (W18)
              Sonata on a Motet (W32)
              Stabat Mater (W125)

1977   Come back, little Sheba (W151)
              Concerto for Clarinet and Orchestra (W12)
              Jubilee Suite (W28)
              Lute-book Lullaby (W115)
              Reflections of a Summer Night (W123)

1977-78   Images (W171)
              Symphony No.3 (W35)

1978   Landscape (W49)
              Shadow of Light (W31)
              Star Preludes (W104)

1979   Concerto No.2 for Violin and Orchestra (W20)
              Hypotheticals (W157)
              Leo Soirs bleus (W134)
              Motet (W116)
              Paraphrase on Mary Queen of Scots (Study No.5)
              (W53)
              Quartet No.3 for Strings (W96)

1979-83   Mangan Triptych (W116)

1980   Dances for Trumpet and Piano (W145)
              Hammer House of Horror: 13th Reunion   )
                                      Growing Pains   ) (W155)
                                      Guardian of the)
                                      Abyss   )
              Mosaic (Study No.6) (W50)
              Portraits for Flute and Piano (W147)
              Siberia (W116)

1981   Afternoons and Afterwards (W144)
              Desert I : Lizard (W81)
              Desert II : Horizon (W169)
              Good Soldier (W154)
              Music's Empire (W120)

1982   All for Love (W150)
              Concerto for Orchestra (W15)
              Desert III : Landscape (W82)
              Lamentation Rag (W48)
              Quartet No.4 for Strings (W97)
              Young Musicians of the Year (W165)

1982-83   Haydn Variations (W46)

1983   Desert IV : Vista (W83)
              Michelin MX Tyres (W160)
              Visions (W116)

1984   Hammer House of Mystery and Suspense:
                  Czech Mate   )
                  The Sweet Scent of Death)   (W156)

1984-85   Tuning (W36)

1985   Cloudcatcher Fells (W168)

1986   Pueblo (W93)
              Scenes in America Deserta (W124)
              Sort of Fanfare (W58)

1987   Centennial Fanfare (W167)
              Rainforest II (W101)

1987-88   Caravan (W77)
              Double Concerto (W24)

1988   Fire at Durilgai (W26)
              Nothing to it (W52)
              These Foolish Things (W164)

1989   Proud Songsters (W121)
              Quartet No.5 for Strings (W98)
              SAM Variations (W102)

1989-90   Concerto for Flute and Orchestra (W13)

1990   January Sonatina (W174)

Index

Page number references refer to pages in the "Biography"; other entries refer to individual items in the "Works and Performances" list (W), the "Discography" (D) and the "Bibliography" (B).

Since the Bibliography is alphabetical by author, index entries for those items have not been included under the author's name (although, of course, other references to those authors are indexed).

About the Author

STEWART R. CRAGGS is Reader Services Librarian at the Sunderland Polytechnic Library in the United Kingdom. He is also the author of two bio-bibliographies, *Arthur Bliss* (Greenwood Press, 1988) and *Richard Rodney Bennett* (Greenwood Press, 1989), and is currently working on two future bio-bibliographies for Greenwood.